The *New* Ukrainian Cookbook

A Blend of Tradition and Innovation

THE HIPPOCRENE COOKBOOK LIBRARY

Afghan Food & Cookery
Alps, Cuisines of the
Aprovecho: A Mexican-American Border Cookbook
Argentina Cooks!, Exp. Ed.
Belarusian Cookbook, The
Bolivian Kitchen, My Mother's
Brazil: A Culinary Journey
Cajun Cuisine, Stir the Pot: The History of
Calabria, Cucina di
Chile, Tasting
China's Fujian Province, Cooking from
Colombian Cooking, Secrets of
Corsican Cuisine
Croatian Cooking, Best of, Exp. Ed.
Czech Cooking, Best of, Exp. Ed.
Danish Cooking and Baking Traditions
Danube, All Along The, Exp. Ed.
Emilia-Romagna, The Cooking of
Egyptian Cuisine and Culture, Nile Style:
English Country Kitchen, The
Estonian Tastes and Traditions
Filipino Food, Fine
Finnish Cooking, Best of
Germany, Spoonfuls of
Greek Cooking, Regional
Haiti, Taste of
Havana Cookbook, Old (Bilingual)
Hungarian Cookbook, Exp. Ed.
India, A Culinary Journey
India, Flavorful
Iraqi Family Cookbook
Jewish-Iraqi Cuisine, Mama Nazima's
Kerala Kitchen, The
Laotian Cooking, Simple
Lebanese Cookbook, The
Ligurian Kitchen, A

Lithuanian Cooking, Art of
Malaysia, Flavors of
Middle Eastern Kitchen, The
Naples, My Love for
Nepal, Taste of
New Hampshire: from Farm to Kitchen
New Jersey Cookbook, Farms and Foods of the Garden State:
Ohio, Farms and Foods of
Persian Cooking, Art of
Pied Noir Cookbook: French Sephardic Cuisine
Piemontese, Cucina: Cooking from Italy's Piedmont
Polish Cooking, Best of, Exp. Ed.
Polish Country Kitchen Cookbook, The
Polish Heritage Cookery, Ill. Ed.
Polish Holiday Cookery
Polish Traditions, Old
Portuguese Encounters, Cuisines of
Punjab, Menus and Memories from
Romania, Taste of
Russian Cooking, The Best of
Scottish-Irish Pub and Hearth Cookbook
Sicilian Feasts
Slovenia, Flavors of
South Indian Cooking, Healthy
Spain, La Buena Mesa: The Regional Cooking of
Trinidad and Tobago, Sweet Hands: Island Cooking from
Turkish Cuisine, Taste of
Tuscan Kitchen, Tastes from a
Ukrainian Cookbook, The New
Ukrainian Cuisine, Best of, Exp. Ed.
Uzbek Cooking, Art of
Warsaw Cookbook, Old

C1

The *New* Ukrainian Cookbook

A Blend of Tradition and Innovation

Annette Ogrodnik Corona

Illustrated by Laurette Kovary

HIPPOCRENE BOOKS, INC.
New York

For further information, contact:
HIPPOCRENE BOOKS, INC.
171 Madison Avenue
New York, NY 10016
www.hippocrenebooks.com

Library of Congress Cataloging-in-Publication Data

Corona, Annette Ogrodnik.
 The new Ukrainian cookbook : a blend of tradition and innovation / Annette Ogrodnik
Corona ; Illustrations by Laurette Kovary.
    p. cm.
 Includes index.
 ISBN 978-0-7818-1287-0 (hardcover) -- ISBN 0-7818-1287-9 (hardcover)
1. Cooking, Ukrainian. I. Title.
 TX723.5.U38C67 2012
 641.593477--dc23

                                                          2012016805

Printed in the United States of America.

Nareshti!

This book is dedicated to Team Corona:
Kevin, Laurette, Stacey, and Frankie

Acknowledgments

Writing this cookbook was a highly personal venture, yet could never have happened without the behind-the-scenes support of a wonderful range of acquaintances. I know it takes more than an author to create a book, but in this case, it took a multitude. When I stop and think of all the people who made this cookbook happen, I feel giddy with gratitude.

For starters, I would like to thank my husband Kevin for lending essential substance to my quirky visions and lifestyle. This book would not have made the jump from dream to reality without his immense patience, positivity, prudence, and spiritual companionship. He is to be kissed and commended for never questioning my insatiable culinary curiosity and for his unselfish expansion of both taste buds and waistline during all of my copious dinner tastings.

Thanks to my longtime pal, Laurette Kovary, for believing we could create an awesome cookbook and for warming the interior pages with delightful illustrations. Thanks also to my best friend, Stacey Butkowski, for her long humorous phone calls and the ability to calm me down during my many computer freak-outs. And a special blessing for Frankie, my pesky, well-fed Jack Russell terrier (the buddy who loves me no matter what), "let bones rain from the sky!"

Special thanks to Orysia Tracz, for working steadily and conscientiously on the transliterations and whose attention to cultural detail brought certain liveliness to the project. I would have never been able to overcome my considerable Ukrainian language obstacles without you!

Blessed are all the venders and farmers at the Emmaus, Easton, and Steel Stacks Farmer's Markets and those farmers everywhere who tend to animals, dig in the dirt, and then stand in the hot sun and drizzling rain to sell us the fruits of their labors. To all you angelic creators, thank you.

Heartfelt thanks to Lori Stansberry, owner of Pure Sprouts Organic Delivery, for making it possible to cook and share my ideas and recipes for a healthy planet before an audience.

A thanksgiving of appreciation to The Ukrainian Museum in New York City; the Ukrainian Homestead in Lehighton, Pennsylvania; Natalie Kononenko of the Peter and Doris Kule Centre for Ukrainian and Canadian Folklore, University of Alberta; and Wilton S. Tifft for the countless suggestions and thoughtful candor during the years of writing this book.

Stockpots of love to all my treasured friends and extended family for their enthusiasm and appreciation thus motivating me to continue to cook and share my Ukrainian food recipes with the world—and for allowing my numerous home visits to take the form of friendly kitchen takeovers.

And at long last, I would like to express my immense gratitude to Priti Gress, my wise and wonderful editor, for the vision to see a book within me waiting to be born, Barbara Keane-Pigeon who guided me through the production process, Wanda España for her brilliant design, and the entire team at Hippocrene for their unwavering excitement and marketing savvy.

Finally, to all culinary savants, what can be said? Cheers to all those hungry for more cookbooks, recipes, and cultural adventures—keep cooking and enjoying new foods, for as the old Ukrainian proverb says: *S'ohodni khoch vola z'yish, a zavtra znovu skhochesh* ("Even if you eat a whole bull today, you'll be hungry again tomorrow").

Contents

Introduction   Ukrainians and Their Food   *ix*

Ukraine at a Glance   *xi*

A Brief Culinary History of Ukraine   *xiii*

A Collection of Soul Nourishing Recipes   *xv*

A Blend of Tradition and Innovation   *xvi*

Chapter 1   Appetizers   *1*

Chapter 2   Borshch and Soups   *31*

Chapter 3   Salads, Pickles and Preserves   *57*

Chapter 4   Sauces, Vegetables and Grains   *79*

Chapter 5   Meats and Poultry   *113*

Chapter 6   Fish and Game   *147*

Chapter 7   Breads, Buns and Rolls   *169*

Chapter 8   Dumplings, Noodles, and Griddlecakes   *189*

Chapter 9   Omelets and Other Egg Dishes   *209*

Chapter 10   Desserts   *217*

Chapter 11   Beverages and Libations   *245*

Holiday Specialties of Easter and Christmas Eve   *257*

Index   *260*

Introduction

Ukrainians and Their Food

I was born in southeastern Pennsylvania. It was there I took my first steps and it is there my palate was awakened. Some of my earliest memories are of food. I remember walking shoeless through the vines of our garden searching out the plumpest cucumber. I remember walking through the woods picking berries to make wine. I remember beautiful braided onions and garlic hanging in our cellar next to slabs of cured pork belly bacon we made from our own pigs. I remember trips to various farmer's markets and sampling piquant marinated chanterelles and soused cherries. I remember sitting under the apple trees watching pasture cattle graze, swooning over the thought of how their creamy milk would be turned into cheese. I remember gathering eggs from our barnyard chickens and ducks to make some of the best omelets and pancakes I ever tasted. But my fondest memories are of time spent with Baba, my grandmother Theodosia, in her farmhouse kitchen.

Baba emigrated from the Ternolpil region of northwestern Ukraine in 1909 and settled in the Lehigh Valley countryside of Pennsylvania. It was there my family ran a 54-acre farm. It was a beautiful and vibrant place. Money was not plentiful, but life on that farm was rich and flavorful—a place of high spirits and good health. We were for the most part self-reliant, producing most of the things we ate. Baba raised beef cattle, dairy cows, pigs, chickens, ducks, geese, and rabbits. Wheat was milled at a communal mill. We picked grapes from our own arbors, and apple, pear, mulberry, plum, and cherry trees filled an extensive orchard. Baba's large gardens behind the barnyard delivered a wide array of fresh vegetables and salad greens. Cascades of melons and squash and fresh herbs like parsley, dill, chives, and purple basil graced our kitchen counters. Alongside them rested rainbows of bell peppers, bulbous green onions, and chubby crimson-colored beets. And when I looked up, baskets of berries and sacks of spices peered down at me from the shelves above. Baba and I jarred, dried, or cured the majority of produce that wasn't eaten in the summertime to save and use during winter months. Any surplus was sold roadside. Memories of these precious times are definitely my reference library when I prepare meals today.

Cooking was also a social activity in our house. Baba's kitchen was not only beautiful, it had a soul. Her kitchen welcomed everyone—not only other Ukrainians. She had a reputation for great culinary prowess and convivial hospitality, so her kitchen was often a gathering place for the hungry and weary, and definitely for those who were in search of a memorable meal. Besides remarkable food, there was always loud singing and storytelling. Baba's kitchen was a learning place for children, a place where political philosophies were expounded, histories examined, and sometimes scandals unearthed. The profusion of scents and smells erupting from that kitchen coupled with the crescendo of color, the din of voices, and the vigor of friends and family was all so stunning it took my breath away.

Ukrainians, whether at home in Ukraine or abroad, believe that food is wedded heart and soul to the land, to the homestead and its ancient traditions. Cooking is seen as an art that evolves from raw materials that must be respected, nurtured, prepared, and then shared. My grandmother used her familiar recipes to remember people at home, in the "Old Country," to remind herself of who she was and to keep in touch with her cultural identity. She approached cooking with abandon and saw food as an organic connection to the planet's magnificent gifts. It is my grandmother, Theodosia Zakamarco Ogrodnik, whose spirit and memory are truly the backbone of this book and from whom I learned the love of cooking and entertaining. These basic lessons started when I was five years old and have been feeding my hungry soul ever since.

As its reputation as "the breadbasket of Europe" suggests, Ukraine has always had a strong agricultural economy. But besides its production of formidable grains, the breeding of hardy livestock and poultry also holds great significance in the Ukrainian way of life. This, coupled with the unusual richness of the soil, creates agricultural commerce worthy of admiration worldwide. Even today family farms in Ukraine often produce more than enough fresh fruit and vegetables, so any extra is made available at farmer's markets in even the smallest of villages. The constraints of modern life have brought about change, but Ukrainians are still prepared to faithfully pursue the freshest and most healthy products that form the cornerstone of Ukrainian cuisine. I am lucky that I developed an appreciation for real, homegrown food early in life. I encourage you to also seek out "good stewards" of the land. Take time to get to know your local farmers and those who use organic growing practices. I use dairy products, eggs, meat, and poultry from pasture-fed, hormone-free livestock raised by farmers whose personal styles I have come to know. The grains and flours I use are grown without pesticides and milled without bleaching or other chemicals. I use raw, unprocessed honey whenever I can as a sweetener and it is supplied by a local beekeeper. I sincerely hope you'll consider doing the same wherever you live and cook.

Preparing Ukrainian food is a rewarding, sensory experience. Smell your food, touch it and mix it with your hands. Look around and enjoy the sights and sounds in your kitchen and share your food and recipes with others. I think the best Ukrainian food is home-cooked and Ukrainian hospitality is legendary, so if you are lucky enough to be invited into a Ukrainian home to eat, you are in for a real treat, and if not try making these wonderful dishes in your home and you do the inviting.

To all of you interested in Ukraine and Ukrainian cuisine, *"Laskavo prosymo v moyu kukhnyu!"* ("Welcome to my kitchen!")

—Annette Ogrodnik Corona
Bethlehem, Pennsylvania

Ukraine at a Glance

Ukraine is bordered by Russia in the east and northeast; Belarus in the north; Poland, Slovakia, and Hungary in the west; and Romania and Moldova in the southwest. With a population of over 45 million, Ukraine is the largest European country in the region after Russia. Kyiv, the capital, is located on the Dnipro River in north-central Ukraine. The country is divided into twenty-four oblasts or regions with the autonomous republic of Crimea with the cities of Kyiv and Sevastopol having the same rights as the oblasts.

The topography of Ukraine consists mainly of fertile steppes or plains and plateaus. The Carpathian Mountains are found only in the western part of the country and the Crimean peninsula (known as Crimea) in the extreme south has both lowlands and low mountains. Ukraine is situated in two climate zones. A moderate climate covers the steppes and mountains while a Mediterranean subtropical climate covers the southern shore of Crimea.

Overall, the center of Ukraine is grain-rich, while the fringes of the country vary dramatically. To the north are forests and marshlands; rivers teeming with fish, such as pike, carp, and salmon, just to name a few; the woods and steppe lands providing plenty of wild game. The cuisine is rich in wild edibles and farm animals are raised in nearly every courtyard of village farms. The east is home of the famed loam, *chornozem*, the rich black soil that produces grains that put bread on the table and provide Ukraine with the eminence of being called "the breadbasket of Europe." Here, in the more Russian-speaking east, Ukrainian cooking is much more influenced by Russian styles and Jewish traditions. Traveling westward, the Carpathian foothills and mountains bring forth succulent berries and strong-flavored mushrooms, and in the higher elevations, sheep herding is often a way of life. Southward along the coast of the Black Sea and the Sea of Azov, the climate is much more temperate and a second planting of vegetables each year is common practice and more varied. Port cities, such as Odesa along the southern coast and Yalta which sits along the southwestern shore of Crimea, enjoy a more cosmopolitan type of seaside cuisine, reminiscent of the Mediterranean.

A Brief Culinary History of Ukraine

It is important to review some of the country's history, for Ukraine's history has written her recipes.

Ukraine is an overwhelmingly agricultural nation and given its strategic location (linking Russia and Europe), it was plundered and fought over for centuries. Numerous bloody wars were fought over the fertile Ukrainian soil, tearing the country and its culture to pieces. Ukraine's culinary history reflects this turbulent history and the blended heritage of its people is vibrant.

During the course of history, Ukrainians gallantly fought off some raids with success, but at the same time accepted and adopted some of their invaders rather strange and unusual cooking habits, techniques, tastes, and styles, while vehemently rejecting others. For example, the stuffed vegetable dishes so significant to Ukrainian cookery are actually modifications of Turkish *dolmas*, which when translated means "stuffed dishes." During the course of Ukraine's history and while fending off attacks by the Ottoman Empire, Ukrainians eagerly adopted this culinary technique and skillfully adapted it by using their own ubiquitous ingredients, namely cabbage or beet leaves, with a stuffing of meat or grain and sour cream as flavoring. As a result, *holubtsi* (page 97) or Ukrainian "stuffed cabbage" is probably the best example of how a foreign dish was skewed to Ukrainian tastes and has long been considered an essential element of Ukrainian cuisine.

Let us not forget the humble eggplant. This versatile vegetable was all but rejected in much of Ukraine, with the exception of the southern regions, until the 1900s because of its association with Ottoman domination. And among the meat dishes, vigorous consumption of pork and wild boar was considered a symbol of resistance to the Muslims, to whom any kind of pork was forbidden.

A popular stew of plump pork sausages in sauerkraut called *bigos* and the love for breaded meats and desserts such as cheesecakes and puddings are associated with the days of Polish and Austro-Hungarian rule. But whenever Ukrainians adopted a dish, they always made an earnest attempt to retain their own social and religious customs in incorporating it into their cuisine.

Up until the beginning of the twentieth century, religious influences—primarily of the "Eastern Rite" (both Ukrainian Catholic and Ukrainian Orthodox Churches)—also helped to determine popular eating habits. The Church made a virtue out of what was economic necessity. Food was divided into two groups. For over half the year only Lenten fare was allowed, namely fish, vegetables, wild mushrooms, and fruits. Milk, eggs, and meat were permitted on the remaining days of the year.

Generally, however, there was opposition to outside influences and Ukrainian palates always preferred the more traditional foods such as hardy root vegetables, potatoes, meats, fish, poultry, wild mushrooms, and berries along with grains like buckwheat and millet and stews and soups, especially the beet soup *borshch*.

A Note on Culinary Transliterations

The Ukrainian terms used in this cookbook are not necessarily present-day terms being used in Ukraine. During the many decades of Soviet rule, the Ukrainian language was russified, with many traditional Ukrainian words disappearing from use. Pressure to use only the Russian language permeated the Ukrainian culture. However, the Ukrainian pioneers and later immigrants to North America did manage to retain a Ukrainian language without too much Russian influence. These are the words used in this cookbook, the words our babas and mamas used and passed on to us.

A Collection of Soul-Nourishing Recipes

Traversed by countless types of people through the ages, today's Ukraine is a cultural tapestry and home to over 100 nationalities. Farmers and city dwellers, young and old, and a fascinating underlying mix of numerous ethnic groups all live together peacefully, yet all seem to have an opinion or attitude about what is typically Ukrainian. There also remains a remnant of Soviet mentality. However, most describe themselves as Ukrainian and of Slavic origin. The largest ethnic group is Russian and mainly concentrated in eastern Ukraine. Other minorities include, in order of size, Belarusians, Moldovans, Bulgarians, Hungarians, Romanians, Poles, and Jews. Indigenous Hutsul communities are seamlessly integrated into the wider community and Kozak influences are evident throughout the land. Almost all of the country's Tatars live in Crimea. This cookbook offers a tempting range of recipes from all over Ukraine. One need not live in Ukraine to cook and eat "the Ukrainian way." There are no qualifications needed other than a desire to try something new. One need only keep in mind that Ukrainian gastronomic culture is tightly interwoven with historical and religious events, geographical conditions, and social peculiarities.

Since the northern and southern regions of Ukraine are climatically and geographically different from each other, the products, as well as the people, are also distinct and therefore one can find that a specialty that originated in a certain region evolves from place to place. Each region and its inhabitants continue to shade and color their dishes differently, but the end results are always genuine and delicious.

Ukraine has had a long tradition of regional peasant cooking defined by the tart flavors of sourdough rye bread, sauerkraut, and pickles, and complemented by fish such as carp, herring, and salmon. Onions and mushrooms are heavily used for flavoring and there is great love of meats, especially pork. Hardy root vegetables, potatoes, greens like spinach and sorrel, fruits like plums and cherries, and a variety of whole grains prevail. Dishes are accented with the flavors of fresh garlic, mustard, or horseradish, and dairy products like buttermilk, sour cream, and yogurt are all the most classic of Ukrainian ingredients and staples.

A Blend of Tradition and Innovation

It is true that some traditional Ukrainian dishes require a little extra creative coaxing, but most are uncomplicated, everyday fare that do not take a long time to prepare. Many even taste better after sitting a day or two in your refrigerator. Please take liberties as you wish: add something of your own to a dish, or simplify it, or prepare only the part that interests you. Never feel like you must do all or nothing. I revised some dishes to be fast and modern, geared toward those who choose to live life in the fast lane, while other dishes require slow braising, stewing, and roasting—building the appetite for what is yet to come. Having a repertoire of useful recipes such as these can prove indispensable to any household and Ukrainian fare lends itself well to family life. I parallel this trend by introducing (or reminding) readers that Ukrainian dishes naturally elicit a sense of returning to a monogamous relationship with meals, instead of relying on processed, packaged foods. A cook of any culinary level will be able to singlehandedly take foods all the way from the market, to the counter's chopping block, to the stove, to the table.

You will notice that classic holiday dishes are notably rich in dairy products and eggs. I made a calculated effort to include traditional ingredients and methods of preparation whenever I could, but also suggest substitutions that would help modernize the recipes and offer lower-fat options. In most cases it is possible to do this without losing the dish's true Ukrainian essence. For example, I use extra-large eggs in all recipes, and unsalted butter or sunflower oil in nearly all recipes that call for some kind of fat, but any quality vegetable oil will do. Lard, *salo* (cured pork belly bacon), and bacon drippings are used religiously for their unique flavor, but feel free to use your own preference. Eggs, as well as dairy products, can be replaced with vegan or vegetarian alternatives in several recipes if one so chooses.

Long ago (pre-World War I), meat was not part of the everyday menu in Ukraine, with the exception of Sunday when poultry was the desired choice. Pork, beef, and lamb were saved for special occasions, feasts, and weddings. Today though, there is no escaping the Ukrainian tendency to make meat the focal point of one's meals. However, I do keep in mind the importance of vegetables and point out vegetarian dishes or dishes where meat can be entirely eliminated if one so desires. There is an extensive list of poultry and fish dishes, many of which are old family recipes that I hope will entice and inspire not only home cooks, but culinary savants, cooking instructors, and restaurant chefs to tread safely and happily into unknown territories.

Pickles, relishes and preserves are Ukrainian specialties and I think recipes like rose petal preserves (page 75) and fruity concoctions like *kysil* (page 219) will be tantalizing memory awakeners for some readers. Perhaps family recipes once thought lost will now be secured in this cookbook. Dough products and pastry dishes are cited and no good Ukrainian cookbook would be worth its salt without an ample collection of baked goodies, dried fruit and nut desserts, and refreshing beverages and libations.

Because of its storied history and great variety, Ukrainian food can be enjoyed by all who have an opportunity to become acquainted with it. It is my hope that people will read this cookbook in two ways: first, as a resource for how to make a wide selection of well-balanced, healthy Ukrainian dishes; and second, as an interesting assembly of illuminating insights into Ukrainian culture and society.

While Ukrainian food has suffered from some negative stereotypes in the past, this lovely patchwork culinary tradition is finally being rediscovered as a national cuisine with wholesome appeal and gastronomic zing. I hope this journey will bring you much satisfaction and that you'll be inspired to bring the new and glorious flavors of Ukraine to your table!

"*Rukavychka*" ("The Mitten")

There is a popular Ukrainian folktale that tells the story of a little mouse who finds a lost mitten in the frozen woods, and decides to make it a home. Other animals, from a tiny frog to a wild boar to a huge bear, in turn also find the mitten, and the mouse welcomes each and every one of them and invites all to stay. The mitten stretches to provide shelter, warmth, and protection for all. It is a wonderful tale that reflects two very basic Ukrainian values: hospitality and community spirit. Even in the hardest times, past and present, the spirit of hospitality always remains. The best food is always for the guest, as is the best room and the best linen.

Chapter 1

Appetizers

Please be seated...

As a prelude to dinner in most Ukrainian households, there is a separate, beautifully set table offering striking platters of tidbits. These informal yet often sophisticated appetizers are called *zakusky*. Ukrainians are grand connoisseurs of *zakusky* and since aperitifs are not common, they begin by helping themselves to *zakusky*. To Ukrainians, this attractive mélange, along with pre-dinner mandatory shots of vodka, make up the very heart of the meal.

The origin of the *zakusky* table is somewhat unclear. Some food historians believe it is a variation of the Scandinavian smorgasbord, a plausible thought considering some of the earliest rulers of the land were of Scandinavian stock. Others are convinced it has long been a peasant tradition and the perfect answer to the unexpected arrival of guests from the cold. First the guest is offered a hearty shot of *horilka* (vodka) followed by some tempting food to "quiet it down." Customarily, Ukrainians believe one should never drink a shot of vodka without eating something immediately. This way the vodka behaves itself, imparting the guest with a pleasant glow and not a sledgehammer aftereffect!

Once upon a time, the *zakusky* table courted the opulence and splendor of the era in which whole stuffed salmon in aspic garlanded with fresh flowers may have presided. Silver bowls heaped with costly caviars surrounded composed salads and only the best silver was displayed. Carved vegetables garnished most dishes as did elaborate butter rosettes. A more frugal table has replaced these efforts in everyday households today, but one can still sample lively, colorful, and eclectic appetizers that also make excellent light suppers and nourishing lunches.

If a family is entertaining, a typical *zakusky* spread can consist of one or two fish and vegetable caviars; chilled fish and herring dishes; garnished hard-cooked eggs; patés and canapés or jellied meat, vegetable, or fish aspics. An assortment of pickles and marinated mushrooms are a must, as well as a few fresh vegetables and perhaps a salad, which may be more formally scooped into hollowed-out vegetables. A selection of mustards, pickled horseradish relish (page 68), and plenty of sourdough rye or dark bread and crackers are staples and sometimes there may be a platter of warm, filled dumplings called *varenyky* (page 192), accompanied by decorative bowls of sour cream or *smetana*, or buttery fried onions. There is always a decanter or two of vodka and even a plate of tiny, sweet-filled pastries to round out the selection. The choice is huge and anything goes as long as you like it. And even when entertaining informally, Ukrainians still take pride in artfully decorating finished dishes, so a pretty herb or flower to garnish any one or two of the previous examples is acceptable.

This chapter features several popular Ukrainian appetizers. It also includes a few recipes for the pastry dough needed to make certain appetizers and other Ukrainian dishes, and those will be cited again and again on the pages of this book. I have also taken the liberty of including some of my own creative versions of all-time favorite sauces and relishes that traditionally accompany particular appetizers.

Potato-digging Parties

Ukrainian community spirit is not only evident at times of hardship, but also at times of joy … To this day many Ukrainian villages keep alive the tradition of helping each other by lending a hand during harvest—with a potato-digging party. Often times farm work has to be rushed in order to gather crops at their prime and in good weather. In poorer villages, harvesting potatoes may still be done by hand, thus all able-bodied friends, relatives, and neighbors, both young and old, volunteer to help, including women and teenagers. This crop-digging party in the dirt begins in the early dawn hours, continues all day, and usually well into the evening. What follows after this hard toil is a community dinner and merrymaking because of a job well done! It is an expression of appreciation for all the help and of gratitude for a good crop on which people depend.

Garnished Eggs

Nachyniuvani yaitsia

"Garnished or stuffed eggs" is an appetizer widely enjoyed in Ukraine. The fillings are varied and can be made from finely chopped mushrooms, grated cheese, chopped smoked ham, anchovies, or leftover chicken. As a general rule, use one tablespoon of softened, unsalted butter or mayonnaise for every two hard-cooked egg yolks and flavor with freshly grated horseradish, mustard, lemon juice, chopped parsley, or chives depending on the filling.

Caviar is the roe (eggs) of a large fish eaten salted, and most often served on its own, but alternatively, it may be used sparingly as a garnish. Caviar is nutritious, low in fat, and has only 73 calories per ounce. When serving caviar, only a spoon from a natural source should be used, like bone, wood, horn, or mother-of-pearl. If sterling silver is used it will impart a metallic taste to the caviar and the caviar will discolor the silver. In the United States, as long as the species of fish precedes the word "caviar," it is considered caviar; pike caviar, golden whitefish caviar, etc. This pretty dish uses salmon caviar which is relatively inexpensive and makes a lovely garnish. (Please see note below.)

- 6 hard-cooked eggs, peeled and halved lengthwise
- 2 scallions, including some greens, finely chopped
- 2 tablespoons mayonnaise
- 1 tablespoon Dijon mustard
- 1 tablespoon fresh lemon juice
- Salt and freshly ground black pepper to taste
- 4 ounces salmon caviar
- Lettuce for serving plate
- Small sprigs of fresh dill for garnish

Remove the yolks from the halved eggs and place in a small bowl. Mash the yolks to a smooth paste and add the scallions, mayonnaise, mustard, and lemon juice. Mix well and season to taste with salt and black pepper. Spoon the mixture back into the egg whites.

Line a platter with lettuce and artfully arrange the eggs on the serving plate. Refrigerate for at least one hour.

When ready to serve, top each egg with 1 teaspoon caviar and garnish with a small sprig of dill. Serve immediately.

. . . .

NOTE: *As of the printing of this book, the Beluga sturgeon, source of much of the world's caviar, is critically endangered! Other sturgeon species are also endangered. All of these species live in the Caspian Sea. When you are buying caviar, please be aware that if you see a tin of caviar marked only "caviar," it is processed from the eggs of a sturgeon.*

Pickled Herring

Herring is a much beloved fish in Ukraine. No *za-kusky* spread is imaginable without at least one herring dish. Often herring dishes are served on a long oval plate accompanied by rye bread, freshly boiled potatoes, or cooked beets. Personally, I love to eat pickled herring with small squares of buttered rye or pumpernickel bread. The choice is certainly yours.

Although the common practice in Ukraine is to buy the herring whole and fillet it yourself, it is much easier to buy either "*schmaltz*" or "*matjes*" herring fillets from any reputable delicatessen. Known by the German or Swedish name, schmaltz herring are higher-fat herring that are filleted and preserved in salt brine. Schmaltz herring fillets must be soaked in water or milk to remove some of the salt before using in recipes. Another choice is the more reddish matjes fillets (the Dutch name) which are fresh, young herring that are not as salty as schmaltz fillets.

2 salt (schmaltz) herring fillets

1 cup milk

1 large onion, thinly sliced into rings

½ cup white vinegar

1 tablespoon sunflower oil

4 black peppercorns

1 bay leaf

1 teaspoon granulated sugar

Chopped fresh parsley or dill for garnishing

Soak the herring in the milk, covered, in the refrigerator for at least 3 hours.

Rinse the herring fillets with cold water (discarding the milk) and pat dry with a towel. Cut the fillets into 2-inch pieces and place in a glass dish, along with the onions.

Bring the vinegar, oil, peppercorns, bay leaf, sugar, and ½ cup of water to a boil in a small, non-reactive saucepan. Remove the pan from the heat and set aside to cool.

When the vinegar mixture is cool, pour it over the herring and onions. Cover the dish and refrigerate for at least 24 hours before serving. Serve with a sprinkling of chopped fresh parsley or dill.

··

VARIATION: *Another popular version is* **Pickled Herring with Sour Cream**. *Just prepare pickled herring as described above and after marinating for 24 hours add ½ cup of thick sour cream that has been blended with 1 tablespoon of vinegar and 1 teaspoon of granulated sugar. Make sure all of the herring is covered and refrigerate several more hours before serving. Garnish the dish if you like with some slices of hard-cooked eggs and chopped scallions just before serving. Delicious!*

Herring Roll Mops Stuffed with Pickles, Mushrooms, and Capers

Zavyvani oseledtsi, nachyneni kvashenymy obirkamy, hrybamy ta kaparamy

Makes 6 servings

Roll mops, or stuffed herring rolls, can be made with matjes herring fillets from any good delicatessen. Serve roll mops on a large platter of ornate curly greens with sprigs of fresh dill and fresh tomato wedges—do not forget plenty of crackers or rye bread on the side to complete your presentation.

1 cup red wine vinegar

6 black peppercorns

1 bay leaf

10 allspice berries

½ teaspoon yellow mustard seeds

1 tablespoon granulated sugar

1 white or yellow onion, coarsely chopped

2 pounds matjes herring fillets (do not substitute salt herring fillets)

⅓ cup prepared mustard

1 red onion, finely chopped

½ cup chopped dill pickles (page 65)

½ cup chopped marinated mushrooms (page 18)

1 tablespoon small capers, rinsed and drained

Bring the vinegar, black peppercorns, bay leaf, allspice berries, mustard seeds, sugar, white onion, and ½ cup of water to a boil in a medium, non-reactive saucepan. Remove the pan from the heat and let cool.

Rinse the herring fillets under cold water and pat dry with a towel. Spread the skinless side of each fillet with some of the prepared mustard. Put some red onion, pickles, mushrooms, and capers on each piece, then roll up and secure with a toothpick. Put the rolls in a glass jar with a tight-fitting lid and pour the marinade over top.

Cover the jar and refrigerate the roll mops for at least 5 days. If the marinade does not completely cover the rolls, turn the jar once a day.

Serve the roll mops on top of a lettuce-lined platter as part of *zakusky* hour or as a light lunch.

Vegetable Caviars

Piquant vegetable side dishes or "vegetable caviars" made from eggplants, mushrooms, or beets are eagerly enjoyed by Ukrainians. Tasty and nutritious, these "mock" caviars, as they are called, also make delicious canapé spreads. In Ukraine, they are served in colorful rustic bowls, but can be more formally scooped into hollowed-out vegetables like zucchini, yellow squash, cucumbers, or tomatoes, or spooned onto lettuce or radicchio leaves. Offer crackers, cocktail slices of rye bread, or toasted pita triangles on the side. The following versions are of utmost importance at my *zakusky* hours.

Eggplant Caviar

"Ikra" z baklazhana

Makes about 1½ cups

Savory eggplant caviar, or *"ikra"* as it is called in Ukrainian, is very popular in the southern region of the country where eggplant grows in abundance.

Preheat the oven to 400°F. Pierce the eggplant in several places with a knife and place on a baking sheet. Bake until very soft, turning it midway through, about 45 minutes. Set aside and let cool.

When cool enough to handle, cut the eggplant in half lengthwise, scoop out all the pulp and finely chop. Put the eggplant pulp in a medium bowl along with the onion, garlic, oil, vinegar, salt, and black pepper. Mix thoroughly.

Cover and refrigerate for at least 2 hours or longer. Scoop the "caviar" into a decorative decanter and serve sprinkle with some toasted sunflower seeds and parsley.

1 large (about 1½-pound) eggplant

1 onion, finely chopped

2 cloves garlic, crushed

¼ cup sunflower oil

2 tablespoons red wine vinegar

½ teaspoon salt

¼ teaspoon freshly ground black pepper

Toasted sunflower seeds and parsley sprigs for garnishing (optional)

Champignon Caviar

Ukrainians are mushroom fanatics! "Champignon" refers to any edible mushroom. I use portabella mushrooms for this recipe, but feel free to experiment with fresh wild mushrooms for a more traditional flavor.

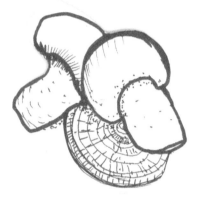

¼ cup (generous) sunflower oil

2 pounds fresh portabella mushrooms, coarsely chopped

1 onion, coarsely chopped

1 clove garlic, coarsely chopped

2 tablespoons mayonnaise

1 tablespoon white vinegar or fresh lemon juice to taste

½ teaspoon salt

½ teaspoon freshly ground black pepper

Parsley sprigs to garnish

Heat half the oil in a large skillet over medium heat. Add the mushrooms and keep stirring until the mushrooms start to give off their own juices. Turn up the heat to medium-high and continue cooking until most of the liquid is evaporated, about 8 to 10 minutes. Remove the mushrooms to a plate to cool.

Using the same skillet over medium heat, add the remaining oil and the onions and garlic, adding a little more oil if necessary. Cook the mixture just until the onions are golden, but not browned. Put the onion mixture in a food processor, along with the mushrooms, and pulse until finely chopped but not pureed.

Put the mixture into a medium bowl and add the mayonnaise, vinegar, salt, and black pepper. Mix well, cover, and refrigerate for at least 1 hour to let the flavors marry and settle. Taste and adjust the seasonings if necessary just before serving. Scoop the "caviar" into a decorative bowl and garnish with sprigs of fresh parsley.

Beet Caviar

"Ikra" z buriakiv

Makes about 2 cups

Savory beet caviars are served in nearly every household, especially in western Ukraine. Ever the cook, I could not help experimenting with the traditional recipe. In my beet caviar, there is a delicate balance between the tartness of the lemon and the sweetness of the raisins, followed by a little jolt from the horseradish. Served warm or at room temperature, this caviar is particularly good with meats.

2 large whole red beets (skins and tap root intact)

¼ cup fresh lemon juice or more to taste

¼ cup seedless raisins

1 clove garlic

1 tablespoon freshly grated horseradish

2 tablespoons mayonnaise

½ teaspoon salt

¼ teaspoon freshly ground black pepper

Preheat the oven to 375°F. Wrap the beets in aluminum foil and bake until tender, about 1½ hours. Remove from oven and allow to cool.

Meanwhile, bring the lemon juice almost to a boil in a small saucepan. Put the raisins in a small bowl and pour the hot lemon juice over top. Let the raisins soak for 20 minutes, then remove, reserving the liquid. Finely chop the raisins and set aside.

When cool enough to handle, peel and chop the beets. Put them in a food processor along with the garlic and pulse until the mixture is finely chopped but not pureed. Transfer the beet mixture to a decorative bowl, add the raisins and lemon juice and grate about 1 tablespoon of horseradish over the bowl. Toss the mixture with the mayonnaise and season with salt and black pepper. Taste and add more lemon juice if desired. Serve.

Cooking Oils

In the earliest of times hemp oil, linseed oil, and olive oil were most often used for culinary purposes. Sunflower oil appeared in Ukraine during the eighteenth century, replacing more costly olive oil (olives only growing along the Black Sea coast). Nowadays, sunflower oil has supplanted nearly all other oils. There are two types of sunflower oil used throughout the country: a hot type that has the smell of fried sunflower seeds preferred with salads, and a cold-pressed type used for frying and most other culinary needs.

Jellied Pig's Feet

Drahli

Drahli, *kholodets*, or *studynets* all refer to any sort of meat (or fish) in aspic and are held in high esteem in Ukrainian cookery. Historically, aspic-covered dishes were seen as specialties of the aristocracy. What we have here with *drahli* is the peasants' attempt to emulate that technique but using a more frugal approach—that is using every part of the beloved farm animal for consumption. I am happy to say that many modern chefs and home cooks alike have a renewed interest in this practice, calling it nose-to-tail eating.

Lucky for us much of the uncertainty has been removed in preparing aspics today by the use of unflavored gelatin. Bones and knuckles, and plenty of them, were once needed to produce the congealing quality, but now if you prefer firmer aspic, just use some gelatin in its preparation.

As a young girl, I remember helping my grandmother cook pig's feet. I grew up on a farm and I never felt any sort of aversion to them as so many people do who were not raised with them. *Drahli* is a very old-time dish and a true favorite of mine. We ate this dish often with plenty of vinegar drizzled over top, hunks of bread, a small bowl of sweet pickles, and fresh radishes. Delicious!

- 3 pig's feet, split
- 2 pounds pork neck bones
- 1 pork shank
- 5 teaspoons salt
- 2 onions, quartered
- 2 carrots, peeled and cut into thick rounds
- 3 cloves garlic
- 2 bay leaves
- 10 black peppercorns
- 5 allspice berries
- 2 tablespoons vinegar
- 1 tablespoon unflavored gelatin (optional)
- Vinegar or fresh lemon juice to serve

Place the pig's feet, neck bones, pork shank, and 4½ teaspoons of salt in a large pot and cover with cold water. Bring the mixture to a boil over high heat, skim off all the foam and discard. Add the onions, carrots, garlic, bay leaves, black peppercorns, and allspice berries. Cover, reduce the heat to low and simmer for 3 hours or until the meat is very tender. Check the pot periodically and add more boiling water if the level gets low, making sure all the meat is covered.

When the meat is ready to fall off the bones, remove with a slotted spoon and let cool. Strain the broth, discarding all solids except the carrots. Scrape all the meat off the bones. Arrange the carrots slices in the bottom of a large oblong dish and scatter the meat over top.

Add the 2 tablespoons vinegar to 1 cup of hot broth and stir in the remaining ½ teaspoon salt. Stir in the gelatin to dissolve and pour over the carrots and meat. Pour enough of the remaining broth over top to cover the meat by at least one inch. Taste and adjust the seasonings if necessary. Cover the dish with plastic wrap and refrigerate at least overnight or until set and the flavors marry.

Before serving, scrape off any fat from the top and invert onto a lettuce-lined platter (optional), slice and serve vinegar or lemon juice on the side to accompany.

Duck in Aspic

Kholodets' z kachky

Duck meat is immensely popular in Ukraine and fresh free-range birds are highly prized. I like to make this aspic, studded with parsnips just kissed by the first frost, in the fall. The sweet, nutty taste of parsnips, along with the lovely anise flavor of fresh fennel nicely compliments the richness of the duck meat. Prepare this dish in advance, two or three days before planning to serve it is best. This way all the flavors marry and you will have better tasting aspic.

2 pounds smoked pork bones or smoked ham bones

1 (4-to-5-pound) duck, quartered, leaving the breast whole

5 teaspoons salt

2 onions, quartered

4 parsnips, peeled and cut into thick rounds

2 ribs celery with leaves

6 black peppercorns

1 bay leaf

2 cups dry white wine

Juice and grated zest of 1 lemon

1 tablespoon unflavored gelatin

2 tablespoons finely chopped fennel fronds

6 finely chopped scallions, including green tops

Roast the pork bones in a 350°F oven for 1 hour.

Place the roasted bones, duck, and 4½ teaspoons salt in a large pot and add enough cold water to cover. Bring to barely a boil over high heat, skimming off and discarding all foam. Add the onions, parsnips, celery, black peppercorns, and bay leaf. Cover, reduce the heat to low and simmer for 2 hours or until the duck meat is falling off the bones.

Remove the duck with a slotted spoon and let cool. Strain the rest of the broth and discard all solids except the parsnips. When cool enough to handle, clean the duck meat off the bones. Dice the breast meat and put all the meat, along with the parsnips in a large bowl.

Pour 2 cups of broth into a measuring cup and allow to cool; then pour off any fat that has risen to the top and put the broth into a large saucepan. Add the wine, lemon juice, lemon zest, and the remaining ½ teaspoon salt. Bring the mixture to a boil and stir in the gelatin, mixing well. Taste and adjust the seasonings if necessary. Remove the pot from the stove and let the mixture cool slightly.

Pour the broth mixture over the duck and parsnips and add the fennel and scallions and gently stir to combine. Cover the bowl with plastic wrap and refrigerate for at least 24 hours or longer.

Before serving, scrape off any fat from the top and invert onto a platter lined with greens. Offer individual plates and plenty of vinegar, pickles, and an assortment of fresh vegetables, such as thinly sliced fennel or young turnips, radishes, or carrot sticks, on the side for each guest to choose from at their discretion.

Garden Vegetables in Lemon Aspic

Horodyna v tsytrynovim kholodtsiu   Makes 6 to 8 servings

Glistening vegetable aspics are very popular in Ukraine and slices can be served on cutout pastry or in baked puff pastry shells (making sure the pastry is completely cooled or it will melt the aspic). Use the freshest vegetables you can find and mix and match as you please. For a dramatic presentation, unmold the aspic onto a chard-lined platter surrounded by Garnished Eggs (page 3) and a variety of small blocks of cheese. If you want to add meats, serve cold cuts on the side, along with some Tartar Sauce (page 13).

3 tablespoons unflavored gelatin

1 tablespoon granulated sugar

1 teaspoon salt

2½ cups very hot water

3 tablespoons white vinegar

Grated zest and juice of 1 lemon

1 small yellow bell pepper, cut into julienne strips

1 small green bell pepper, cut into julienne strips

2 scallions, chopped (including the greens)

5 small red radishes, thinly sliced

¼ cup grated carrot

½ cup finely shredded tender green cabbage

½ cup shredded spinach

½ cup fresh parsley, finely chopped

Put the gelatin, sugar, and salt in a medium bowl. Add the hot water and stir to dissolve the ingredients. Mix in the vinegar, grated zest, and lemon juice.

Pour about ½ cup of the gelatin mixture into an oiled 8½-inch x 4½-inch x 3-inch loaf pan and let set for about 10 to 15 minutes. (Keep the rest of the gelatin mixture lukewarm so it doesn't set.) On the gelatin layer arrange an interesting pattern with a few strips of yellow and green pepper, scallions, radish slices, and grated carrot. Spoon a little more of the gelatin mixture over top of the vegetables to "anchor" them and let set either at room temperature if not too warm or in the refrigerator, about 10 to 15 minutes.

Put the rest of the bell pepper strips, scallions, radishes, and carrot, as well as the cabbage, spinach, and parsley in the remaining gelatin mixture and stir to combine. Spoon it over the set mixture in the loaf pan and lightly press down with the back of the spoon to smooth it out evenly. Put the loaf in the refrigerator and chill several hours or overnight, so the flavors marry and the gelatin sets. Unmold onto a serving platter and serve.

Losos' v kholodtsiu

Makes 8 servings

A whole fish with a glistening aspic coating makes an impressive centerpiece on a *zakusky* table any time of year, but this dish in particular is a favorite choice for those Ukrainians who observe Lent. Fish in aspic is also often part of the very holy Christmas Eve supper known as "*Svyata Vechera*" in which several meatless courses are offered. There is always a great demand for fish at this time of year, so feel free to substitute whole trout or pike if salmon is not available. Sometimes I dress several smaller trout in this way and lay them side-by-side on a lettuce-lined platter garnished with hollowed out vegetables filled with various salads and topped with a dab of caviar for a very dramatic presentation.

I have also included two recipes that I feel are a great accompaniment to this dish: *Traditional Tartar Sauce* and *Mayonnaise Relish*. Both have held a prominent place in Ukrainian kitchens for hundreds of years.

1 (5-pound) whole salmon, fins removed, but head and tail intact

Salt and freshly ground black pepper to taste

2 tablespoons sunflower oil

2 bay leaves

6 black peppercorns

1 lemon, thinly sliced

2 cups dry white wine or water

1 to 2 tablespoons unflavored gelatin

2 medium cucumbers, very thinly sliced

Lemon wedges and sprigs of dill to garnish

Season the inside of the fish with salt and black pepper. Brush the entire fish generously with oil to protect it from heat while poaching. Put the fish on a large, double piece of cheesecloth and lay it in a large covered pot or poaching tin with the cheesecloth slightly overlapping the sides. Add the bay leaves, black peppercorns, and lemon slices. Pour the wine into the pan, adding cold water if needed to cover the entire fish. Cover (use an oiled piece of aluminum foil if your pan does not have a lid) and bring the liquid to a boil. Reduce the heat to low and gently simmer for 10 minutes. Turn off the heat and let the fish cool in the pan with the lid on. When cooled, remove the lid and gently lift the fish out of the pan and place on a kitchen board or any flat surface (reserving the poaching liquid). Gently peel off the skin, leaving the head and tail intact. Discard the fish skin. Gently place the fish on a platter.

Strain the poaching liquid and bring 1 cup to a boil in a small saucepan. Stir in the gelatin and mix well. Let the gelatin cool slightly, and then brush over the <u>entire</u> fish. Arrange the cucumber slices over the fish's body, slightly overlapping (do not put any cucumber slices over the head or tail of the fish), and then brush gelatin over the top of the <u>entire</u> fish again. (If you need more gelatin mixture, heat another cup of poaching liquid and dissolve another tablespoon of gelatin in it to finish glazing the fish.)

Chill the fish in the refrigerator for several hours or until the gelatin is set. Serve garnished with plenty of lemon wedges, sprigs of fresh dill, and tartar sauce or mayonnaise relish.

Traditional Tartar Sauce

Tradytsiyna tatars'ka pryprava

Makes about ⅔ cup

The proportions and ingredients may vary slightly in recipes for this ever popular condiment. Some cooks add finely chopped hard-cooked egg yolks to their tartar sauce and some add a bit of horseradish. This is my version. This sauce can be served as an accompaniment to Whole Salmon in Aspic (page 12) and also with roasted and smoked meats (not just fish), cooked vegetables, and salads.

Put the egg yolks in a small bowl and mash with a fork. Add the remaining ingredients and mix well. Pour the sauce into a covered container and keep refrigerated until ready to use. This mixture keeps for about 3 days.

6 hard-cooked egg yolks

½ teaspoon dry mustard

2 tablespoons sunflower or olive oil

½ teaspoon salt

¼ teaspoon freshly ground black pepper

½ teaspoon honey

2 tablespoons apple cider vinegar

2 teaspoons finely chopped onion

2 teaspoons finely chopped dill pickle

2 teaspoons finely chopped green bell pepper

Mayonnaise Relish

Pryprava z mayonezu

Makes about 1¼ cups

I think my version of this popular condiment is especially good over lightly steamed or boiled vegetables like green beans, cauliflower, or broccoli. It is also a delicious spread for canapés and makes a delicious accompaniment to Whole Salmon in Aspic (page 12).

Put the eggs in a small bowl along with the rest of the ingredients except the horseradish and mix well. Pour the relish into a glass container and stir in freshly grated horseradish to taste. Cover and keep refrigerated until ready to use. This mixture keeps for about 3 days.

3 hard-cooked extra-large eggs, finely chopped

½ teaspoon dry mustard

½ teaspoon salt

2 tablespoons sunflower or olive oil

3 tablespoons fresh lemon juice

¼ cup sour cream

1 tablespoon finely chopped red bell pepper

1 tablespoon finely chopped green bell pepper

1 tablespoon finely chopped green olives

1 tablespoon finely chopped dill pickle

Freshly grated horseradish to taste

Ukrainian Party Etiquette

What is important to remember as a guest invited into a Ukrainian home for a dinner party is that there is an unspoken protocol of hospitality that exists in Ukrainian culture. There are age-old traditions that endure as to introductions, toasts, and even the consumption of food. Any breach will be considered rude and disrespectful.

For instance, upon arrival do not shake hands across the threshold. Step inside the doorway, remove gloves if wearing, and follow your host's lead when it comes to a handshake—handshakes are not obligatory in Ukrainian culture and your host may simply nod his head. If this is the case, let that be enough for you, too. A good friend may give you a hug. As for the hostess, do not kiss her unless she is a close friend, and then let it be a triple cheek kiss upon arrival and departure. *Khrystosuvannia* or the triple kiss is actually an Easter tradition, but considered an acceptable greeting anytime. Bring a bottle of something other than Ukrainian libations for the host and lots of candy for any children—they will expect it. Be prepared to remove your shoes as Ukrainians like to wear slippers in the house, and do not be surprised if you are offered a pair to wear, especially in the wintertime.

Since a Ukrainian dinner party is always a "sit-down" affair, at this time, all will go to a table set with a wonderful array of appetizers or *zakusky*. As a guest you will be expected to eat … and eat … and eat. Overfeeding guests is a national tradition! Keep in mind refusing food is seen as insulting and graceless. There will likely be several courses and a series of toasts throughout the meal. Ukrainians see drinking as an integral part of socializing, so if you do not imbibe for any reason or you do not want to get drunk, use the state of your health as an excuse. This way no one will be offended and everyone will understand. The mood will be light and relaxing and inevitably there will be singing, so just do your best to join in!

By the end of dessert and after coffee, guests will be expected to make a toast to the host, their friendship, and the skills of the hostess. The final toast at the end of the evening may well be "*Na Konya!*", which translates as "On to the horse!". It is likely this toast comes from the times when mighty Kozak warriors had one last drink before galloping away.

It certainly will be an evening to remember, and the day after, while one may feel a card or thank-you note appropriate, do not follow through, for Ukrainians consider friends part of the family and such a gesture would seem too stiff and formal.

Ukrainian Cod Fish with Tomato Sauce

Triska v pomidorovomu sosi

Ukrainians love tomato sauces with a little tang and this traditional fish dish is no exception. Flavored with allspice, cloves, and capers, the tomato sauce is also slightly sweet. This is a fish dish served chilled as part of *zakusky* hour, but do not let this stop you from serving it hot as a main course with fluffy buttered rice and perhaps a green vegetable.

2 pounds cod fillets, cut into equal-size portions

¼ cup sunflower or olive oil

Juice of 1 lemon plus 2 additional tablespoons

½ teaspoon salt

3 tablespoons unsalted butter

4 leeks (white parts only), finely chopped

1 clove garlic, sliced

½ cup tomato paste

2 cups fish stock

Bouquet garni (1 bay leaf, 6 black peppercorns, 6 allspice berries, 4 cloves tied in a piece of cheesecloth to make a pouch)

1 tablespoon capers, rinsed and drained

1 tablespoon honey or more to taste

Chopped fresh parsley to garnish

Preheat the oven broiler. Rub the pieces of cod on both sides with oil, juice of 1 lemon, and salt. Broil the fish approximately 3 minutes on each side until flaky, basting with pan juices. Remove the fish to a serving dish and set aside.

Melt the butter in a medium skillet over medium heat and add the leeks. Gently sauté the leeks until soft, about 5 minutes. Add the garlic and tomato paste and continue cooking another 5 minutes or just until the tomato sauce starts to brown, adding a little more butter if necessary. Increase the heat to high, add the fish stock and bouquet garni and bring to a gentle boil. Cover and reduce the heat to medium-low and simmer the sauce for 20 minutes.

Remove the bouquet garni and discard. Add the remaining two tablespoons lemon juice, capers, and honey. Continue cooking another 2 minutes. Taste and adjust the seasonings, adding more honey if necessary. Pour the sauce over the fish, cool, and then refrigerate a few hours before serving garnished with chopped fresh parsley.

NOTE: *Haddock fillets also work well in this dish.*

Country Pate

Pashtet

A *pashtet* is a meatloaf similar to a country pate. Combinations usually consist of two or three meats, vegetables, and spices mixed together, baked, and served cold with an assortment of mustards and perhaps warm crusty bread. Every Ukrainian family has its own version of this dish.

This is a delicate *pashtet* which uses strips of bacon, a boneless, skinless chicken breast, ground veal, and young leeks, yielding a fresh and light result. The smokier the bacon the better! Beer goes nicely with this dish if you serve it for lunch, or perhaps take my lead and opt for some fresh apple cider—a choice not unheard of in many Ukrainian homes.

Preheat the oven to 325°F. Stretch the bacon in overlapping slices over the bottom and up the sides of a 2-pound loaf pan. Cut the chicken breast into 2-inch long strips, sprinkle with lemon juice and set aside.

Put the ground veal in a large bowl and gently mix in the leeks, carrot, parsnip, and celery. Add the eggs, garlic, thyme, allspice, salt, black pepper, and parsley and gently mix again until well blended.

Spoon half the veal mixture into the loaf pan and level the surface. Arrange the chicken slices on top, then spoon in the rest of the veal mixture. Gently press down on the mixture and smooth the top. Sharply tap the pan a few times to release any pockets of air. Cover the pan with a sheet of buttered aluminum foil and place in a roasting pan. Pour hot water into the roasting pan halfway up the sides of the loaf pan. Bake 1 hour or until the loaf is firm.

Allow the loaf to cool completely in the pan before turning it out. Chill for several hours. Serve sliced alongside radishes, halved tomatoes, and plenty of lemon wedges to squeeze over top.

8 ounces smoked bacon slices

1 whole boneless, skinless chicken breast (about 8 ounces)

2 tablespoons fresh lemon juice

8 ounces ground veal

3 young leeks including some of the greens, trimmed and finely chopped

1 small carrot, peeled and finely chopped

1 small parsnip, peeled and finely chopped

1 small rib celery (preferably with some leaves), finely chopped

2 extra-large eggs, beaten

1 clove garlic, crushed to a paste

1 teaspoon ground thyme

1 teaspoon ground allspice

1 teaspoon salt

½ teaspoon freshly ground black pepper

2 tablespoons chopped fresh parsley

Whole radishes, halved tomatoes, and lemon wedges for garnish (optional)

16   Chapter 1 Appetizers

And then there are mushrooms ...

In Ukraine, mushroom picking is a popular national pastime. August is mushroom-picking time and is something everyone looks forward to because it means plenty of fresh mushrooms then and plenty of dried mushrooms for use all winter long. Most kinds of boletus, those with the brownish caps and sponge-like texture under the caps, are the preferred pick. They are superb cooked fresh, but also dry very well. But if you decide to try picking them yourself, beware, some types of wild mushrooms can make you very sick or even cost you your life! Precautions are necessary and if you have never picked wild mushrooms, find someone reliable who has, since the adventure can be dangerous.

Do not despair, if picking is not for you or you don't have access to their growing areas, there are many varieties of wild and domestic mushrooms available fresh and dried at any good market, including porcini, chanterelles, portabella, shiitake, and the common champignon, or as they are more commonly called, white button mushrooms. Domestic mushrooms can be substituted for wild mushrooms in any of the recipes in this book, however, if you do have a chance to try wild mushrooms do so, for they impart an earthy, lusty flavor to dishes.

Marinated Mushrooms

Marynovani hryby

Marinated or pickled mushrooms are eaten anytime in Ukraine, but they are of particular importance during the *zakusky* hour, especially when served with small pieces of buttered rye bread and shots of vodka! My marinated mushrooms can be eaten after marinating for just a few hours, but their flavor will improve still more if you wait a few days. They will keep in your refrigerator for up to a month.

2 pounds small champignon (button) or cremini mushrooms

2 tablespoons fresh lemon juice

1 teaspoon salt

⅔ cup white wine vinegar

6 black peppercorns

2 bay leaves (preferably fresh)

½ teaspoon granulated sugar

12 small stalks fresh tarragon leaves

Put the mushrooms in a large bowl, sprinkle with lemon juice, and let stand for 10 minutes.

Put the mushrooms in a medium non-reactive saucepan and add ¾ cup water. Bring to a boil and add the salt, stirring to completely dissolve. Reduce the heat to medium-low and gently cook the mushrooms for 10 minutes. Remove them with a slotted spoon, rinse under cold water, and set aside.

Strain the mushroom cooking liquid and rinse out the saucepan. Return the liquid to the rinsed out saucepan. Add the vinegar, black peppercorns, bay leaves, and sugar. Bring the mixture to a boil, reduce the heat to medium-low and simmer uncovered for 5 minutes. Let the mixture cool to room temperature.

Pack the mushrooms into a quart jar, putting tarragon stalks in between layers. Add the cooled marinade. Cover the jar with a vinegar-proof (non-reactive) lid and refrigerate. The mushrooms are ready to eat in 6 hours but ideally they should marinate at least 3 days or longer.

Mushroom Patties

Sichenyky z hryby

Crispy "patties," or *sichenyky* as they are called in Ukrainian, are a favorite standby in Ukrainian homes. Made from meat, poultry, fish, hard-cooked eggs, fruits, or vegetables, these croquette-type of appetizers are really worth the effort and you will surely not be disappointed. This dish is a good choice for your *zakusky* table since a few warm dishes do tend to make an appearance there. However, it can also be served as an entrée.

2 thick slices stale white bread, crusts removed

¼ cup milk

4 tablespoons bacon drippings or sunflower oil

1 onion, finely chopped

2 cloves garlic, crushed

2 pounds fresh mushrooms, chopped

1 extra-large egg, slightly beaten

1 tablespoon mayonnaise

½ teaspoon salt

½ teaspoon freshly ground black pepper

1 tablespoon finely chopped fresh dill

½ cup fine dry breadcrumbs

Lemon wedges for garnishing (optional)

Tear the bread into pieces and put in a small bowl with the milk. Let soak for 5 minutes, and then squeeze the bread to remove any excess liquid. Discard milk.

In a large skillet over medium heat, melt 2 tablespoons of the bacon drippings, add the onion and garlic and gently sauté until the mixture is golden, about 5 minutes. Add the mushrooms and continue cooking until the mushrooms start giving off their own liquid, then turn up the heat to high and continue cooking until the mushrooms are golden and the mixture is dry. Spoon the mushroom mixture into a large bowl and let cool slightly.

Add the soaked pieces of bread, egg, mayonnaise, salt, black pepper, and dill to the mushroom mixture. Mix thoroughly and shape into 8 patties.

In the same skillet over medium heat, melt the remaining 2 tablespoons bacon drippings. Dip the patties into the dry breadcrumbs, carefully coating both sides, and fry in the drippings until crisp and golden, about 3 to 4 minutes on each side. Drain the patties on paper towels and serve warm garnished with lemon wedges.

The Complexity of Crimean Tatar Cuisine and its Place in Ukrainian Culture

Crimean Tatars are the indigenous people of Crimea. They possess a diverse background with their ethnic core coming from Europe, Turkey, and Mongolia. Historically, this makes Crimean Tatar cuisine rich and intriguing due to contact with Greek, Italian, Turkish, Russian, and Ukrainian cuisines. Over the decades, this culture was subjected to crimes and atrocities and eventually deported from Crimea to Central Asia by the Stalinist regime in 1944. As of the printing of this book, the rights of the Crimean Tatar people are being restored within the Crimean Autonomous Republic (Ukraine) and since their resettlement back into Crimea, the restoration and preservation of their culture and cuisine has been a top priority.

Ukraine is a large country and it is evident that its cuisine is wedded heart and soul to the land and all that has happened there through the ages. Many Tatar specialties, whether by ingredients or in preparation methods, are today considered essential elements of Ukrainian cuisine as a whole, and for this reason they are included in this book. Some second and third generation Ukrainians here in the United States may not even be familiar with some of these dishes. So it is my hope that for many readers this will be a new and wonderful experience.

Crimean Tatar specialties include: flaky-crusted pies filled with meat, potato, pumpkin, rice, cheese, or nuts; meat dumplings; boiled noodles with beans; and small scones made from yeast dough served plain. Yogurt and cottage cheese are staples and saffron, olives, cilantro, onion chives, and ever-present sour cream are used to flavor many dishes. Persimmons, melons of all kinds, figs, and grapes are made into syrups and thick jams along with apples, pears, plums, cherries, and mulberries. Nuts, especially walnuts which are available all year long in Crimea, are used extensively in baking or as a filling for pies and sweet dishes.

Even sub-ethnically, there are regional differences and subtle differences within Crimean Tatar cuisine depending on whether settlements are along the coastlines or in the steppes. For example, those Tatars who are living in the foothills and mountains eat more meat, especially mutton and beef, and milk and milk products, as compared to those living along the coastlines who eat mostly fish, fruits, and vegetables.

Crimean Tatar Biber Dolmas

Biber dolma po kryms'ko-tatars'ky

Small stuffed peppers are a favorite Ukrainian appetizer and there are many versions. I am including one popular in Southern Ukraine, primarily in Crimea. Tatar people call this dish "*dolma*" when small bell peppers are stuffed with meat and spices and stewed in a mixture of tomato and broth. It is a nutritious dish. Traditionally, this dish is served hot, but room temperature is also acceptable.

3 tablespoons white rice

1 small onion, finely chopped

1 carrot, peeled and finely chopped

1 tablespoon finely chopped fresh parsley

1 tablespoon finely chopped fresh dill

8 ounces ground beef chuck, or any "fattier" meat

½ teaspoon salt

½ teaspoon freshly ground black pepper

8 small red, green, or yellow bell peppers or sheep's nose sweet peppers, stems and seeds removed

2 tablespoons unsalted butter

¼ cup tomato paste

2 cups boiling meat broth or water

Sour cream to serve

Put the rice, onion, carrot, parsley, dill, ground beef, salt, and black pepper in a medium bowl and mix well. Fill each pepper as compactly as possible with some of the mixture and set aside.

In a medium casserole dish, melt the butter over medium heat and add the tomato paste. Cook the paste for 2 minutes, stirring well to blend with the butter. Stand the stuffed peppers in the dish in a single layer and pour in the boiling meat broth to almost come to the tops of the peppers.

Cover the dish, reduce the heat to low, and gently simmer for about 30 minutes or until the peppers are tender and the rice and meat are cooked.

Remove the peppers with a slotted spoon and serve in a shallow decorative bowl with a little of the broth and garnished with a generous dollop of sour cream.

Crimean Fish Cakes

Kryms'ki sichenyky z ryby

Makes 4 servings

Here is an example of seafood served in Crimea. These fish cakes feature finely chopped skate and shrimp. I have paired them with a great yogurt sauce.

1 (8-ounce) skate fillet

Salt and freshly ground black pepper to taste

3 tablespoons unsalted butter or sunflower oil

2 scallions including green tops, finely chopped

1/3 cup fine dry breadcrumbs

2 tablespoons milk

8 ounces fresh small shrimp, shelled and finely chopped

2 extra-large egg yolks

1 to 2 tablespoons sour cream

Season the skate fillet on both sides with salt and black pepper. Melt 1 tablespoon butter in a medium skillet over medium heat, and gently sauté the skate until golden brown, about 2 minutes on each side. Remove the skate from the pan, let cool, shred, and reserve.

Sauté the scallions in the same skillet over medium heat until soft, about 5 minutes; let cool and reserve.

Put the breadcrumbs in a medium bowl, add the milk and let stand for 5 minutes. Add the shredded skate, scallions, shrimp, egg yolks, and sour cream. Mix very gently with a fork, cover, and refrigerate for 1 hour.

Preheat the oven to 350°F. Shape the skate mixture into 8 patties. Melt the remaining 2 tablespoons butter in a large skillet over medium heat and fry each fish cake until golden brown, about 2 minutes on each side. Transfer the fish cakes to a lightly greased baking sheet, cover lightly with aluminum foil and bake for 12 to 15 minutes. Serve immediately with *Crimean Yogurt Sauce* (recipe next page).

Crimean Yogurt Sauce

Kryms'ka pidlyva z yogurtu

Makes about 2 cups

This sauce has definite Turkish and Mediterranean roots. Besides being a great accompaniment to seafood, this sauce is excellent poured over a medley of steamed or grilled vegetables or makes a lovely dip for fresh vegetables as part of a *zakusky* spread.

1 cup very thick (Greek) plain yogurt

¼ cup ground walnuts

2 cloves garlic, smashed with ½ teaspoon salt

1 cup stale Turkish bread pieces (see Note), crusts removed and torn into very small pieces

2 tablespoons olive oil

1 tablespoon (or more to taste) finely chopped fresh cilantro

Put all the ingredients into a small bowl and mix well. Let stand for 15 minutes for all the flavors to come together and stir before serving.

Keep any extra in a covered container in your refrigerator where it will keep for up to 1 week.

VARIATION: *Sometimes this sauce is made with half yogurt and half sour cream.*

NOTE: *If you do not have access to a Turkish market that sells fresh bread, any type of white sourdough bread may be used instead.*

Pastry Doughs

Dough and pastries are an integral part of Ukrainian cuisine and for this reason I have included two recipes for yeast dough: *Basic Yeast Dough* and *Quick Yeast Dough* and one recipe for *Sour Cream Pastry Dough* (page 27) early on in this book, for all three recipes are called for again and again throughout.

Both *pyrizhky* and *pyrih* are popular Ukrainian pastries with a filling, served warm, often as part of *zakusky* hour. Made from either yeast-raised dough or on special occasions a short crust or puff pastry and stuffed with a savory filling, *pyrizhky* and *pyrih* (often just a larger version of *pyrizhky*) are also served as a side dish to many Ukrainian soups, especially the beet soup called *borshch*.

The traditional shape of these pastries is small and oblong, about the size of a small egg, with tapering ends. The fillings are innumerable and include: cabbage, sauerkraut, dried peas, cottage cheese, buttery onions, dilled rice, hard-cooked eggs, scallions, ground meat or buckwheat, or bits of bacon and onion. *Pyrizhky* can also be stuffed with a sweet filling.

The first recipe is for traditional yeast dough. I am also including a recipe for yeast dough that can be ready to use in 15 minutes. Both recipes are easy to make and I urge readers to try both ways.

NOTE: Both dough recipes make enough for about 3 dozen filled *pyrizhky* or 1 large *pyrih*.

Basic Yeast Dough

1 cup warm milk (about 110°F)
2½ teaspoons active dry yeast
1 tablespoon granulated sugar
2 extra-large eggs, well beaten
4 tablespoons unsalted butter, melted
1 teaspoon salt
4½ cups unbleached all-purpose flour

Pour the warm milk into a small bowl and add the yeast. Stir in the sugar, mix well and let sit until frothy, about 10 minutes.

Put the eggs, melted butter, and salt in a large bowl and mix well. Stir in the yeast mixture. Add the flour 1 cup at a time, stirring well after each addition. Turn out the dough onto a lightly floured board or counter and knead the dough for about 10 minutes; or use a dough hook on an electric mixer for about 5 minutes, until smooth and elastic.

Lightly coat another bowl with some butter or oil and put the dough in it, turning it over to coat evenly. Cover the bowl with a kitchen towel and put in a warm, draft-free place until the dough is doubled in volume, about 1½ hours.

After rising, punch the dough down in the bowl and turn it out onto a lightly floured board or counter and knead for about 30 seconds. The dough is now ready to use in any recipe.

Quick Yeast Dough

⅔ cup scalded milk
2½ teaspoons active dry yeast
2 teaspoons granulated sugar
16 tablespoons (2 sticks) unsalted butter, melted and cooled to lukewarm
2 extra-large egg yolks, slightly beaten
1 teaspoon salt
4½ cups unbleached all-purpose flour

Pour the warm milk into a large bowl and stir in the yeast and sugar. Let the mixture stand until foamy, about 10 minutes.

Add the butter, egg yolks, and salt and mix well. Stir in the flour, 1 cup at a time, stirring well after each addition, adding just enough flour to make a soft, loose dough.

Transfer the dough to a lightly floured board or counter and knead gently until the dough is soft and satiny, about 4 to 5 minutes. Shape the dough into a ball, cover with a cotton kitchen towel and let stand in a warm, draft-free place for 15 minutes. The dough is now ready to use in any recipe.

Pyrizhky with Cabbage

Pyrizhky z kapustoyu

Make the filling:

Bring 8 cups of salted water to a boil. Add the cabbage and cook for 10 minutes. Drain the cabbage well, squeezing it to remove any excess moisture.

Melt the butter in a large skillet over medium heat. Just as the butter starts to brown, add the cabbage and cook until very soft, about 25 minutes, adding more butter if necessary. Transfer the cabbage to a large bowl and add the chopped eggs, dill, and parsley and mix well. Season the cabbage to taste with salt and black pepper and let filling cool to room temperature before using.

Assemble pyrizhky:

Preheat the oven to 350°F and grease two large baking sheets.

Divide the dough into two pieces and cover the half you are not using with a kitchen towel (if using quick yeast dough, refrigerate the dough you are not using). On a lightly floured board or counter, cut off a small, egg-size piece of dough and flatten to 1/3-inch thickness. Put a teaspoon of filling in the center, bring the edges together and seal securely, making sure all the edges are free from filling. Shape the pyrizhky into an oblong with tapering ends and place seam-side down on the baking sheet. Continue assembling pyrizhky until all the dough and filling are used. If all do not fit on the baking sheets, bake in batches, keeping the unbaked ones covered (or refrigerated if using quick yeast dough). Brush the pyrizhky with egg wash and bake for 30 minutes or until golden brown. Serve warm.

1 recipe Basic Yeast Dough (page 24) or Quick Yeast Dough (page 25)

Egg wash: 1 beaten egg mixed with 1 teaspoon milk

FILLING:

1 (3-pound) head of cabbage, finely chopped

3 tablespoons (generous) unsalted butter or oil

2 hard-cooked extra-large eggs, finely chopped

1 tablespoon finely chopped fresh dill

1 tablespoon finely chopped fresh parsley

Salt and freshly ground black pepper to taste

Sweet Pyrizhky with Cranberries

Solodki pyrizhky iz zhuravlynoyu   Makes about 2 dozen

Sweet pastries are also part of *zakusky* hour. The addition of sour cream gives this short pastry dough a creamier texture and a distinctive flavor. This sour cream pastry dough (minus the sugar) can also be used with any other savory pastry or tart. But I usually use this pastry when cranberries are in season and I want to serve sweet *pyrizhky*.

SOUR CREAM PASTRY DOUGH:

3 cups unbleached all-purpose flour

½ teaspoon salt

2 tablespoons granulated sugar (omit if making savory pastry)

¾ teaspoon baking powder

14 tablespoons chilled unsalted butter, cut into small pieces

2 extra-large egg yolks, lightly beaten

⅔ cup thick sour cream

FILLING:

3 cups fresh cranberries, coarsely chopped

1 tablespoon unbleached all-purpose flour

1 cup loosely packed brown sugar or more to taste

Sweetened sour cream or honey to serve (optional)

Make dough:

In a large bowl, combine the flour, salt, sugar, and baking powder. Cut the chilled butter into the flour mixture using a pastry blender or by quickly using your fingertips. Combine only till the mixture resembles coarse crumbs. Mix the egg yolks with the sour cream and add to the flour mixture a little at a time, working quickly with your hands. Transfer the dough to a cold (if possible) lightly floured surface and knead for only 30 seconds. Divide the dough into two balls, wrap in plastic wrap and refrigerate for at least 1 hour before using.

Make the filling:

Put the cranberries, flour, and sugar in a large bowl and stir to combine.

Assemble pyrizhky:

Preheat the oven to 350°F.

Retrieve one ball of pastry from the refrigerator. Pinch off a small amount of dough and roll into a 4-inch round on a lightly floured surface. Place 1 tablespoon cranberry mixture in the center and pleat the dough around the center to make a tart, leaving the filling exposed. Place on a baking sheet. Repeat the process with the remaining dough and cranberry mixture. (Keep any extra pastry dough refrigerated until needed.)

Bake the sweet *pyrizhky*, in batches if you have to, until bubbly and golden, about 20 minutes. Serve with sweetened sour cream or a drizzle of honey.

Ukrainian Potato Bread

Pyrih z baraboleyu

This is a delicious potato-stuffed pastry suitable for *zakusky* hour or as a brunch dish. Some regional variations include sautéed cabbage in the filling.

3 large potatoes, peeled and chopped

2 tablespoons sunflower oil

1 onion, chopped

½ teaspoon salt

½ teaspoon freshly ground black pepper

2 tablespoons milk

4 ounces mild cheddar cheese, shredded

½ recipe Quick Yeast Dough (page 25)

Coarse salt

Preheat the oven to 375°F. Put the potatoes in a medium saucepan and cover with cold water. Bring to a boil over high heat and cook the potatoes until tender, about 10 minutes. Drain, put the potatoes in a large bowl and cover with a kitchen towel.

Warm 1 tablespoon of the oil in a medium skillet over medium heat. Add the onion and sauté until soft and fragrant, about 5 minutes. Add the onion to the potatoes along with the salt, black pepper, milk, and cheese. Using a potato masher or large fork, mash together all the ingredients until completely combined. Let the mixture cool.

Remove the dough from the refrigerator and divide into two equal portions. On a lightly floured board or counter, roll out one of the portions in a rectangle to about a ¼-inch thickness and place on a baking sheet. Pile the potato mixture on top of the dough leaving a 2-inch margin around the edges. Roll out the remaining dough in the same way and carefully place it on top of the potato mixture. Pinch the edges of the dough together all around and crimp with your fingers to seal or use the tines of a fork.

With a small, sharp knife, cut three slits in the top dough for the steam to escape. Brush with the remaining 1 tablespoon of oil and sprinkle with coarse salt. Bake 20 to 25 minutes or until golden brown. Let cool slightly before slicing.

Ukrainian Snack Foods

While it is a bit difficult to identify traditional Ukrainian snack foods, there are some preferred choices. Peanuts, while not a traditional snack, are now popular roasted and salted, as are roasted chestnuts which are sold from kiosks on the streets of many cities. Unadulterated thick and rich ice cream is also sold street-side. Boiled and salted corn-on-the-cob is another popular street food in large cities and even in smaller villages. *Deruny* (potato pancakes) and small canapé sandwiches topped with assorted goodies like cucumber slices, anchovies, shrimp, or cheese are prepared for picnics or when visiting family in the countryside. Other Ukrainian snacks include confections, baked goods, and cookies, and there are also commercially produced preparations and snack foods, such as mushroom-flavored potato chips, sold throughout the country.

Chapter 2

Borshch and Soups

Winter and summer pleasures ... popular hot or cold

Ukrainian soups are honest, spontaneous energy-builders and taste as rich as the Ukrainian soil itself. Soups reflect the country's diversity and copiousness to an extent that it was difficult to decide which ones to include. Subtle regional variations seem endless, but all are extraordinary and delicious.

At lunchtime, soup is a must, or it is served at home as a starter for dinner. Red beet soup or *borshch*, eaten all year long, satisfies cravings for the bounty of fresh produce available during the spring and summer months and sustains through the winter. A borshch including pork, ham, and other meats, along with an ample supply of beets and vegetables like cabbage and potatoes is usually filling enough to serve as a meal, while soups such as Wild Mushroom Soup and Fresh Pea Soup are light and elegant starters, often followed by potato pancakes (page 84) and a more substantial dessert. While meat or meat stock is incorporated into most Ukrainian soups, vegetarian soups are popular during Lent.

Soups are always served with plenty of bread to sop up all the juices, or fortified with healthy cooked grains such as barley or rice. Borshch is often accompanied by delicious small buns served drizzled with sunflower oil, crushed garlic, and coarse salt or small filled-pastries called *pyrizhky* (page 26). *Lokshyna* (homemade noodles, page 202) or small "drop" dumplings called *halushky* (page 200) are popular additions, as are leftover thinly sliced pancakes called *nalysnyky* (page 205). Plenty of fresh herbs are used in Ukrainian cooking—the more fresh herbs one adds to a soup, the better it gets.

Revitalizing chilled soups, an excellent way to fight a summer's thirst when even chewing seems difficult, are popular in Ukraine. Cold borshch, served with a splash of red wine, sitting in an outer bowl of crushed ice and accompanied by a platter of garnished eggs or various canapés makes a great lunch or brunch dish.

Chilled fruit soups are standard summer fare and most often are served solo, perhaps as a mid-afternoon snack. However, served with a dollop of honey-sweetened sour cream, whipped cream, or a few sprigs of fresh mint, fruit soup also makes a lovely and acceptable dessert.

"Borshch: The center of everything"
—Ukrainian proverb

Borshch is the quintessential soup of Ukraine. Probably better than any other traditional dish, borshch reflects the Ukrainian national character and to some extent Ukrainian ethnic history. To a great many Ukrainians living in Ukraine, borshch continues to be their staple food, the principle dish on their daily menu.

There is an old Ukrainian saying that goes, "there are as many variations of borshch as there are Ukrainian cooks." In spite of the great varieties of borshch, the commonality in all is the presence of the luscious red beet, in one form or another, some cooked beforehand and grated and chopped, and some added directly giving the soup its characteristic crimson color and flavor. Ukrainian connoisseurs of good borshch insist on plenty of meat, usually pork, and perhaps some smoked meat to nicely perfume the stock. Some cooks take the meat out before serving and present it as a separate course, while others put a few slices in each diner's bowl and pour soup over top. Still others chop the bigger pieces of meat or pull the meat off the bones and put it all back into the borshch pot. And if one observes Lent, the borshch will be meatless during that season.

Traditionalists and old country cooks rely on *beet kvas* (page 35) or *rye kvas* alone for imparting acidulant to the soup, giving the borshch its own unique personality. *Beet kvas* is the fermented liquid of red beets, slightly tart in taste. Many Ukrainians make their own at home. *Rye kvas* is another fermented mixture made of rye flour, yeast, and water, though it is not used as frequently as *beet kvas*.

The finishing touches to borshch also vary with regions, cities, or cooks. Some Ukrainians add *zapravka* (a paste of crushed garlic and cured pork belly bacon), bacon fat, or salt pork fried with onions. *Zapravka* is stirred into the soup just before serving and without it some say the borshch lacks character. In neighboring regions, *zapravka* is not made in a skillet, but is ground in a mortar and pestle and called *zatovka*. In still other regions, *zapravka* is made from fried millet or flour which is stirred into the soup near the finale. Those who have a passion for dill use it liberally in borshch. And unless the borshch is meatless for Lent, a few tablespoons of *smetana* (sour cream) is the chief-of-all-accompaniments and is always swirled into each bowl tableside (never in the borshch pot), adding a unique finishing flavor all its own.

In the end, borshch may be served hot or cold, clear or with many vegetables. One thing is for certain—you should always make plenty because borshch tastes better the next day and even better the day after that!

Borshch Geography

Varieties of borshch reflect specific geographical areas in Ukraine. For instance, Ukrainians in the western part of the country like the predominance of red beets, while those in the central region like a good amount of cabbage with the beets. It would not be unusual to find grated eggplant, beans, apples, bell peppers, tomatoes, and carrots included in addition to the beets and cabbage in the southern regions. Still others add potatoes, insisting it gives the final product a more velvety consistency. There is even "green" borshch made with lemony-tasting sorrel leaves or nettles that grow wild in the countryside and are enjoyed by all.

In the southern region around the city of Odesa, among the ingredients one may find in borshch are duck, chicken, and even fish and shellfish. Taking another geographical jump, in the river-sliced woodsy region of Polissya, wild mushrooms come to the borshch forefront. Further west in the romantic Carpathian Mountains, mushrooms and beans take center stage in the list of borshch ingredients; and in the villages higher up in the mountains, beans take precedent.

But somehow, regardless of all these variations, the essence of borshch always remains the same.

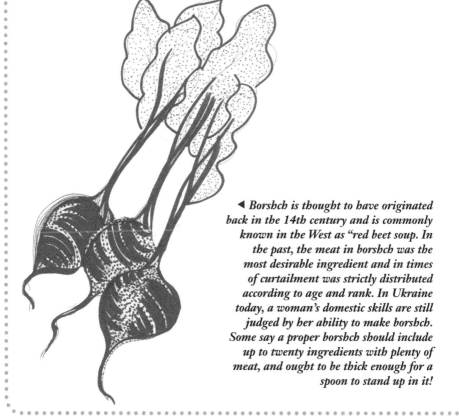

◀ *Borshch is thought to have originated back in the 14th century and is commonly known in the West as "red beet soup. In the past, the meat in borshch was the most desirable ingredient and in times of curtailment was strictly distributed according to age and rank. In Ukraine today, a woman's domestic skills are still judged by her ability to make borshch. Some say a proper borshch should include up to twenty ingredients with plenty of meat, and ought to be thick enough for a spoon to stand up in it!*

Country-Style Ukrainian Borshch

Selians'kyi borshch

A rustic borshch such as this one always has plenty of ingredients, and sometimes I add even more meat, beans, and additional root vegetables like turnips or rutabagas. I also lean towards adding more fresh dill than most people. This is how my grandmother made borshch in the U.S. She believed one should make use of all that is available wherever it is that you live. By her own admission, she always liked borshch thick with ingredients and on the sweeter side, which always seems to be a point of contention. I say, if you like it tart or sweet, who cares—it is always delicious!

Put the pork butt and pieces of beef in a large pot and cover with cold water or stock. Slowly bring to a boil over medium-high heat, skimming off and discarding any foam that rises to the top. Add the salt, black peppercorns, allspice berries, sprigs of dill, and bay leaves. Cover, reduce the heat to medium-low and gently simmer for 2 to 2½ hours or until the meat is very tender. Remove the meat from the stock with a slotted spoon and when cool enough to handle, chop the meat into bite-size pieces. Strain the stock and reserve. Discard the spices and dill.

In another large pot, melt the bacon drippings over medium heat and add the onion. Gently sauté for 3 minutes. Add the carrots, parsnips, parsley root, and celery, stirring to combine. Continue cooking over medium heat until the vegetables start to give off their own juices. Add the reserved meat stock and vinegar and bring to a boil. Stir in the beets, potato, cabbage, tomatoes, tomato paste, raisins, and pieces of meat. Bring the soup back to barely a boil, cover, reduce the heat to low and simmer the soup for about 1 hour. At this point, turn off the heat and let the covered pot sit for at least 10 minutes for the flavors to mingle.

When ready to serve, stir in the crushed garlic and fresh dill. Taste and add more salt and black pepper if needed. If you prefer a sweeter borshch, stir in some honey, 1 tablespoon at a time, or if you like a tart (but not sour) borshch, add more vinegar, 1 tablespoon at a time, until the desired taste is achieved. Ladle the borshch into individual bowls and serve with plenty of sour cream on the side.

1 (3-pound) smoked pork butt, or 2 large smoked ham hocks

1 (3-pound) beef chuck roast, cut into chunks

8 cups cold water (or reserved meat stock)

1 tablespoon salt

10 black peppercorns

6 allspice berries

3 sprigs fresh dill

2 bay leaves

2 tablespoons bacon drippings

1 large onion, chopped

2 carrots, peeled and chopped

2 parsnips, peeled and chopped

1 small parsley root, peeled and chopped

1 rib celery, chopped

2 tablespoons vinegar

3 large red beets, peeled and grated

1 large potato, peeled and coarsely chopped

2 cups shredded green cabbage

1 cup chopped fresh or canned tomatoes with juices

½ cup tomato paste

1 tablespoon raisins, or 3 chopped pitted prunes

2 cloves garlic, crushed

¼ cup finely chopped fresh dill

Additional salt and freshly ground black pepper to taste

1 tablespoon or more honey (optional)

2 cups (generous) sour cream to serve

Homemade Beet Kvas

Buriakovyi kvas

Makes about 1½ quarts

Beet *kvas* is simply the liquid of fermented red beets that is used to flavor soups, especially borshch, and in braising meats. It is touted as an overall health tonic. It's slightly tart, effervescent qualities are an acquired taste to some. Old-fashioned beet *kvas* recipes call for stale rye bread, yeast, or whey (a by-product of cheese-making from raw milk), but I found only three ingredients are really necessary and the result is quite good. Use organic or naturally grown red beets, coarse sea salt (Celtic salt is preferable), and filtered water, not tap water because of added chemicals, etc. I also like to mix this beet *kvas* with sparkling mineral water and a drizzle of honey for a refreshing and healthy beverage.

2 to 3 large unpeeled organic red beets, root tops and tap roots removed

1 teaspoon coarse sea salt

6 cups filtered water

One 2-quart glass jar

Cheesecloth and string

Cut beets into small wedges of equal size and place in glass jar. Add the salt and water and mix well. Cover the jar with a piece of cheesecloth and secure with some string. Leave sit in a warm place for 3 days to ferment.

Taste the kvas after 3 days. It should be pleasantly tart, somewhat salty, and slightly effervescent. If it tastes more salty than sour, let the kvas sit for another day or two and taste again. Strain the kvas and store in the refrigerator until ready to use.

NOTE: *See recipe for* Meatless Kvas Borshch *on page 36. Add beet* kvas *to borshch towards the end of cooking to retain its flavor and color.*

Chapter 2 *Borshch and Soups* **35**

Meatless Kvas Borshch

Pisnyi borshch z kvasom

Here is a meatless borshch that includes tender beet greens and beet *kvas*.

4 red beets, peeled and grated, plus the green tops, shredded

1 onion, chopped

1 carrot, peeled and chopped

1 potato, peeled and chopped

1 cup finely shredded green cabbage

6 cups vegetable stock

1 cup tomato juice

½ cup beet *kvas* (page 35)

2 tablespoons finely chopped fresh dill

Salt and freshly ground black pepper to taste

Sour cream to serve

Put the beets, beet greens, onion, carrot, potato, and cabbage in a large pot. Add the vegetable stock and bring to a gentle boil over medium-high heat. Cover, reduce the heat to medium-low, and simmer until the vegetables are tender, about 20 to 30 minutes.

Pour in the tomato juice and enough beet kvas to give desired tartness. Stir in the dill and season to taste with salt and black pepper.

If possible, let the borshch stand for a few hours before serving. When ready to serve, ladle into bowls and serve with sour cream on the side.

Zaporizhzhya-Style Borshch

Borshch po-zaporizhs'ky

This regional variation of borshch is named for the city of Zaporizhzhya in eastern Ukraine. Historically, this city was home to the most famous band of Kozaks (see page 38). This flavorful borshch gets its tang from sauerkraut versus fresh cabbage and its hardiness from meat left on the bone. The ribs are usually removed from the soup and served separately on a platter sprinkled with chopped fresh parsley.

3 pounds beef or pork spareribs, separated

1 tablespoon salt

6 black peppercorns

1 bay leaf

2 tablespoons unsalted butter

1 large onion, chopped

2 cloves garlic, sliced

3 large red beets, peeled and chopped into bite-size pieces

1½ cups sauerkraut

3 tablespoons tomato paste

Juice of 1 lemon

2 tablespoons sugar or honey

½ cup or more chopped fresh parsley

Sour cream to serve

Put the spareribs into a large pot and pour in about 8 cups cold water (enough to cover the spareribs). Slowly bring to a boil over medium-high heat, skimming off and discarding any foam that rises to the top. Add the salt, black peppercorns, and bay leaf, cover, and reduce the heat to medium-low. Simmer for about 1 hour or until the spareribs are tender.

Melt the butter in a medium skillet and add the onion and garlic. Gently sauté for about 5 minutes and then add to the soup pot along with the beets, sauerkraut, and tomato paste. Stir to dissolve the tomato paste while bringing the soup to nearly a boil over medium-high heat. Cover, reduce the heat to low and simmer for 30 minutes.

Stir in the fresh lemon juice and sugar. Taste and adjust the seasonings with additional salt and black pepper.

To serve, remove the ribs from the soup pot with a slotted spoon and serve separately on a platter garnished with half of the chopped parsley. Add the remaining parsley to the borshch and serve ladled into bowls with plenty of sour cream on the side.

The Kozaks

Also known as adventurers or freedom-fighters, Ukrainian Kozaks ("Cossacks" in English refers to Russian and Central Asian Cossacks) were a version of the Ukrainian military formed to fight for Ukraine's independence.

They arose out of the steppes in the mid-fifteenth century in the country's sparsely populated mid-south, initially as a group of hunters foraging for food. This same area attracted runaway serfs trying to escape feudal oppression from Polish lords, Orthodox refugees, and bandits, along with a few semi-independent Tatar bands. These hard-living, brave inhabitants formed self-governing militaristic communities known as *kozaky*, from a Turkic word meaning "outlaw or free person." The most famous and fiercest band of Kozaks was based below the rapids of the Dnipro River, in a fortified island community called Zaporizhzhs'ka Sich.

The Kozaks' powers of endurance on land and sea, ability to withstand pain, horsemanship, and ability to drink were legendary. Their mystique lives on today by virtue of proverbs, songs, and legends.

▲ *For hundreds of years Ukrainian Kozaks carried small cooking stoves with them to cook food on their marches.*
Based on the drawing by M.S. Samokysh, 1900.

Poltava Borshch with Chicken and Dumplings

Poltavs'kyi borshch z kurkoyu ta halushkamy

Makes 8 servings

Poltava is a pretty, quaint city on the Vorskla River in eastern Ukraine. Chicken and *halushky* (small "drop dumplings") come to the borshch forefront in this region. Cured pork belly bacon (*salo*) is traditionally used to sauté the vegetables, but melted bacon drippings, butter, or even oil can also be used if *salo* is not available. When served, a piece of chicken is put into each diner's bowl along with a few *halushky*, and then the soup is ladled over top. I have to admit, this is one of my favorite borshch variations. Unfortunately, it is not well known outside of Ukraine.

Put the chicken into a large pot and add about 8 cups cold water. Slowly bring to a boil over medium-high heat, skimming off and discarding any foam that rises to the top. At the boiling point, stir in the salt, cover, reduce the heat to low and gently simmer for 1 hour or until tender.

Melt the bacon drippings in a large skillet over medium heat and add the onion, carrot, and beets. Drizzle with vinegar and braise the vegetables for about 10 minutes, adding a little of the chicken broth to keep the vegetables moist. Add these vegetables to the soup pot, along with the potatoes, tomatoes, and cabbage and bring to nearly a boil. Reduce the heat to medium and continue cooking until all the vegetables are tender. Stir in some black pepper, dill, and parsley. Taste and adjust the seasonings if necessary.

Turn off the heat and let the borshch sit, covered, for 15 minutes for the flavors to marry. To serve, put a piece of chicken in each diner's bowl, along with a few *halushky*, and ladle soup over top. Offer sour cream on the side.

1 (4-pound) chicken, cut into serving pieces

1 tablespoon salt

4 tablespoons bacon drippings

1 onion, chopped

1 carrot, peeled and chopped

3 large beets, peeled and grated

¼ cup vinegar

4 large potatoes, peeled and chopped

6 large tomatoes, peeled, seeded, and coarsely chopped

2 cups finely shredded green cabbage

Freshly ground black pepper to taste

¼ cup or more finely chopped fresh dill

¼ cup or more chopped fresh parsley

Halushky (page 200)

Sour cream to serve

Ukrainian Lenten Borshch

Pisnyi borshch

This traditional Lenten borshch is a refreshing fish soup that is a bit unusual. Good hot and also tasty chilled in the summertime, it is thick and rich with flavors.

Put the mushrooms in a strainer and rinse well under cold water. Place them in a small saucepan along with 2 cups of vegetable broth and bring to a boil. Remove the pan from the heat and let the mushrooms soak for 30 minutes.

Meanwhile, warm the oil in a large pot over medium heat and add the onion. Gently sauté until very soft, about 5 minutes. Add the carrots and celery. Stir in the tomato paste, making sure all the vegetables are coated. Continue cooking the mixture another 5 minutes. Add the mushrooms and their soaking liquid, the remaining 6 cups of vegetable broth, beets, cabbage, potatoes, bay leaf, and salt. Bring to a boil, cover, reduce the heat to low and simmer for 30 minutes.

Break the fish into pieces and add to the soup along with the tomato sauce. Stir in the vinegar. Taste and adjust the seasonings and add black pepper to taste. Add more vinegar at this point if you like a tart borshch. Stir in the crushed garlic and dill when ready to serve.

4 dried porcini mushrooms

8 cups vegetable broth

3 tablespoons sunflower oil

1 large onion, finely chopped

2 carrots, peeled and finely chopped

1 rib celery, finely chopped

¼ cup tomato paste

3 large red beets, peeled and grated

2 cups shredded green cabbage

2 large potatoes, peeled and finely chopped

1 bay leaf

2 teaspoons salt

12 ounces canned herring fillets or sprats in tomato sauce

1 tablespoon apple cider vinegar or more to taste

Freshly ground black pepper to taste

2 cloves garlic, crushed

2 tablespoons chopped fresh dill

VARIATION: *Fresh fish fillets can also be used in this variation of borshch. Any firm-fleshed fish will do. Just sprinkle the fish with salt and black pepper and pan fry in oil until crisp and golden. Serve the borshch with a piece of fish in each bowl.*

NOTE: *Sprats are small European herrings.*

Meatless Chernivtsi Borshch

Pisnyi borshch po-chernivets'ky

Makes 6 to 8 servings

This variation of borshch is named after the ancient city of Chernivtsi located in the Bukovyna region of northwest Ukraine, home of the Carpathian Mountains. It is a lighter than usual borshch and I have opted to make it vegetarian-style. Most variations do contain meat, usually beef chuck or meaty beef shins, but I like my version since there is an unexpected twist from the borshch norm by the addition of beans, tart apples, and squash (usually zucchini). This borshch is quick and easy to make and can be whipped up in just 30 minutes. However, it is always better to let borshch sit for a few hours for the flavors to marry, or easier yet, make it the day before. I like to serve this borshch with a bowl of cooked rye kasha (rye berries).

Melt the butter in a large pot over medium heat. Add the onion, carrots, parsnips, and celery and cook until the vegetables are soft and fragrant, about 5 minutes. Add the vegetable broth, bay leaves, beets, cabbage, potatoes, tomatoes, and paprika and bring to a boil. Cover, reduce the heat to low and simmer for 20 minutes.

Add the apples, zucchini, and beans and continue cooking another 10 minutes. Stir in the garlic, honey if using, dill, and parsley. Taste and adjust the seasonings by adding salt and black pepper to taste. Let the borshch stand for a few hours if possible, before serving with plenty of sour cream on the side.

4 tablespoons unsalted butter

1 large onion, chopped

2 carrots, peeled and chopped

2 parsnips, peeled and chopped

1 rib celery, chopped

8 cups vegetable broth

2 bay leaves

3 large red beets, peeled and grated

2 cups shredded green cabbage

2 large potatoes, peeled and chopped

1 pound fresh tomatoes, peeled, seeded, and coarsely chopped with juices

1 tablespoon sweet Hungarian paprika

2 Granny Smith apples, cored, peeled, and chopped

1 medium zucchini, chopped

1 cup cooked red or white beans

2 cloves garlic, crushed

1 to 2 tablespoons honey (optional)

2 tablespoons chopped fresh dill

2 tablespoons chopped fresh parsley

Salt and freshly ground black pepper to taste

Sour cream to serve

Shchavlevyi abo zelenyi borshch

Makes 6 servings

This soup features sorrel, or as it is sometimes called "sour leaf," a hardy perennial that is found growing wild and in abundance all over the world. Sorrel's sharp, almost lemony flavor is said to have a "cleansing effect" on the body, so it is no wonder that many Ukrainians serve this soup in the springtime, after a long, cold winter.

3 tablespoons unsalted butter

1 large onion, peeled and grated

1 carrot, peeled and chopped

8 cups *Rich Ukrainian Chicken Broth* (page 44)

2 potatoes, peeled and chopped

6 cups finely shredded sorrel

2 tablespoons finely chopped fresh dill

2 tablespoons finely chopped fresh parsley

½ cup light cream

½ cup sour cream

1 tablespoon unbleached all-purpose flour

Slices of hard-cooked eggs and sprigs of dill for garnishing

Melt the butter in a large pot over medium heat. Add the onion, reduce the heat to medium-low, and gently sauté until soft and golden but not browned, about 10 minutes. Add the carrot and continue cooking another 5 minutes. Add the chicken broth and potatoes and bring to a boil. Reduce the heat to medium-low and simmer until the potatoes are tender, about 15 minutes.

Bring the soup back up to barely a boil and add the sorrel, dill, and parsley. Cook just until the sorrel has wilted, about 5 minutes. Turn the heat back down to low and remove 1 cup of soup and pour it into a medium bowl. Set aside.

Pour the light cream into a small bowl and add the sour cream and flour and whisk until smooth and creamy. Stir this mixture into the reserved cup of soup, and then add mixture to the pot, stirring all the while. Continue cooking the borshch another 2 minutes. Serve ladled into individual bowls garnished with slices of hard-cooked eggs and sprigs of fresh dill.

Cold Peasant Borshch

Makes 5 to 6 servings

Cold borshch is served during the summer months with some raw vegetables added—only the beets and potatoes are cooked.

½ cup chopped dried fruit
(apples, plums, cherries, raisins, apricots, etc.)

4 large beets, boiled, peeled, and chopped

2 tablespoons (generous) apple cider vinegar

2 large potatoes, baked, peeled, and chopped

2 cups shredded scallions, including green tops

1 large cucumber, peeled and chopped

2 hard-cooked extra-large eggs, grated

3 cups beet kvas (page 35)

2 tablespoons chopped fresh dill

Salt and freshly ground black pepper to taste

1 tablespoon honey (optional)

Sour cream to serve

Pour 2 cups of water into a small saucepan and add the dried fruit. Simmer over low heat just until the fruit is softened, about 5 minutes. Remove the pan from the heat and chill for several hours.

Put the beets into a large bowl, sprinkle with the vinegar and let sit 2 to 3 hours.

Put the potatoes, scallions, cucumber, and eggs in another large bowl and add the chilled fruits with their soaking liquid, and all of the beets and any liquid in the bowl. Stir in the beet kvas and dill. Taste and add salt and black pepper to taste. Add more vinegar and some honey if desired. Chill at least 1 hour so the flavors come together before serving with plenty of sour cream on the side.

Rich Ukrainian Chicken Broth

Kuriachyi rosil

Makes about 3 to 3½ quarts

Chicken broth is almost as popular as borshch in Ukraine. In days gone by, chicken broth was special, usually served at Sunday supper, while borshch was everyday fare. Ingredients should be simple as to not rob the broth of its subtle flavor. I think chicken feet, backs, and necks make the best broth—rich-tasting, gelatinous, and enough fat for a lot of flavor and little cash output. Any extra broth I portion into pint containers. This broth will keep for one week in your refrigerator and up to one month in your freezer.

2 pounds chicken feet

2 pounds chicken backs and necks

1 onion, peeled and cut into wedges

1 large carrot, broken into pieces

2 celery ribs with leaves, broken into pieces

2 sprigs parsley

1 bay leaf (preferably fresh)

1 tablespoon salt

Put the chicken feet into a large pot, add enough cold water to cover and bring to a boil. Boil for 5 minutes, skimming off and discarding any foam that rises to the top. Drain the feet and rinse with cold water so they can be handled. Snip the tips of the claws off at the joint and discard (this process allows the marrow and gelatin from the bones to flow).

Put the chicken feet back into the rinsed pot, along with the backs and necks, onion, carrot, celery, parsley, and bay leaf. Add enough cold water to cover and bring to a boil, skimming off and discarding any foam that rises to the top. Reduce the heat to low and stir in the salt. Cover and gently simmer on low for 3 hours. Check the pot occasionally, and skim off and discard any foam that has risen to the top.

Remove the cover, turn up the heat to medium and let the broth begin to reduce. Simmer another hour to intensify the flavors. Strain the broth twice and serve.

NOTE: *When cool, the broth will firm up nicely into a gel. Scrape off some fat, but leave some for flavor. Refrigerate or freeze your chicken broth for future use.*

Hetman-Style Short Ribs Soup

Yushka z reber, po-het'mans'ky

Makes 6 servings

This is a rustic, homestyle dish that is perfect for a company meal instead of a more elaborate preparation. Wine is sometimes used to enhance the flavor of meat in Ukrainian cookery, and stirring a small amount of sour cream into this soup at the end of cooking will enrich the broth even more. Remember, whisking a little flour with the sour cream will help keep it from curdling when adding it to a simmering stew, soup, or sauce. Use the very best quality sour cream money can buy, preferably direct from a dairy farmer, and do not be shy about its culinary possibilities.

Preheat the oven to 325°F. Rub each rib with the crushed garlic and dredge in the seasoned flour. Melt the bacon drippings in a large covered casserole or Dutch oven over medium heat and brown the ribs on all sides. Add the ham and burgundy wine and bring to a gentle boil over medium heat. Cover and braise in the oven for 1½ hours or until the ribs are nearly tender.

Add the onion, mushrooms, potatoes, tomatoes, meat stock, salt, and crushed black peppercorns. Cover and continue braising in the oven for another hour, or until the vegetables are cooked and the ribs are very tender. Taste and adjust the seasonings with additional salt and black pepper if needed.

Whisk the tablespoon of flour into the sour cream and stir into the soup. Ladle into bowls making sure each diner has some meat and serve sprinkled with chopped fresh parsley.

2 pounds lean and meaty beef short ribs, cut into pieces

2 cloves garlic, crushed

½ cup unbleached all-purpose flour seasoned with salt and freshly ground black pepper

2 tablespoons bacon drippings, unsalted butter, or oil

½ cup finely chopped smoked ham

2 cups burgundy wine or any dry wine

1 large onion, chopped

2 cups fresh wild or cultivated mushrooms, sliced

1 large potato, peeled and chopped

1 cup stewed tomatoes

2 cups meat stock

1 teaspoon salt

6 black peppercorns, crushed

1 tablespoon unbleached all-purpose flour

2 tablespoons sour cream

¼ cup chopped fresh parsley to serve

Spicy Beef Soup with Herbs

Kharcho

Georgian in origin, this soup has proliferated in Ukraine for over 40 years due to Russian influence. You can find *kharcho* everywhere, from humble cafeterias and street-side cafes, to the most exclusive restaurants in major cities. The recipe has gone through countless changes as it made its way across Ukraine, but the most significant is the tendency of Ukrainians in the east to substitute lamb for the original beef in the soup. Beef seems to be the preference in western Ukraine. My version has a thicker base, beef, and a little more robust flavor. It also incorporates many fresh herbs thereby striking a nice balance between spicy, tart, sweet, and exotic. Delicious!

1 (3½-pound) beef brisket, cut into small chunks

2 teaspoons salt

2 tablespoons unsalted butter

1 large onion, chopped

3 tablespoons tomato paste

4 large plum tomatoes, peeled, seeded, and coarsely chopped

1 bay leaf

¾ teaspoon crushed coriander seeds

1 teaspoon sweet Hungarian paprika

2 cloves garlic, crushed

1 cup white rice

Juice of 1 lemon

2 tablespoons chopped fresh celery leaves

1 cup chopped fresh herbs in any combination: basil, parsley, dill, tarragon, etc.

Rub the pieces of brisket with 2 teaspoons of salt. Cover and refrigerate overnight.

Put the brisket pieces in a large pot, add 8 cups cold water, and bring to slow boil over medium-high heat. Skim off any foam that rises to the top and discard. Cover, reduce the heat to medium-low and simmer until the meat is tender, about 2 hours.

Melt the butter in a medium skillet over medium heat. Add the onion and sauté until softened and fragrant, about 5 minutes. Stir in the tomato paste, fresh tomatoes, bay leaf, coriander seeds, paprika, and garlic and continue cooking another 5 minutes.

Whisk the tomato mixture into the soup pot with the brisket and increase the heat to medium-high. As the soup nears a boil, add the rice and lemon juice and turn the heat down to low. Cover and simmer for 20 minutes or until the rice is tender.

Remove the pot from the heat and add the celery leaves and half of the fresh herbs. Cover and let sit for an additional 10 minutes. Taste and adjust the seasonings with additional salt and black pepper if needed. Just before serving, stir in the remaining herbs.

Traditional Ukrainian Fish Soup

Tradytsiyna yushka z ryby

Makes 6 to 8 servings

This soup can be made with any freshwater fish and is enjoyed throughout Ukraine. Carp is the preferred choice, but feel free to substitute trout, pike, bass, or even young catfish. It is usually served as a clear fish broth or sometimes with the addition of dumplings. The poached pieces of fish are served as a separate course accompanied by one's favorite sauce. Mashed potatoes are the preferred accoutrement.

1 (3-pound) whole carp, scaled and cleaned

Salt and freshly ground black pepper to taste

1 onion, cut into wedges

1 parsley root, broken into pieces

1 carrot, broken into pieces

1 rib celery, broken into pieces

2 bay leaves

1 tablespoon salt

10 black peppercorns

2 sprigs fresh dill

Chopped fresh parsley to garnish

Cut the head, tail, and fins off the carp and put them into a large pot. Slice the remaining carp into 1-inch-thick steaks, sprinkle with salt and black pepper, and refrigerate until ready to use.

Add 8 cups of cold water to the pot with the carp trimmings and add the onion, parsley root, carrot, celery, bay leaves, salt, black peppercorns, and sprigs of dill and bring to a boil. Cover, reduce the heat to medium low, and simmer for 1 hour.

Strain the fish broth (discarding all solids) and pour into a clean pot. Bring the broth to a boil over medium heat. Remove the carp steaks from the refrigerator and add to the simmering fish broth. Reduce the heat to low and gently poach the carp steaks for about 20 minutes or until tender.

Gently remove the carp steaks and place on a warmed platter. Keep the fish broth hot. This soup is served as a clear broth with a sprinkling of fresh parsley. Serve the carp steaks as a separate course with your favorite sauce.

Ukrainian Milk Soup with Rice

Molochna yushka z ryzhom

Makes 4 to 6 servings

Some years ago I ran a small catering company. I had no real business scheme in mind except to cook the foods I liked the most. I figured if I approached this task with passion and integrity, other food lovers would share an appetite for my culinary whims. When I sold off the business in 2006, the following soup was the unanimous favorite among those who helped with the task of tasting my latest creations.

My grandmother made the most delicious soup and she would let me help when I was just a little girl. She would take cooked, seasoned rice, form it into little balls and then let me drop them into simmering milk. I also had the job of seasoning the soup simply with a little butter and salt—under Baba's careful tutelage of course. Leave it to my grandmother to have such a way of making starchy excess ever so satisfying!

As it turns out, cooking various grains in milk or serving grains cooked in milk, affectionately called "milk soups," is common practice in Ukraine. "Milk soups" were the result of making the most of whatever ingredients were available at the time. Buckwheat, barley, millet, cornmeal, rice, or even cooked noodles were added to milk soups. It is also a favored way of using up any extra fresh vegetables from the garden. Variations are limitless.

2 cups leftover cooked rice

1 tablespoon finely chopped onion

2 tablespoons unbleached all-purpose flour

1 extra-large egg, slightly beaten

1 tablespoon mayonnaise

4 tablespoons unsalted butter, softened

2 teaspoons salt

6 cups creamy whole milk or light cream

1 cup finely shredded fresh spinach (optional)

Freshly ground black pepper to taste (optional)

Push the rice through a potato ricer (a handheld gadget that forces food through a disk with holes making food creamier) and into a small bowl. Add the onion, flour, egg, mayonnaise, 1 teaspoon butter, and ½ teaspoon salt. Mix thoroughly and refrigerate the mixture for 30 minutes. Form the rice mixture into small balls about the size of marbles.

Pour the milk into a medium saucepan and bring to a gentle boil over medium heat, stirring constantly. Add the remaining butter and salt. Reduce the heat to medium-low and carefully drop the rice balls, one-by-one, into the simmering milk. After 2 minutes, carefully stir in the spinach, if using, and continue cooking another 3 to 5 minutes. Taste and add more salt and butter if necessary and some black pepper if you like. Ladle the soup into bowls and serve immediately.

Ukrainian Potato Soup

Kartoplianka

Makes 8 to 10 servings

While in some towns and villages in western Ukraine this soup is called "white borshch," it is more of a potato soup with a little shredded cabbage in it. I grew up eating this soup. Since we lived on a farm and had access to fresh milk on a daily basis, my family—perhaps completely out of traditional context—finished this soup off with buttermilk. Thick and creamy, the buttermilk and sour cream add just the right amount of tartness and improve the flavor still further. I always serve this soup with rye bread croutons or *pyrizhky* (page 26).

2 tablespoons unsalted butter

1 large onion, chopped

2 ribs celery with leaves, finely chopped

4 large potatoes, peeled and chopped

1 cup finely shredded green cabbage

4 cups Rich Ukrainian Chicken Broth (page 44)

1 teaspoon salt

2 cups buttermilk, whole milk, or light cream

½ cup sour cream

3 tablespoons unbleached all-purpose flour

½ cup chopped scallions including green tops

Freshly ground black or white pepper to taste

Melt the butter in a large pot over medium heat. Add the onion and sauté until soft, about 5 minutes. Add the celery and continue cooking another 5 minutes. Add the potatoes, cabbage, chicken broth, and salt and bring to a gentle boil. Cover, reduce the heat to medium-low, and simmer until the vegetables are tender, about 20 minutes. Uncover, reduce the heat to low and leave the soup to simmer.

Meanwhile, pour the buttermilk into a large bowl and whisk in the sour cream and flour, making sure there are no lumps. Add a few tablespoons of hot soup and stir. Slowly pour the buttermilk mixture into the simmering soup, stirring all the while. Add the scallions and cook another 5 minutes. Taste and add more salt if necessary and some black or white pepper. Ladle the soup into bowls and serve.

Wild Mushroom Soup

Yushka z dykykh hrybiv

Makes 6 servings

I n Ukraine many people pick their own wild mush-rooms and they are used in all sorts of amazing and delicious dishes. Using dried mushrooms insures one can enjoy this dish all year long—but if you are able to use freshly picked wild mushrooms, by all means do.

1 ounce dried wild mushrooms, such as porcini, cepes, morels, etc., or 6 ounces fresh wild mushrooms

6 cups Rich Ukrainian Chicken Broth (page 44)

2 tablespoons unsalted butter

1 large onion, chopped

1 clove garlic, chopped

2 carrots, peeled and cut into julienne strips

2 pounds cultivated mushrooms (such as portabella, champignon, etc.), stems trimmed and sliced

1 teaspoon salt

½ teaspoon freshly ground black pepper

3 tablespoons chopped fresh parsley

3 tablespoons unbleached all-purpose flour

2 tablespoons cognac

Sour cream to serve

Put the dried wild mushrooms, if using, in a strainer and rinse under cold water. Put them in a medium saucepan with 1 cup of chicken broth and bring to a boil. Remove the pan from the heat and set aside 45 minutes to soak.

Meanwhile, in a large pot, melt the butter over medium-low heat, add the onion and sauté until fragrant and golden, about 10 minutes (do not brown). Add the garlic, carrots, and fresh mushrooms. Increase the heat to medium and continue cooking another 5 minutes or just until the mushrooms start to soften.

Add the salt, black pepper, and 2 tablespoons of the parsley and sprinkle the entire mixture with the flour, stirring to coat evenly. Continue cooking another 5 minutes.

Add the cognac, remaining 5 cups chicken broth, and the dried mushrooms and their soaking liquid. Stir well, cover, reduce the heat to low and simmer 40 minutes or until the mushrooms are very tender. Sprinkle the soup with remaining 1 tablespoon fresh parsley and serve each bowl with a dab of sour cream.

"The *dacha* is a way of life"

The *dacha* or summer house is a concept left over from Soviet times when the state allocated 0.6-acre plots to particular factories, farms, and research centers for distribution to selected workers. As a result, many Ukrainians received *dachas* outright without paying for them. However, most *dachas* today are privately owned and the difference between those of earlier times and those of today is well-manicured lawns have replaced what once were rose bushes, ample gardens, and fruit orchards—signs that the owners can afford not to grow their own food. Nevertheless, this does not mean Ukrainians do not enjoy their *dachas* or love spending time outdoors. Weekend activities often include going to the *dacha* and throwing an informal party or barbecue is a favorite activity. Time spent at the *dacha* is a great way to observe grilling techniques—considered a "man's activity" and an acquired skill.

Fresh Pea Soup

Yushka iz svizhoho horokhu

Makes 6 servings

This satisfying soup captures all the flavors of summer in Ukraine. The fresh peas give it exquisite color. If fresh peas are not available, use frozen peas, but thaw before using.

6 scallions including green tops, chopped

2 tablespoons sunflower oil

4 cups shelled peas (about 4 pounds fresh or frozen)

3½ cups water or Rich Ukrainian Chicken Broth (page 44)

1 teaspoon salt

½ teaspoon freshly ground black pepper

2 tablespoons chopped fresh parsley

2 tablespoons heavy whipping cream

Snipped chives for garnishing

In a large saucepan over medium heat, gently sauté the scallions in the sunflower oil until soft, about 5 minutes. Add the peas, water or broth, salt, and black pepper. Bring to a boil, reduce the heat to medium-low and simmer about 10 minutes for younger peas or about 20 to 25 minutes for larger or older peas, stirring occasionally.

When the peas are tender, remove the pot from the heat and let cool slightly. Ladle the soup into a food mill or blender, or use an immersion blender, and puree or pulse until almost smooth.

Return the soup to the saucepan and stir in the cream. Reheat to a gentle simmer over medium-low heat. Taste and adjust the seasonings if necessary. Serve each bowl garnished with some snipped chives.

VARIATION: *Cooked smoked ham is delicious added to this soup.*

52 Chapter 2 *Borshch and Soups*

Sauerkraut Soup

Kapusniak

Sauerkraut is a staple throughout Ukraine and this soup is an old-time favorite. In my version, the stock is made first, and then ladled over the cooked sauerkraut before serving. Someone once asked me: "Why in this order?" And my reply was that it was the way my Baba did it! Serve *kapusniak* with plenty of warm crusty rye bread or cooked buckwheat kasha (page 105).

2 pounds smoked ham bones, skin, and any leftover scraps from a smoked ham

1 unpeeled onion, cut into wedges

2 carrots, broken into pieces plus a few sprigs of carrot greens

2 parsnips, broken into pieces

1 parsley root including some of the green tops, coarsely chopped

2 teaspoons salt

10 black peppercorns

2 tablespoons unsalted butter

6 cups sauerkraut, drained and squeezed dry

1 tablespoon ground caraway seeds

Put the ham bones and scraps into a large pot and add 8 cups of cold water. Bring to a boil, skimming off and discarding any foam that rises to the top. Add the onion, pieces of carrot and carrot greens, parsnips, parsley root and parsley greens, salt, and black peppercorns. Cover, reduce the heat to low and simmer 2 hours. Strain the stock (discarding all solids), pour it back into the rinsed-out pot and keep hot over medium heat.

Melt the butter in a large skillet over medium heat and add the sauerkraut and ground caraway seeds. Reduce the heat to low and sauté the sauerkraut until soft and tender, about 30 to 40 minutes, adding a few tablespoons of stock if the mixture becomes too dry. Divide the sauerkraut among six serving bowls. Cover with hot stock and serve immediately.

. . . .

VARIATION: *Cooked dried peas or kidney beans can be added to make this a heartier soup.*

Zaporizhzhya-Style Sauerkraut Soup

Kapusniak po-zaporizhzhs'ky

Zaporizhzhya is a city with a rich history located along the banks of the Dnipro River in eastern Ukraine. *Kapusniak* is made a little differently in this region. Millet, allspice, and salt pork figure prominently in this version, along with lean pork. It is very tasty.

1 (2 to 3-pound) pork loin

2 teaspoons salt

1 bay leaf

2 large cloves garlic, coarsely chopped

1 parsley root, broken into pieces including some finely chopped greens

4 cups sauerkraut

2 tablespoons unsalted butter

1 carrot, peeled and finely chopped

1 parsnip, peeled and finely chopped

1 rib celery, finely chopped

2 large potatoes, peeled and finely chopped

2 tablespoons finely chopped salt pork

¼ cup millet

Pinch of ground allspice

Freshly ground black pepper to taste

Sour cream and freshly chopped parsley to serve

Put the pork loin into a large pot and add 8 cups of cold water. Bring to a boil, skimming off and discarding any foam that rises to the top. Add the salt, bay leaf, garlic, and parsley root. Reduce the heat to medium-low and cook, uncovered, for 1½ hours or until the pork is very tender.

Remove the meat from the pot and set aside. Strain the stock, discarding the solids, and return it to the rinsed-out pot. Bring the stock to a gentle simmer over medium heat and stir in the sauerkraut. Continue cooking until the sauerkraut is partially cooked, about 20 minutes.

Meanwhile, melt the butter in a large skillet over medium heat and add the carrot, parsnip, celery, and potatoes. Gently sauté the vegetables just until they start to soften, about 5 minutes. Mix the salt pork with the millet. Add to vegetables and stir in the allspice.

Remove vegetable mixture from the heat and add to the simmering sauerkraut. Reduce the heat to medium-low, cover, and continue cooking 30 minutes longer or until the sauerkraut and millet are tender. Taste and adjust the seasonings with additional salt and black pepper if necessary.

Pull the pork off the bone and put a few slices in each diner's bowl. Ladle some soup over top and add a generous dollop of sour cream. Sprinkle with some fresh parsley and serve hot.

Chilled Fruit Soup

Kholodnyy sup frukty

I cannot think of anything more refreshing than a bowl of chilled fruit soup on a sizzling August afternoon. Any fresh fruit or berries in season may be used. The amount of honey used depends upon how sweet one likes their soup, and whether one uses a thickener or not really depends upon personal preference. This soup features fresh peaches.

2 pounds fresh peaches

Juice of 1 lemon

¼ cup honey (more or less to taste)

2 teaspoons potato flour or cornstarch

Whipped cream or sour cream to serve (optional)

Peel and pit the peaches, coarsely chop, and put into a medium saucepan. Add the lemon juice, honey, and 3 cups of cold water. Cook the fruit gently over medium-low heat, just until the honey is dissolved and the fruit is soft, about 5 to 7 minutes. Puree the soup in a blender and pour it back into the rinsed-out saucepan and reheat over medium heat.

In a small bowl, blend the potato flour with 3 tablespoons of cold water to make a smooth paste. Pour the mixture into the simmering soup, stirring all the time until the soup thickens. Remove the pan from the stove and let the soup cool.

Taste and add more honey if desired. Pour the soup into a large bowl and chill for several hours. Serve the soup ladled into chilled bowls garnished with whipped cream or a small dollop of sour cream.

....

VARIATION: *On special occasions, I add a few drops of cognac, vodka, or Port wine to my chilled fruit soup before serving.*

Chapter 3

Salads, Pickles and Preserves

Simplicity at its finest ...

Ukrainian salads are almost as diverse as the soups and can make an appearance at almost any stage of the meal. Heartier salads are often combinations of cooked vegetables, smoked meats, fish, or shredded duck or goose, and often accompany an entrée. But because such an enormous premium is placed on fresh vegetables, most times salads are simple, bound with a dollop of sour cream or mayonnaise (which Ukrainians love almost as much as sour cream), yogurt mixed with a splash of cream, or a mere drizzle of vinegar and oil. Other times a vegetable is simply blanched in salted water, cut into strips, combined with mayonnaise and served warm as the ever popular more Europeanized composed salad.

Homemade pickles add a delightful touch of luxury to a meal, yet are both easy and satisfying to make. One of the most beloved national domestic chores in Ukraine is pickle-making. Pickled cucumbers, brined cabbage or sauerkraut, marinated mushrooms (page 18), and pickled fruit are Ukrainian staples, satisfying their taste for sours. Many a cupboard is lined with jars of every shape and size filled with these tantalizing jewels set in brine. Sometimes a dish of pickled vegetables replaces a fresh salad, especially in the wintertime, when there may be a shortage of fresh vegetables to accompany an entrée.

And on the sweet side, spiced fruit and sugarless fruit preserves, made from only the freshest and unblemished fruits, are used to fill a number of traditional Ukrainian pastries. A variety of fruit preserves are a must at tea time where they are used in place of sugar to sweeten one's tea. If a family is lucky enough to have an abundance of fruit trees and bushes at one's *dacha* or country home, a cheap source of fruit is available and Ukrainians often give extra jars of fruit preserves away as hospitality gifts.

In the springtime, Ukrainian villages are completely pink and white—because of all the fruit and berry trees in bloom around each house. What a beautiful site! Orchards in bloom are sung about in many Ukrainian folk and ritual songs.

Mixed Vegetable Salad with Vinaigrette

Salata z mishanoyi horodyny, prypravlena vinegretovoyu polyvkoyu   Makes about 6 servings

This country-style salad is popular all over Ukraine where it is synonymous with the term *"vinegret."* There are as many versions of this salad as there are Ukrainians, but most often if *"vinegret"* is offered on a menu, whether at a restaurant or home, one will be served a beautiful mixed vegetable salad dressed with either mayonnaise or vinaigrette and garnished with fresh herbs such as parsley, basil, or dill. Below is a typical combination—however, ingredients are always dependent upon availability.

2 cups shredded green cabbage

2 potatoes, peeled and cut into ½-inch pieces

1 carrot, peeled and cut into ½-inch pieces

1 teaspoon salt

1 dill pickle, cut into ½-inch pieces

1 cucumber, peeled and cut into ½-inch pieces

½ cup fresh peas or thawed frozen peas

6 red radishes, thinly sliced

1 medium red beet, cooked, peeled, sliced and cut into julienne strips, or 1 16-ounce can red beets, drained and chopped

Chopped fresh dill, tomato wedges, and coarse salt for garnishing

VINAIGRETTE:

2 tablespoons red wine vinegar

1 teaspoon prepared mustard

1 tablespoon granulated sugar or honey

½ teaspoon salt

¼ teaspoon freshly ground black pepper

⅓ cup sunflower oil

Put the cabbage, potatoes, and carrot in a deep skillet with just enough cold water to cover (about 2 cups) and add 1 teaspoon of salt. Bring the mixture to a boil, reduce the heat to medium-low and simmer gently, uncovered, just until the vegetables are tender, about 10 minutes. Drain the vegetables in a colander and let cool.

In a large salad bowl, gently toss together the dill pickle, cucumber, peas, radishes, and beets. Set aside.

In a small bowl, whisk together the vinegar, mustard, sugar, salt, and black pepper. Slowly pour in the sunflower oil, whisking constantly until the dressing is creamy-thick.

Add the cooked vegetables to the vegetables in the salad bowl and toss with the vinaigrette, being careful not to crush the vegetables—do not over mix.

Serve garnished with chopped fresh dill, tomato wedges, and a generous sprinkling of coarse salt.

Warm Onion Salad with Smoked Salmon Vinaigrette

*Tepla salata iz tsybuli, prypravlena
polyvkoyu z vudzhenoho lososia*   *Makes 4 servings*

I firmly believe a salad should be as memorable as the main course of a meal. The dressing in this recipe is an adaptation of a very old recipe in the grand Russo-French tradition popular throughout what is now Ukraine in the early part of the nineteenth century. It is Slavic simplicity at its finest and the perfect choice when elegant fare is in order.

8 ounces smoked salmon, sliced ⅛-inch thick

¾ cup white wine

4 small leeks (whites only), cleaned and thinly sliced

1 sweet onion, quartered and thinly sliced

1 red onion, quartered and thinly sliced

2 teaspoons red wine vinegar

1 tablespoon finely chopped fresh dill

1 tablespoon finely chopped fresh tarragon

Pinch of salt

1 teaspoon small capers, rinsed and drained

¼ cup (generous) olive oil

Freshly ground black pepper to taste

Butter crunch lettuce leaves and salmon caviar for garnishing

Cut the salmon into ¼-inch pieces and set aside.

Bring the white wine to a boil in a medium saucepan and add the leeks and onions. Boil 1 minute and then remove the vegetables with a slotted spoon and place in a colander to drain. Reserve the white wine boiling liquid.

In a medium bowl, whisk together 2 tablespoons of the cooled white wine, the red wine vinegar, dill, tarragon, salt, and capers. Slowly add the olive oil, whisking gently.

Add the leeks and onions to the vinaigrette and then the salmon and toss gently with two salad spoons so the salmon does not tear. Arrange the salad on individual lettuce-lined plates, sprinkle with a few grinds of black pepper, and top with a dab of salmon caviar. Serve immediately.

Chilled Onion Salad

Kholodna salata z tsybuli

Makes 4 servings

This salad is the perfect accompaniment to any kind of meat or fish.

Put the slices of onion in a medium bowl, sprinkle with vinegar and season to taste with salt. Cover and refrigerate for 1 hour.

Arrange the lettuce leaves on a small serving platter. Drain the onion slices and scatter on top of the lettuce. Just before serving, put the sour cream in the center of the platter on top of the lettuce and sprinkle with paprika.

2 onions, sliced paper-thin

3 tablespoons white vinegar

Salt to taste

1 head butter crunch lettuce, torn into small pieces

2 tablespoons sour cream

Sweet Hungarian paprika

Beet Pickle Salad

Taratuta

Makes 6 servings

This is a very old beet salad recipe, typically served during the first week of Lent. It is usually scooped onto lettuce leaves to serve. You can save time by using canned organic beets.

Put the red beets, pickles, and slices of onion in a large bowl. In a small bowl, whisk together the oil and horseradish relish, and add salt and black pepper to taste. Drizzle the dressing over the beet mixture and toss gently.

Serve by scooping a single portion into an individual lettuce leaf and place side-by-side on a serving platter. Simple and delicious!

6 red beets, cooked, peeled, and sliced

3 dill pickles, sliced

1 onion, thinly sliced

2 tablespoons sunflower oil

1 teaspoon Pickled Horseradish Relish (page 68)

Salt and freshly ground black pepper to taste

6 large single lettuce leaves to serve

Cucumbers with Sour Cream

Mizeria

Makes 6 servings

This popular Ukrainian dish is an ideal accompaniment to a summer meal. Some cooks use diluted vinegar flavored with sugar to dress this salad, while others choose sour cream as a binder. This is my variation. Salting the cucumbers draws out their natural moisture, thereby making them firmer. Make sure you pat dry the cucumbers with a paper towel before dressing the salad so it will not be too salty.

Put the cucumber slices in a colander set over a bowl and sprinkle with salt. Leave to drain for at least 20 minutes, then pat dry with a paper towel.

Put the cucumbers in a large salad bowl and add the onion, dill, vinegar, and sour cream and toss gently. Cover and refrigerate 1 hour, then toss again and season to taste with black pepper. Serve garnished with sprigs of fresh dill.

2 large cucumbers, thinly sliced

1½ teaspoons salt

1 small onion, thinly sliced

2 tablespoons finely chopped fresh dill

1 tablespoon white vinegar

½ cup (generous) sour cream

Freshly ground black pepper to taste

Sprigs of dill to garnish

Country-Style Cucumber Salad

Selians'ka salata z ohirkiv

Makes 6 to 8 servings

This old-fashioned cucumber salad is very good served with sliced cold chicken, duck, or pan-seared fish.

Put the cucumber slices in a colander set over a bowl and sprinkle with salt. Leave to drain for at least 20 minutes, then pat dry with a paper towel. Put the cucumber slices into a large bowl and set aside.

Remove the yolks from the hard-cooked eggs and mash with a fork. Slice the egg whites and set aside.

Pour the sour cream into a small bowl and whisk in the dill, parsley, black pepper, honey, mustard, and mashed egg yolks until the mixture is smooth and creamy. Gently stir in the egg whites.

Pour the entire mixture over the cucumber slices, toss gently and chill for at least 1 hour before turning into a decorative shallow bowl. Serve garnished with small sprigs of parsley.

3 large cucumbers, thinly sliced

1½ teaspoons salt

2 hard-cooked extra-large eggs

⅔ cup sour cream

1 teaspoon finely chopped fresh dill

1 teaspoon finely chopped fresh parsley

¼ teaspoon freshly ground black pepper

1 tablespoon honey

2 teaspoons prepared mustard

Small sprigs of parsley to garnish

Radishes with Lemon and Honey

Red'ka prypravlena tsytrynoyu i medom Makes 6 servings

This is a refreshingly cool and tangy salad, best eaten immediately after it is made.

Put the radish slices in a medium bowl and gently toss with salt and parsley. Set aside.

In a small bowl, whisk together the sunflower oil, lemon juice, and honey. Pour over the radishes, toss gently and serve on individual salad plates garnished with a few grinds of black pepper and a dollop of yogurt.

20 large red radishes, thinly sliced

½ teaspoon salt

¼ cup chopped fresh parsley

2 tablespoons sunflower oil

2 tablespoons fresh lemon juice

1 tablespoon honey

Freshly ground black pepper to taste

¾ cup plain yogurt

Sauerkraut Salad

Salata z kvashenoyi kapusty Makes 6 servings

Sauerkraut is usually served stewed, but this raw cabbage salad is more popular in warmer summer months.

Coarsely chop the sauerkraut and put into a large salad bowl. Add the scallions, bell pepper strips, oil, and honey. Toss gently and taste. Add some salt if necessary. Cover and refrigerate for at least 1 hour. Serve with a generous sprinkling of black pepper and paprika.

1 pound sauerkraut, rinsed with cold water and squeezed dry

6 scallions (including green tops), chopped

1 small red bell pepper, seeded and cut into julienne strips

2 tablespoons sunflower oil

1 tablespoon honey

Freshly ground black pepper to taste

Sweet Hungarian paprika to taste

Creamy Shrimp Salad

Salata z krevetok v smetani

Makes 6 to 8 servings

M ost Ukrainians crave that little something with a tangy flavor. There is also a national weakness for poached fish and shellfish in a creamy sauce. This zesty salad brings together the best of both worlds.

Prepare shrimp:

In a large shallow bowl, whisk together the vinegar, oil, mustard, and honey for the marinade. Add the shrimp and toss to coat. Cover and refrigerate 2 hours.

Preheat the broiler or fire up the grill or barbecue. Remove the shrimp from the marinade and sprinkle with salt and black pepper. Broil or grill the shrimp 4-inches from the heat for about 4 minutes, turning once and basting with any leftover marinade. Set the shrimp aside to cool.

Assemble salad:

Meanwhile, thoroughly combine all the dressing ingredients in a small bowl. Pour the dressing over the cooled shrimp and toss gently. Refrigerate for at least 1 hour. Serve the shrimp salad on individual salad plates garnished with a sprinkling of coarse salt and a few cornichons.

NOTE: *Cornichons are pickled gherkin cucumbers traditionally served with pashtet (recipe on page 16), smoked meats, and many fish dishes.*

2 pounds extra-large shrimp, peeled, deveined, tails left attached if desired

Salt and freshly ground black pepper to taste

Coarse salt and cornichons to garnish

MARINADE FOR SHRIMP:

2 tablespoons white vinegar

¼ cup sunflower oil

1 tablespoon prepared mustard

1 tablespoon honey

DRESSING:

¼ cup sour cream

½ cup mayonnaise

1 tablespoon tomato paste

1 tablespoon honey

2 tablespoons apple cider vinegar

2 tablespoons chopped fresh dill

1 large dill pickle, finely chopped

2 ribs celery, finely chopped

Fish Salad Mimosa

Salata z ryby Mimosa

Makes 12 servings

O ften making an appearance on the *zakusky* table, this very rich layered sardine salad is reserved for big holiday celebrations and special occasions like birthdays or anniversaries. It is not for the faint of heart—but then Ukrainians are not calorie-conscious when it comes to celebrations and this is a favorite dish throughout the country.

If possible, use a large, deep glass bowl so you can see all the layers, making sure you spread each layer evenly and all the way to the rim of the bowl. If you prefer, use tinned herring fillets, salmon, or even tuna fish instead of sardines. I like to use raw milk cheddar cheese, but feel free to use your favorite cheddar. Also, freezing your sticks of butter will make them easier to grate. You can even grate the frozen butter directly over the salad.

If you are wondering about the name of this salad, the last layer of the salad is grated hard-cooked egg yolks and their beautiful yellow color is reminiscent of the yellow mimosa flower that grows all over the country.

8 jumbo hard-cooked eggs

2 cups grated sharp cheddar cheese

3 tins sardines (about 8-ounces total), drained

2 cups mayonnaise

1 cup (2 sticks) chilled unsalted butter, grated

1 large onion, grated

Sprigs of fresh dill for garnish

Gently separate the egg whites from the egg yolks, being careful to keep the egg yolks whole. Set the egg yolks aside. Grate the egg whites directly into a large glass serving bowl making the first layer of the salad. Make a second layer with the grated cheese.

Put the sardines on a plate and smash with a fork until mixed up and very soft. Lay half of the sardines in the bowl, making the third layer. Cover with half of the mayonnaise, making the fourth layer. Sprinkle the grated butter directly on top of the mayonnaise, making the fifth layer. Add the grated onion, making the sixth layer.

Add the rest of the sardines, making the seventh layer, then cover with the rest of the mayonnaise, making the eighth layer. Grate the egg yolks directly over the salad bowl and spread evenly over the top, making sure not to mix any into the mayonnaise. The grated egg yolks are the ninth and final layer.

Cover the bowl with plastic wrap and refrigerate several hours or overnight so all the flavors marry. Garnish the salad with a few sprigs of parsley just before serving. Serve the salad in the bowl it is prepared in with a large spoon on the side so each person can scoop a portion of it onto their plate.

Crocked Dill Pickles

Kvasheni ohirky

To satisfy their taste for sour foods, the quantity of cucumbers grown in Ukraine is startling—for come late summer it is pickle-making time! Every Ukrainian household has their own recipe for pickle-making. My recipe yields crunchy dill pickles that are ready to eat in two days and will keep one week in your refrigerator, with the flavor becoming stronger the longer the cucumbers sit in the brine. I use an old stone crock to hold my cucumbers, but a one-gallon jar with a wide mouth or an enamel-lined pot will work just fine, too. You will also need a saucer slightly smaller than the crock, some cheesecloth, a weight or heavy can, and some kitchen string.

- 30 fresh pickling cucumbers (3 to 4-inches long), washed and dried
- 5 stalks fresh dill with the dill heads if possible
- 2 pieces (1-inch each) horseradish root
- 4 cloves garlic, cut in half
- 10 black peppercorns
- 1 teaspoon caraway seeds
- 4½ tablespoons kosher salt

Trim both ends off the cucumbers and pack upright in the crock, interspersing them with the stalks of dill, horseradish root, garlic, peppercorns, and caraway seeds.

Pour 8 cups of water into a medium saucepan and stir in the salt. Bring to a boil and stir to make sure the salt is completely dissolved. Pour the salt water over the cucumbers, covering them completely. Let the mixture stand for 20 minutes.

Place the saucer inside the crock and put a weight on top to hold the pickles down and keep them submerged in the brine. Cover the top of the crock with water-dampened cheesecloth and secure with some string. Let the crock sit at room temperature overnight.

Rinse out the cheesecloth the next day and cover the crock again. Let the cucumbers stand for one more day, then transfer the pickles and brine to a clean jar and refrigerate. These pickles will keep for one week in your refrigerator.

Pickles lift ordinary meals above the commonplace, as a piquant accompaniment to a crackling roast or a steaming platter of kasha or as a treat in their own right. Various pickles are an absolute must on the *zakusky* table.

Pickled Red Beets

Kvasheni buriaky

Makes about 1 quart

This is my favorite way of preparing pickled beets. It is a quick and easy recipe and will keep in your refrigerator for three weeks. It is not terribly sweet as I use just a small amount of honey. Using red beets at the peak of their growing season will yield naturally sweet beets. When I serve my pickled beets, I sprinkle them with coarse salt and freshly ground black pepper and sometimes add a dab of sour cream. If you want to make this dish more elegant, use whole, small baby beets and add a cinnamon stick and grated orange zest to the basic recipe. If you like cloves, add a few. Sometimes I also add thinly sliced onions. Delicious!

3 medium whole red beets with stems and tap root intact, washed

⅓ cup apple cider vinegar

¼ cup buckwheat honey or more to taste

If the greens are still attached to the beets, break them off and use in other recipes. Put the beets into a large saucepan and cover with 6 cups of cold water. Bring to a boil, reduce the heat to medium-low and simmer, uncovered, until the beets are tender, about 35 to 45 minutes. Remove the beets with a slotted spoon and let cool. Reserve the boiling liquid.

Ladle 4 cups of the hot beet cooking liquid into a large glass bowl or jar fitted with a lid. Stir in the vinegar and honey. Adjust the amount of sweet and sour to suit your taste. When the beets are cool enough to handle, cut off the tops and tap roots and slice the beets in half. Peel the beet halves—the skins should slip right off. Slice the beets and put into the marinade. All the beet slices should be covered with the liquid. When cooled, cover the bowl or jar and refrigerate.

The pickled beets will be ready to eat in about 3 days and the flavor will become stronger the longer they sit in the marinade. These pickles will keep in your refrigerator for 3 weeks.

Sterilizing Jars for Pickles and Preserves

To sterilize jars or containers, wash them thoroughly in hot water or run them through the hot cycle of your dishwasher and dry them off in a cool oven set at 275°F. Fill the jars while they are still warm, handling them as little as possible.

To close, use special preserving lids with metal screw bands and flat metal lids edged with sealing compound. Wipe the jars after filling while still warm. Let the jars cool completely before labeling.

Fresh Homemade Sauerkraut

Kvashena kapusta

Makes about 3 quarts or about 4¾ pounds

Sauerkraut has always had a special place in the Ukrainian diet as an adjunct to making other foods more agreeable, as well as for its own taste and nutritional value. It is made in huge quantities in Ukraine for winter use, when fresh cabbage may not always be available.

5 pounds fresh green or red cabbages

¼ cup fine dry salt

Choose fresh, firm, mature heads of cabbage when making sauerkraut. A general rule is to use two teaspoons of salt for every one pound of cabbage. You will also need a one-gallon stone or ceramic crock with a wide mouth, a saucer smaller than the top of the crock, a weight or jar filled with water, cheesecloth, and some kitchen string.

Adding a few black peppercorns, caraway seeds, or a small quantity of mixed whole spices is common when preparing sauerkraut. Some people add shredded carrots, onion, red or green bell peppers, lingonberries or cranberries, or a few whole small apples to the cabbage, the latter being a particular favorite. Apples fermented with cabbage make a wonderful addition to meat and especially game dishes.

This is my basic recipe for sauerkraut. If I am making sauerkraut in late summer or early fall, I add fresh cranberries to the cabbage and maybe a few Granny Smith apples that have been peeled, cored, and chopped. I also make sauerkraut with red cabbage in the same way and its vibrant, deep purple color looks stunning next to a roast chicken or ham. Try serving either one as you would a winter salad with roast beef, goose, or cold slices of pork roast.

Remove the outer leaves of the cabbages and set aside. Quarter the heads and shred (including the core) by hand or in a food processor.

Mix the cabbage and salt in a large bowl, working the salt into the cabbage by hand, distributing it evenly. Put about 2 cups of cabbage into a crock and press down firmly with your hands, or use a potato masher as I do, to expel air and start the juices flowing. Continue to add layers of cabbage to the crock, pressing down firmly on each layer.

When all the cabbage has been added to the crock, cover the top with some of the large outer cabbage leaves you have set aside, put the saucer on top and put a weight on the saucer. Cover the crock with cheesecloth and secure with some kitchen string. Store the crock in a dark place at a temperature of about 60 to 72°F.

After one day, check the cabbage. Enough water should have been drawn out of the cabbage to cover it, but not the plate. Check the mixture every other day. Rinse off the large cabbage leaves on top of the sauerkraut and wipe around the edges of the crock removing any scum or mold (this is normal) that may form. Taste the sauerkraut from time to time. Fermentation will take 1 to 2 weeks and is indicated by the formation of gas bubbles. When no bubbles rise and the kraut tastes clean and bright, fermentation has ended.

Transfer the kraut to sterilized jars and store in the refrigerator where it will keep for several months. Rinse with cold water before serving as is, or add to recipes.

....

NOTE: *Sauerkraut stores well by freezing. Pack the kraut in freezer-safe containers, seal and freeze. If you do not have room in the freezer, keep your crock of sauerkraut in an unheated garage or shed during the wintertime.*

Pickled Horseradish Relish

Khrin v otsti

Makes about 1½ cups

Horseradish is a very pungent root that adds lots of flavor and no fat. When grated raw, it is the perfect accompaniment to balance rich foods. Ukrainians love horseradish!

When picking out fresh horseradish root, look for unblemished ones that are not sprouting. Generally speaking, the whiter the root, the fresher it is. Peel only what you are going to use and grate or shred in a food processor. Horseradish spreads its pungency around, so make sure your kitchen is well ventilated as the oils are volatile. Freshly grated horseradish is best mixed with mild vinegar or the root will darken, lose its pungency, and become unpleasantly bitter.

2 cups grated horseradish

1 tablespoon granulated sugar

1 teaspoon salt

2 cups white wine vinegar

Mix all ingredients in a medium glass bowl. Pack into small sterilized jars leaving some space at the top. Seal and store in a cool, dry place. The pickled horseradish will keep for about one month.

Yet another recipe for horseradish: Horseradish sauce ...

This is the perfect dressing for a fresh vegetable salad. Combine ½ cup cottage cheese in a small bowl with 2 tablespoons sour cream or plain yogurt, 2 teaspoons sunflower oil, ½ teaspoon white wine vinegar, and 1 teaspoon freshly grated horseradish. Mix until creamy. Pour over garden fresh vegetables to serve.

Beet and Horseradish Relish

Tsvikly

This is the traditional Easter relish served with ham or roast suckling pig. It is always best to let fresh relish sit for at least 24 hours before serving, so plan ahead. If there is any relish left over, it is delicious spooned over platefuls of steaming scrambled eggs.

¾ cup apple cider vinegar

½ cup granulated sugar

½ teaspoon salt

½ cup freshly grated horseradish

5 cups finely chopped cooked red beets

Pour the vinegar into a medium glass bowl fitted with a lid. Whisk in the sugar and salt, and then stir in the horseradish. Add the beets and mix thoroughly. Cover tightly and chill overnight. Keep any leftover relish refrigerated.

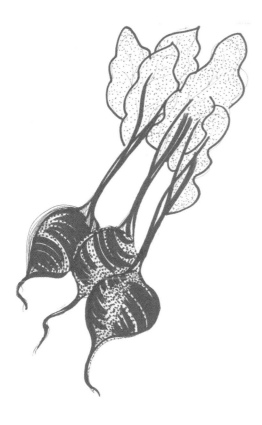

Old Country Cabbage-Beet Relish

Starokrayova pryprava zi svizhoyi kapusty i buriakiv

Makes about 6 pints

This is a very old recipe, an unusual one in fact, used as a condiment or relish or as an accompaniment to roasts and poultry and game dishes.

3 cups apple cider vinegar

¾ cup granulated sugar

1 tablespoon salt

½ teaspoon freshly ground black pepper

4 cups finely shredded green cabbage

4 cups shredded cooked red beets

1 cup freshly grated horseradish

Pour the vinegar into a medium, non-reactive saucepan and stir in the sugar, salt, and black pepper. Bring to a boil and stir, making sure all the sugar is dissolved.

Meanwhile, mix the cabbage, beets, and horseradish together in a large glass bowl. Pour the vinegar mixture over top and mix thoroughly. Pack into sterilized jars and seal with vinegar-proof (non-reactive) caps. Store jars in a cool place where they will keep for up to one month.

Cooked Fruit Pulp

Povydlo

Povydlo is simply fresh fruit that has been cooked down to a very thick consistency. One of the benefits of making your own is that you can usually avoid adding sweetener of any kind. As the fruit cooks down it intensifies in flavor and rarely have I ever had to add honey or sugar.

Povydlo can be made from any kind of fruit, but Ukrainians like to use plums over any other fruit. Pick plums that are very ripe—wrinkling at the stems. At this stage the plums are very sweet and less juicy, yielding an excellent tasting preserve. The end result should be soft and spreadable enough to mound gently and stay in place on a spoon. *Povydlo* should not be syrupy or stiff. Sometimes it takes the place of jam, but most often *povydlo* is used to fill pastries and candies.

5 pounds very ripe plums

A heavy cast iron pot or preserving kettle

Wash, pit, and quarter the plums. Put into the pot and add just enough water to prevent burning, about ½ cup. Bring to a boil, stirring frequently, and reduce the heat to medium-low. Gently simmer, uncovered, stirring occasionally, until the fruit mixture is fairly thick, about 1 hour. Taste and sweeten if desired.

Place the pot in a 300°F oven, uncovered, for 4 to 5 hours. Stir the fruit occasionally, about once or twice an hour. The pulp is ready when you cut across it with a wooden spoon and it stays separated. Remove from oven and cool.

When cooled, pack into sterilized jars and store in the refrigerator where it will keep for several months.

Sweet Pickled Cherries (No-Cook Method)

Starokrayova pryprava zi

Makes about 1½ to 2 quarts

I believe the tart sour cherry to be the garnet jewel of the Ukrainian kitchen. It is truly worthwhile to take advantage of the brief period they are in season. There is hardly anything better to accompany roast poultry or game, lamb, or even pork than these cherries with their sweet-and-sour flavor. Pickled sour cherries are also used in salads and look splendid as a garnish.

3 pounds sour cherries

2½ cups white wine vinegar or apple cider vinegar

2 scant cups loosely packed light brown sugar

Wash and pit the cherries. Put them in a one-gallon stone crock or glass jar with a fitted lid. Pour the vinegar over top and let the cherries sit overnight at room temperature.

Drain the cherries and return to the rinsed-out crock or jar. Mix in the sugar, cover with a piece of cheesecloth, and secure with a string. Let the cherries sit for 5 days at room temperature, stirring them once each day. The cherries can be eaten immediately after this amount of time.

Pack any extra pickled cherries in sterilized pint or quart jars along with some of the liquid. Seal and store in the refrigerator where they will keep for up to one month.

Preserved Pears

Zavareni brushi

Pickled fruit often takes the place of a salad on the Ukrainian table, and sometimes is preferable, especially during the winter months when heartier dishes are served. For this recipe make sure to use firm pears—Bartlett pears are suggested. This is also the traditional way of making pickled crab apples, though it is difficult to find crab apples today unless you know someone with an orchard who grows them.

12 firm Bartlett pears, peeled, cored, and halved

Juice of 1 lemon

1 cup lightly flavored honey (see Note)

1 cup apple cider vinegar

1 4-inch piece cinnamon stick

10 whole cloves

6 tablespoons brandy (optional)

Put the pears in a large bowl and sprinkle with the lemon juice. Let stand for 5 minutes.

Pour 2 cups of water and the honey into a large non-reactive saucepan and bring to a boil over medium heat, stirring to dissolve the honey. Add the pears and gently simmer until barely tender, about 5 minutes. Remove the pears with a slotted spoon and set aside.

Pour the vinegar into the syrup in the pan and add the cinnamon stick and cloves. Bring to a boil over medium heat, stirring constantly. Reduce the heat to low and simmer 5 minutes, stirring constantly. Remove the pan from the heat and let the syrup cool to room temperature.

Strain the cooled syrup. Pack the pears into sterilized quart jars and sprinkle the brandy over them. Spoon some of the syrup into each jar; seal and refrigerate. The pears will be ready to eat in 3 days and will keep for 1 month in the refrigerator.

NOTE: *Examples of lightly flavored honey are clover, wildflower, alfalfa, or orange blossom honey. Darker varieties like buckwheat honey are stronger flavored and more readily used in baking cakes and pastry.*

Honey Huts ... Ukraine has an extensive bee-culture history ...

Petr Prokopovich (1775-1850) was born in Ukraine. He was the inventor of the first mobile hive for gathering honey and the founder of the first apiculture school in the world. But before the development of modern hives, bee-keeping was common practice throughout the country. Separate, free-standing honey huts were erected, often close to one's dwelling, so that swarms could be detected and captured and also so that the bees would get used to human interaction. These beautiful honey huts pay homage to the honey bee's place in Ukrainian legends, beliefs, and folklore.

Rose Petal Preserves

Rozha z tsukrom

Makes about 2 pints

Fragrant, delicate rose petals with a velvety texture make a very exotic preserve that has been eaten for centuries in Ukraine. Considered unequalled as a filling for yeast-raised doughnuts called *pampushky* (page 182), rose petal preserves are traditionally made from a mixture of scented rose petals and sugar, and flavored with fresh lemon juice and a splash of rum. The sweet doughnuts dusted with confectioners' sugar and filled with rose petal preserves are often part of *Sviata Vechera* —the holy Christmas Eve dinner.

8 cups organic red rose petals, tightly packed

8 cups granulated sugar

Juice of 1 lemon

1 tablespoon dark rum

Snip the yellow tips off the rose petals where they have been attached to the crown of the blossom as they have a bitter taste.

Put half the rose petals in a food processor, along with 4 cups of sugar, half the lemon juice, and half the rum. Pulse a few times, stop to scrape the sides of the processor bowl, and then pulse a few more times. Turn the contents into a large glass bowl. Repeat the process with the remaining ingredients and combine with the first batch.

Pack the preserves into sterilized jars, seal and store in a cool, dry place or cupboard. The preserves will keep for up to one year.

Strawberry Preserves

Marmeliada iz sunyts'

Makes about 6 pints

Ukrainian pastries alone place an enormous demand on numerous fruit preserves, but tea time also requires a nice sampling of preserves to be used in the place of sugar. They are usually eaten with a sip of unsweetened tea or small spoonfuls are heaped into a cup or glass of clear tea. Refreshing summer juices may even have a spoonful of preserves added to each glass. Strawberry, raspberry, gooseberry, sour cherry, black currant, peach, and apricot preserves are the most popular.

2 pounds fresh, firm strawberries

3 cups granulated sugar

2 tablespoons apple cider vinegar

Pinch of salt

Put all the ingredients in a large non-reactive saucepan. Bring to a rolling boil over high heat, stirring occasionally with a wooden spoon, being careful not to crush the fruit. Keep at a rolling boil for 15 to 20 minutes or until the mixture reaches 220°F on a candy thermometer. Transfer the mixture to hot, sterilized jars and seal. Jars can be stored for 1 month in your refrigerator.

....

NOTE: *If you want to keep preserves longer, use jars and lids especially made for canning. Process the filled and sealed jars in a hot water bath: set the jars on a rack in a large pot, cover with boiling water by at least one inch, cover and boil or process for 10 minutes. Label jars when completely cooled.*

Spiced Apricot Jam

This jam is delicious scooped into a cup of hot tea.

3 pounds ripe apricots, peeled, pitted, and finely chopped

¼ cup fresh lemon juice

6 cups granulated sugar

¼ teaspoon ground cinnamon

¼ teaspoon ground allspice

¼ teaspoon ground cloves

1 (6-ounce) bottle liquid fruit pectin

Put the apricots in a large bowl and sprinkle with the lemon juice. Let sit for 5 minutes.

Transfer the apricots to a large preserving pan and mix with the sugar, cinnamon, allspice, and cloves. Heat to boiling over high heat and boil hard for 1 minute, stirring constantly. Remove the pan from the heat and immediately stir in the pectin. Cool slightly, about 5 minutes.

Ladle into warm, sterilized jars. Cover and seal when cold. Let the jam sit for about 2 weeks at room temperature before using. Store the opened jars of jam in your refrigerator.

Chapter 4

Sauces, Vegetables and Grains

Ever popular and ingenious . . .

Fresh vegetables are enthusiastically consumed by Ukrainian people. Ukrainian vegetable cookery is very similar to many other cuisines, with the only differences being in the final finishes and garnishes or in the sauces used. Fresh spring vegetables like greens are usually eaten raw in salads or shredded and added to soups. A drizzle of browned butter or a scattering of browned buttered crumbs is the most traditional way of garnishing cooked vegetable dishes. Constituting a large part of the Ukrainian diet are stuffed vegetables, usually with stuffing made of grain or meat or a combination of both, served very simply with a splash of cream or a sprinkling of chopped fresh herbs or chopped salt pork.

The next likely way of serving vegetables is with a thickened cream sauce that suits that particular vegetable (or grain) dish. Often times this basic sauce is enhanced with different seasonings, fresh herbs, or additional ingredients. Milk, meat stocks, mushrooms, or mildly flavored vegetables may be added and will impart their own flavor to the basic sauce, thus creating a new one. This chapter starts with sauces I consider the most useful both as components of vegetable and grain cookery and for serving with other dishes, examples of which are cited.

Flavorful grains have, from times immemorial, sat at the very heart of Ukrainian cuisine. Presented in imaginative ways, grains like buckwheat, cornmeal, millet, and wheat have provided an endless source of folklore and wisdom, and in their methods of preparation an important form of regional self-expression. A nutritious, high-fiber food, grains are made into some particularly healthy dishes, excellent for alternating with richer ones made with meat and eggs to create a balanced diet.

Ukraine is a vast country rich in natural beauty ... fertile soil, plentiful rainfall, and a long growing season favor the growth of lush vegetation, so it is no wonder that Ukrainians are excellent farmers. The beautiful gardens, picturesque orchards, rich pasturage, and flowing grain fields are all worthy of admiration.

Smetankova pidlyva   Makes 2 cups

This basic cream sauce is used often in Ukrainian cookery and is a favorite standby for many meat, vegetable, and grain dishes.

2 tablespoons unsalted butter

2 tablespoons unbleached all-purpose flour

1 cup milk or light cream

1 cup Rich Ukrainian Chicken Broth (page 44), vegetable broth, or water

½ teaspoon salt

¼ teaspoon freshly ground black pepper

Melt the butter in a medium saucepan over medium heat. Stir in the flour making a paste (roux) and continue stirring for 2 minutes (do not let brown). Slowly add the milk and chicken broth and stir steadily over medium heat until the mixture boils and starts to thicken. Reduce the heat to low and continue cooking another 3 minutes. Stir in the salt and black pepper. Serve as is or use as a base for any of the following variations.

DILL SAUCE: Add 2 tablespoons finely chopped fresh dill to the hot cream sauce. *Serve over cooked green beans, red beets, cabbage, carrots, mushrooms, or cauliflower. Dill sauce is a favorite standby for roasted new potatoes, all chicken and fish dishes, halved hard-cooked eggs, grain dishes, and combination meat and grain dishes.*

ONION SAUCE: Add ½ cup finely chopped onions sautéed in unsalted butter or oil, ½ teaspoon dry mustard, and 2 teaspoons white wine vinegar to the hot cream sauce. *Serve over asparagus, cabbage, wilted greens, halved hard-cooked eggs, pork, lamb, or any grain dish.*

MUSHROOM SAUCE: Add 1 cup sliced mushrooms sautéed in unsalted butter or oil, ½ cup sour cream, and 1 tablespoon finely chopped fresh dill or parsley to the hot cream sauce. *Serve over cooked green beans, cabbage, broccoli, cauliflower, Brussels sprouts, or carrots. Mushroom sauce is a favorite standby for meat, egg, fish, grains, and combination meat and grain dishes. Sometimes a clove or two of crushed garlic is added to this sauce.*

TART SOUR CREAM SAUCE: In a small bowl, temper 2 beaten egg yolks by stirring in a few tablespoons of hot cream sauce. Slowly stir the egg mixture into the hot cream sauce and continue cooking 1 more minute. Remove the pan from the heat and whisk in ½ cup sour cream and 1 teaspoon fresh lemon juice. *Serve over cooked potatoes, red beets, cabbage, mushrooms, Brussels sprouts, chicken, pork, or fish dishes, halved hard-cooked eggs, or any grain or combination meat and grain dish.*

HOT HORSERADISH SAUCE: In a small bowl, temper 2 beaten egg yolks by stirring in a few tablespoons hot cream sauce. Slowly stir the egg mixture into the hot sauce and continue cooking 1 more minute. Remove the pan from the heat and whisk in ½ cup sour cream, ¼ cup freshly grated horseradish, 1 tablespoon fresh lemon juice, and 1 teaspoon honey. *Serve over cooked potatoes, red beets, cabbage, wilted greens, broccoli, cauliflower, or Brussels sprouts. Hot horseradish sauce is especially good with beef and fish dishes, halved hard-cooked eggs, grains, and combination meat and grain dishes.*

YELLOW CREAM SAUCE: In a small bowl, temper 2 beaten egg yolks by stirring in a few tablespoons of hot cream sauce. Slowly stir the egg mixture into the hot sauce and continue cooking 1 more minute. If the sauce is too thick, add a few more tablespoons chicken broth or water until you achieve desired consistency. *Serve over any cooked vegetable, halved hard-cooked eggs, chicken or fish, or any grain dish.*

CREAMY CHEESE SAUCE: Add 1 cup shredded or grated cheese to the hot cream sauce. If the sauce is too thick, add a few more tablespoons chicken broth or water until you achieve desired consistency. *Serve over cooked asparagus, broccoli, cauliflower, potatoes, wilted greens, halved hard-cooked eggs, and chicken or fish dishes.*

BROWN CREAM SAUCE: Follow the recipe for basic cream sauce making the following changes: use whole wheat flour instead of all-purpose and cook the paste until golden in color; use a richly-flavored beef broth in place of the chicken broth; opt for light cream instead of milk; sauté ½ cup of onions in unsalted butter or oil and stir into the hot brown sauce. *Serve over cooked green beans, cabbage, mushrooms, halved hard-cooked eggs, or any grain dish. Brown cream sauce is a favorite standby to enhance all meat dishes and combination meat and grain dishes.*

Pork Cracklings   *Shkvarky*

Ukrainians are out-and-out fat fanciers! These crackling little bits of pork are a favorite garnish strewn over cooked potatoes, grains, noodles, or dumplings. Ask your farmer or butcher to score the pork rind as he would for a crackling roast.

TO MAKE PORK CRACKLINGS:

Preheat the oven to 400°F. Wipe the pork rind dry with some paper towels or a kitchen cloth. Rub a generous amount of salt into the pork rind and put into a baking pan. Roast for 15 minutes, keeping a watchful eye on it. During this time the fat will render and the skin will become crispy. Transfer the pork rind to a cutting board and let cool. Chop into small pieces and serve immediately. Store any extra in an air-tight container in your refrigerator where the cracklings will keep for 1 week.

Potato Babka

Kartopliana babka

The word *babka* refers not only to rich cake-like breads but also to various puffy, egg-type dishes such as this one. Make sure you use a good quality whole milk cottage cheese and hot mashed potatoes and this recipe will surely not disappoint. Using Yukon gold potatoes yields a rich, golden result.

2 cups hot mashed potatoes

2 extra-large eggs, separated

½ cup milk

½ cup cottage cheese

½ teaspoon salt

¼ teaspoon freshly ground black pepper

Preheat the oven to 350°F and grease a 9-inch round baking pan with butter.

Put the mashed potatoes in a medium mixing bowl. Beat in the egg yolks. Add the milk, cottage cheese, salt, and black pepper. Beat vigorously until light.

In a separate bowl, beat the egg whites until stiff. Gently fold them into the potato mixture. Spoon the mixture into the greased baking pan and bake for 20 to 25 minutes or until browned and puffy. Serve immediately.

Roasted Potatoes with Caraway Seeds

Pecheni kartopli z kmynom

Makes 6 servings

Goose fat is prized by Ukrainians as are caraway seeds.

2 to 3 tablespoons rendered goose fat (see Note)

3 pounds baking potatoes, peeled and cut into 2-inch pieces

1 teaspoon salt

½ teaspoon freshly ground black pepper

1½ teaspoons caraway seeds

Chopped fresh parsley for garnishing

Preheat the oven to 400°F. Melt the goose fat in a small saucepan. Toss the potatoes with the melted fat and arrange them in a single layer in a casserole dish or baking pan. Sprinkle with the salt, black pepper, and caraway seeds and bake for about 45 minutes or until the potatoes are fork-tender, turning them halfway through the baking process. Sprinkle with chopped fresh parsley and serve immediately.

. . . .

NOTE: *Goose fat can be bought in jars online or in specialty food stores. Duck fat or bacon drippings can be used in place of the goose fat. If observing Lent, use sunflower oil or olive oil instead.*

Deruny

Makes 6 servings

Deruny, pancakes made from coarsely grated potatoes, make an attractive and satisfying dish. Also called *pliatsky*, *terchenyky*, or *kartoplyanyky*, these hot richly-browned potato pancakes are a national obsession in Ukraine and no one ever seems to tire of eating them! *Deruny* are traditionally served with various toppings such as sour cream, cottage cheese, pork cracklings, and sautéed onions.

3 pounds baking potatoes

1 large onion, grated

¼ cup unbleached all-purpose flour

2 extra-large eggs, slightly beaten

1 teaspoon salt

½ teaspoon freshly ground black pepper

⅓ teaspoon baking powder

3 tablespoons (generous) lard or sunflower oil

Preheat the oven to 200°F. Peel and grate the potatoes just before making the pancakes. Put the grated potatoes in a cotton kitchen cloth and squeeze to remove the excess moisture. Wait 5 minutes and squeeze again.

Put the potatoes in a large bowl and add the onion (and any of its juices) and flour and stir well with a fork. Add the eggs, salt, black pepper, and baking powder and mix thoroughly.

Melt the lard in a heavy skillet over medium heat and drop the potato mixture by the tablespoonful into the hot lard, without crowding, and gently flatten each with a spatula. Cook about 2 minutes and then flip to the other side to brown. Keep fried *deruny* warm in the oven while cooking the remaining batches. Serve immediately.

Potato Spirals with Caviar

Kartopliani spirali z ikroyu

Makes about 20 spirals

Ukrainian cooks take great pride in garnishing platters of meat roasts or whole cooked fish in extravagant ways. These potato puffs made from mashed potatoes prove to be a perfect vehicle for that and for indulging in a mouthful of caviar. They also make a substantial nibble on the *zakusky* table. It is a more sophisticated yet easy potato dish to prepare. Use whatever caviar your taste and budget permits.

6 baking potatoes

2 tablespoons unsalted butter, softened

½ cup milk

1 extra-large egg, lightly beaten

2 egg whites, lightly beaten

1 teaspoon freshly grated lemon zest

2 teaspoons finely chopped fresh parsley

½ teaspoon salt

¾ cup thick sour cream

3 ounces caviar

Preheat the oven to 400°F. Bake the potatoes for 1 hour or until tender. Let cool for a few minutes, then cut the potatoes in half and scoop out the insides, discarding the skins. Press the pulp through a ricer or food mill into a large mixing bowl. Beat in the butter, milk, egg, and egg whites. Stir in the lemon zest, parsley, and salt.

Line a large baking sheet with parchment paper. Transfer the potato mixture to a pastry tube fitted with a large tip and pipe 20 2-inch spirals (coils) in rows on the baking sheet. Use a small spoon to press a small, round indentation in the center of each swirl that will be large enough to hold ½ teaspoon sour cream and ½ teaspoon caviar.

Bake the potato swirls about 10 to 15 minutes or until lightly browned and crisp. Transfer the swirls to a serving platter and fill each hollow with some sour cream and some caviar. Serve immediately.

NOTE: *The potato swirls can be baked ahead of time in the morning and kept covered at room temperature until ready to prepare. Reheat them in a 350°F oven for 5 to 10 minutes just before filling and serving.*

Crispy Fried Potatoes with Wild Mushrooms

Prysmazheni kartopli z dykymy hrybamy Makes 4 servings

This intensely-flavored, soul-satisfying combination of crispy fried potatoes and wild mushrooms is the quintessential country dish. Chanterelles, meadow mushrooms, honey mushrooms, or morels are popular choices.

1 pound fresh wild mushrooms

2 tablespoons unsalted butter

3 tablespoons lard or sunflower oil

4 medium white potatoes, peeled and cut into 1-inch x ¼-inch sticks

1 teaspoon salt

½ teaspoon freshly ground black pepper

¼ cup sour cream

Chopped fresh parsley to garnish

Wipe the mushrooms clean with a damp cloth and separate the caps from the stems. Chop up the stems and slice the smaller caps in half and the larger caps into quarters.

Melt the butter in a medium skillet over medium heat. Add the mushrooms and stir until they start to give off their own liquid, then turn up the heat to medium-high and continue cooking until all liquid has evaporated, about 10 minutes. Set the pan aside.

Melt the lard in a heavy skillet over medium heat. Add the potatoes and cook about 7 to 8 minutes on one side. Scraping the bottom of the skillet, turn the potatoes over and cook the other side. Once the potatoes are cooked, stir in the mushrooms, salt, black pepper, and sour cream, tossing everything together well. Turn the heat down to low and cook another 1 to 2 minutes, until everything is heated through. Sprinkle with some chopped fresh parsley and serve immediately.

Dried Wild Mushrooms with Gravy

Makes 4 to 6 servings

A dish such as this is traditionally served over roasted meats, especially pork, or vegetables, grain dishes, or stuffed cabbage leaves called *holubtsi* (page 97).

2 cups dried porcini mushrooms

1 tablespoon sunflower oil

1 onion, chopped

2 cloves garlic, sliced

2 tablespoons unbleached all-purpose flour

4 cups meat broth or water

½ teaspoon salt

½ teaspoon freshly ground black pepper

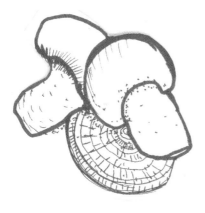

Soak the dried mushrooms in cold water overnight. Drain, rinse, and put in a medium saucepan with enough water to cover. Bring to a boil, reduce the heat to medium and simmer for 20 minutes. Drain the mushrooms (reserving the liquid for soups and sauces), chop, and set aside.

In a medium heavy skillet, warm the oil over medium heat. Add the onion and gently sauté for about 3 minutes. Add the garlic and continue cooking another minute. Sprinkle the flour over the mixture, stirring to coat evenly, and then add the broth. Turn up the heat to medium-high and bring to a boil, stirring constantly.

Add the drained mushrooms, salt, and black pepper. Reduce the heat to low and simmer, uncovered, for 20 minutes, stirring occasionally. Taste and adjust the seasonings if necessary and serve.

Warm Asparagus with Vinaigrette

Tepli shparagy u vinegreti

In Ukraine, fresh asparagus is usually simply pre-pared by poaching in a small amount of salted water and served with a sprinkling of toasted buttered bread crumbs or a dollop of sour cream flavored with a little crushed garlic. Another way to serve asparagus, as well as nearly any other poached vegetable, is with a drizzle of fresh lemon juice and some oil whisked into a vinai-grette dressing.

2 hard-cooked extra-large eggs

1 tablespoon Dijon mustard

½ teaspoon salt

¼ teaspoon freshly ground black pepper

2 tablespoons fresh lemon juice

6 tablespoons sunflower oil

30 to 36 asparagus spears, trimmed

2 tablespoons snipped fresh chives to garnish (optional)

Separate the egg yolks from the whites. Finely chop the egg whites and set aside.

In a small bowl, mash together the hard-cooked egg yolks and mustard to form a paste. Add half the salt, the black pepper, and lemon juice, stirring until smooth. Slowly whisk in the sunflower oil to make a creamy vinaigrette. Taste and adjust the seasonings if necessary. Set aside.

Pour about 1 cup of water into a large skillet and stir in the remaining ¼ teaspoon salt. Add the asparagus and bring to a boil over high heat. Lower the heat to medium and gently simmer for about 5 minutes or just until the spears are tender-crisp. Remove the asparagus with some tongs and place on a kitchen towel and pat dry.

Arrange the asparagus spears on a large serving platter and pour the vinaigrette over top while the asparagus is still warm. Scatter the chopped egg whites and chives over top and serve warm or at room temperature.

. . . .

NOTE: *Poached green beans, carrots, celery root, Brussels sprouts, broccoli, cauliflower, Savoy cabbage cut into small sections, tender baby leeks, wilted spinach, and beet greens are also served in this way.*

Bell Pepper Paprikash

Paprykash z pertsiv

Sweet bell peppers smothered in a piquant tomato sauce and spiked with sweet paprika is a dish with definite Hungarian roots, but one that Ukrainians love dearly as their own. In fact, this vegetable specialty is canned and sold commercially in Ukraine. But one can easily prepare this dish at home. It is meant to be served with cold meats as part of *zakusky* hour. It is also good served warm as a relish with fish dishes or with a simply cooked grain or *kasha* dish. Try to use a combination of sweet bell peppers for contrasting colors and flavors.

2 tablespoons (generous) sunflower oil

1 onion, finely chopped

2 teaspoons sweet Hungarian paprika

2 tablespoons finely chopped carrot

2 tablespoons finely chopped celery

6 large sweet bell peppers (red, orange, green, and/or yellow peppers in combination), seeded and cut into thick strips

3 large plum tomatoes

2 tablespoons tomato paste

½ cup vegetable broth or water

½ teaspoon salt

½ teaspoon freshly ground black pepper

1 tablespoon apple cider vinegar

1 tablespoon honey or more to taste (optional)

Warm the oil in a large skillet over medium heat. Add the onion and sauté until soft, about 5 minutes. Stir in the paprika, carrot, celery, and peppers and continue cooking another 5 minutes, adding a little more oil if necessary. Do not allow the vegetables to brown.

Peel, seed, and chop the tomatoes and add to the skillet along with any juices. Stir in the tomato paste, broth, salt, and black pepper. Allow the mixture to come to a boil over medium heat, then reduce the heat to low, cover, and simmer gently for about 10 minutes, adding a little more broth if liquid evaporates.

Remove the pan from the heat and stir in the vinegar and honey and let rest for a few minutes for the flavors to marry. Serve warm, at room temperature, or chilled.

Cauliflower with Dill Seed

Tsvitna kapusta z kropom

Makes 4 to 5 servings

I think most Ukrainians would agree that a topping of pork cracklings (page 81), while not necessary, could not hurt this dish!

1 medium head cauliflower

1 teaspoon salt

1 lemon, sliced

2 tablespoons unsalted butter, bacon drippings, or sunflower oil

1 teaspoon dill seeds

Sprigs of fresh dill and coarse salt for garnishing

Cut the head of cauliflower into bite-size pieces and put in a large saucepan, along with 2 cups of cold water, the salt, and half of the lemon slices. Bring to a boil, cover, and reduce the heat to medium-low. Simmer about 6 to 8 minutes or until the cauliflower is fork tender.

Meanwhile, melt the butter in a small saucepan over medium heat and just as the butter starts to brown, add the dill seeds and stir. Remove the pan from the heat and let rest.

Remove the cauliflower from the saucepan with a slotted spoon and transfer to a serving platter. Drizzle with the dill seed-infused browned butter and garnish with a few sprigs of dill, the remaining lemon slices, and a sprinkling of coarse salt. Serve immediately.

Sweet and Sour Red Cabbage

Chervona kapusta na kvasno i solodko   Makes 6 servings

This cabbage dish is the perfect accompaniment to meats, especially game meats. Sometimes cooked kidney beans are added to make the dish more substantial.

1 (3-pound) head red cabbage

1½ teaspoons salt

½ cup white vinegar

2 tablespoons unsalted butter or sunflower oil

⅓ cup loosely packed brown sugar

½ teaspoon freshly ground black pepper

2 sprigs fresh dill

Sour cream to garnish (optional)

Remove the outer leaves of the cabbage and discard. Core the cabbage, cut into wedges, and then into shreds. Put the cabbage into a large saucepan along with 3 cups of cold water and 1 teaspoon salt and bring to a boil. Cover, reduce the heat to medium-low, and simmer for about 20 minutes or until the cabbage is tender.

Meanwhile, pour the vinegar and 1 cup of cold water into a small, nonreactive saucepan and bring to a boil. Stir in the butter, brown sugar, remaining ½ teaspoon salt, black pepper, and sprigs of dill. Reduce the heat to medium-low and let simmer for 5 minutes. Remove the pan from the heat. Drain the cabbage and put into a large glass bowl. Pour the marinade over top, cover, and refrigerate for at least 12 hours.

When ready to serve, put the cabbage and its juices into a nonreactive saucepan and warm over medium-low heat. Use a slotted spoon to portion the cabbage into servings and garnish each with a slather of sour cream.

Honey-Glazed Brussels Sprouts and Chestnuts

Bruksel'ka z kashtanamy u medu   Makes 6 to 8 servings

B russels sprouts are to fall what asparagus is to springtime in Ukraine. These miniature cabbages with their green hues and grace of structure make an elegant accompaniment to any meal. Chestnuts are used in various ways—added to soups and casseroles and used as a stuffing for *holubtsi* (page 97). This dish is a sweet and smoky pairing of both and goes well with dramatic meat roasts such as Stuffed Crown Roast of Pork (page 121) or Holiday Stuffed Roast Goose (page 144).

1½ pounds Brussels sprouts

24 whole chestnuts, peeled

2 cups Rich Ukrainian Chicken Broth (page 44)

4 thick slices smoky bacon, chopped

3 tablespoons honey

½ teaspoon salt

½ teaspoon freshly ground black pepper

Make an "X" in the bottom of each sprout to ensure quicker cooking. Put in a medium saucepan with enough cold water to cover and cook until tender-crisp, about 5 minutes. Drain and set aside.

Put the chestnuts and chicken broth in a small saucepan and bring to a boil. Reduce the heat to medium-low, cover, and simmer until the chestnuts are tender, about 20 minutes. Drain, reserving broth.

In the meantime, sauté the bacon pieces in a medium skillet over medium heat until crisp. Remove from pan (reserving drippings), drain on paper towels, and set aside.

Pour off all but 2 tablespoons of bacon drippings and add the sprouts, chestnuts, and a few tablespoons of the chicken broth. Stir in the honey, turn the heat up to medium-high, and cook, stirring frequently, until the liquid is reduced to a glaze, about 5 minutes. Add the bacon pieces, salt, and black pepper and toss. Serve immediately.

Eggplants Stuffed with Shrimp

Nachyniuvani baklazhany

Makes 3 to 6 servings

In Ukraine, the faintly exotic eggplant is usually sliced and fried or oven-roasted, but many times it is served stuffed with equally exotic ingredients, especially in southern Ukraine. In this case, the shrimp stuffing is punctuated with pine nuts, currants, and chopped mint, rendering a rich-tasting succulent yet light entrée. Delicious served hot on a bed of steamed rice or cold with plenty of fresh lemon wedges, it also makes a delightful and different appetizer.

6 small eggplants

2 tablespoons sunflower or olive oil

1 small onion, finely chopped

¼ cup plain dry breadcrumbs

1 tablespoon dried black currants

10 ounces small shrimp, peeled and chopped

1 tablespoon chopped fresh mint

1 tablespoon pine nuts

½ teaspoon salt

¼ teaspoon freshly ground black pepper

12 thick slices fresh tomato

1 tablespoon unsalted butter

Fresh lemon wedges to serve (optional)

Cut the eggplants in half lengthwise and carefully scoop out the insides, leaving a ½-inch shell. Sprinkle the shells with salt and set aside.

Warm the oil in a large skillet over medium heat, add the onion and sauté until softened, about 5 minutes. Add the eggplant pulp, breadcrumbs, and currants and continue cooking another 5 minutes, adding a few tablespoons water if the mixture becomes dry. Take the pan off the heat, stir in the shrimp, mint, pine nuts, salt, and black pepper and let the stuffing cool down for a few minutes.

Stuff the eggplant shells with the filling using a teaspoon. Put a slice of tomato on top of each and top with a small dab of butter. Put the eggplants into a shallow skillet with about 1 cup of water. Bring to a boil over medium heat, cover, reduce the heat to medium-low and cook until the water evaporates and the filling is cooked, about 10 minutes. Carefully remove the stuffed eggplants and place on a serving platter garnished with fresh lemon wedges if desired.

Varya

Makes 6 servings

This is a nutritious beet and bean dish flavored with dried prunes. It is a great way to utilize leftover vegetables. The proportions need not be followed too closely—adjust to your liking.

1 cup chopped cooked red beets

1 cup chopped pickled red beets (page 66)

1 cup cooked red kidney beans

12 dried prunes, poached, pitted, and chopped

½ teaspoon salt

2 tablespoons sunflower oil

Put all the ingredients into a large bowl. Toss and serve at room temperature.

More Party Etiquette ... "The Meaning of Flowers"

The Ukrainian love of nature often manifests itself in the giving of flowers. The type, color, and number of flowers all possess special meaning in Ukrainian culture, so in order to steer clear of an embarrassing gaffe, one needs to know a few basic do's and don'ts ...

- If you are invited to a birthday party, take an odd number of flowers—but no more than nine. Giving more than nine flowers indicates sincere romantic intentions. But if you want to make a real impression on the birthday girl, give her as many flowers as her age, adding or subtracting one to make an odd number.

- An even number of flowers is for funerals *only*, as are chrysanthemums and lilies.

- Yellow flowers symbolize separation or farewell; white is considered the color of innocence so white flowers are appropriate for weddings.

- Red is a symbol of victory and patriotism and red flowers (especially red carnations) may be given to a veteran or to a man on his anniversary.

- In February, bunches of violets and snowdrops are sold on the streets of Ukraine as a sign spring is approaching.

Bean Fritters

Makes 4 to 5 servings

Beans are eaten with great relish in Ukraine. Lightly spiced, moist, and delicious, I like my bean fritters topped with a scoop of creamy cottage cheese or a dollop of thick sour cream. While the flavor of fresh fruit nicely complements beans and legumes, some Ukrainians prefer fruit preserves or syrups with this dish. The choice is certainly yours.

¼ cup warm water (about 110°F)

½ teaspoon active dry yeast

2 tablespoons granulated sugar

⅓ cup canned evaporated milk, warmed

2 cups cooked navy beans or small lima beans

1 cup unbleached all-purpose flour

2 tablespoons sunflower oil

1 extra-large egg, slightly beaten

½ teaspoon salt

½ teaspoon freshly ground black pepper

2 tablespoons lard, unsalted butter, or oil for frying

1 cup (generous) creamed cottage cheese

Sprigs of parsley for garnishing

Pour the warm water into a medium bowl and sprinkle the yeast over top. Add the sugar and milk and stir. The mixture will foam. Leave to rest for 10 minutes.

Puree the beans in a blender or food processor and put into a large bowl. Add the flour, sunflower oil, egg, salt, and black pepper and mix until well blended. Stir in the yeast mixture and let rise for 30 minutes.

Preheat the oven to 200°F. Melt the lard in a large skillet over medium heat. To make fritters, drop 2 tablespoons of batter at a time into the hot lard and fry until set, about 3 minutes, then flip and brown on the other side. Keep the fritters warm in the oven while cooking other batches.

Serve the fritters warm topped with creamed cottage cheese and a few sprigs of parsley as a garnish.

Kvashena kapusta z horokhom

This dish should be quite thick, as it is made with cooked dried peas. It is traditionally served as a vegetables side dish with any meat course, especially pork. A sauerkraut dish of some kind is usually included in the holy Christmas Eve dinner, "*Svyata, Vechera,*" and this dish is a favorite choice with a few changes: omit the bacon and use sunflower or olive oil in preparation; skip the sour cream and garnish with chopped fresh parsley or dill.

3 cups sauerkraut

4 thick slices bacon, chopped into small pieces

1 onion, chopped

2 tablespoons unbleached all-purpose flour

1 cup cooked dried peas

½ cup cooked sliced mushrooms

1 clove garlic, crushed

¼ cup sour cream

Salt and freshly ground black pepper to taste

Put the sauerkraut into a large saucepan, add 1 cup of water and bring to a boil over medium-high heat. Reduce the heat to medium-low and cook, uncovered, for about 30 minutes. Drain, reserving liquid.

In a large skillet over medium heat, fry the bacon pieces until brown and crisp. Add the onion and continue cooking until the onion is soft, about 5 minutes. Sprinkle the flour over the entire mixture and stir to form a paste. Add the liquid from the sauerkraut and stir until the sauce thickens. Add the sauerkraut, cooked dried peas, mushrooms, and garlic and reduce the heat to low. Simmer uncovered for about 15 minutes. The mixture should be quite thick. Remove the pan from the heat and stir in the sour cream, salt, and black pepper. Serve immediately.

Stuffed Cabbage Rolls

Holubtsi Makes 10 to 12 servings (approximately 2 to 3 holubtsi per person)

Holubtsi in Ukrainian literally translates as "little" or "dearest pigeons," though they do not contain pigeon meat at all! *Holubtsi* are simply stuffed cabbage rolls, usually made in great quantities. They may be stewed in a sauce depending on the filling. It is a popular family dish and one that is always served at festive or community dinners. On certain occasions, more than one preparation may be served. It is not what I would call a dainty dish; however, it is incredibly flavorful, inexpensive, and offers an interesting change of pace.

Fillings for *holubtsi* vary, but usually any combination of meat and rice or buckwheat, mushrooms, grain, or vegetables and meat finds the greatest favor. It is a versatile dish capable of a number of variations, depending upon the season, personal preference, and, like so many Ukrainian dishes, regional differences. For instance, in summer, red beet leaves, large spinach leaves, or even lettuce leaves may take the place of cabbage. In places where grape-growing is popular and in the southern region of Ukraine, grape leaves are wrapped around the filling in place of the cabbage. Old-fashioned recipes call for whole pickled cabbage leaves rather than fresh cabbage leaves and some cooks insist that tucking shredded sauerkraut between layers of rolls made from fresh cabbage leaves gives the end result a tart and tangy finish. If eaten during Lent, *holubtsi* are made with a meatless filling and oil is used rather than animal fat in preparation.

Holubtsi may be cooked with liquid or without, depending on the nature of the filling. A fully cooked filling will require very little or no liquid. If one chooses to use a partially cooked grain filling (as is often the case) some liquid will be needed when stewing the rolls. Any filling that is partially cooked will need more moisture to tenderize than a completely cooked one. Tomato sauce, tomato juice, soup stock, mushroom stock, meat drippings, sour cream, or simply water can be used. The end result should never be soggy and sometimes it just depends on what ingredients are available or on hand.

This first recipe for *holubtsi* is a standard one and a number of delicious variations follow.

1 (6 to 7-pound) head green cabbage

1 tablespoon plus 2 teaspoons salt

2 tablespoons apple cider vinegar

4 tablespoons bacon drippings

1 onion, finely chopped

3 cups partially cooked white rice (see note)

1 pound ground beef or veal

1 pound ground pork

½ teaspoon freshly ground black pepper

2 cups chunky tomato sauce

2 tablespoons tomato paste

1 to 2 tablespoons brown sugar (optional)

Additional tomato sauce, sour cream, or crumbled bacon to serve

In a large pot, bring enough water to a boil to cover the cabbage. Mix in 1 tablespoon salt and the vinegar. Cut the core out of the cabbage and remove the larger outer leaves and set aside. Put the cabbage, core-side down, in another large pot and pour in the seasoned boiling water. Cover and let sit for about 30 minutes or until the leaves are soft enough to roll easily. Gently pull away as many leaves as possible and set aside. (*It is likely that after pulling off a few layers you will have to put the cabbage head back into the boiling liquid and let sit again until more leaves are pliable.*)

continued on next page ⇨

In a small skillet over medium heat, melt 2 tablespoons of the bacon drippings and add the onion. Sauté until soft, about 5 minutes, then set aside to cool.

Put the rice in a large bowl and using a fork, separate the grains. Add the beef, pork, 1 teaspoon salt, and the black pepper. Mix gently and set aside.

In a medium saucepan over medium heat, gently warm the tomato sauce and then stir in the sautéed onions plus any fat in the pan, tomato paste, and brown sugar. Cover, reduce the heat to low, and simmer 15 minutes. Make sure the filling is well-seasoned as some of the flavors will be absorbed by the cabbage leaves. Failure to do so will result in a flat-tasting dish.

Preheat the oven to 350°F. Melt the remaining 2 tablespoons bacon drippings and set aside. Place a few of the reserved outer cabbage leaves in the bottom of a Dutch oven or large covered casserole (reserve a few other tougher leaves for the top of casserole).

Begin filling the pliable cabbage leaves by placing 1 to 3 tablespoons meat mixture on the base of each leaf (more filling for larger leaves; less for smaller ones), tuck in the sides and roll up as firmly as you can, continuing to tuck in the sides as you roll. Arrange one layer of the rolls on top of the leaves in the pot. Sprinkle with some of the remaining 1 teaspoon salt, drizzle with some of the tomato sauce and some of the melted bacon drippings (the liquid should barely show between the layers).

Follow with another layer of cabbage rolls and seasonings and continue this process with the remaining ingredients. There will be several layers. Cover the last layer of the *holubtsi* with more of the reserved outer cabbage leaves.

Cover tightly and bake 2 hours or until the cabbage and filling are cooked, removing the lid the last 30 minutes. Serve with additional tomato sauce, sour cream, or crumbled bacon.

NOTE: *I use short medium-grain white rice in this dish which breaks up more easily and clings together when cooking. The rice is considered "partially cooked" when all the liquid is absorbed, but the rice is not tender—in other words, with a "slight bite" when tasted.*

VARIATIONS:

Cured Cabbage Leaf Holubtsi

This is an old-fashioned *holubtsi* dish made from whole cured cabbage leaves. Brined whole cabbage leaves are available packed in jars and sold in Ukrainian or Russian specialty shops, but it is just as easy to do at home. Simply put a few layers of whole cabbage leaves in the middle of the shredded cabbage when making your own sauerkraut (*recipe on page 67*). Rinse the cured cabbage leaves well. Prepare any of the fillings given here and make the *holubtsi* using the same method as in the preceding recipe. The only differences are that you may need to omit any extra salting of layers if your cabbage leaves are well-flavored and *holubtsi* made with cured cabbage leaves will take a slightly longer time to cook than those made with fresh cabbage.

Curing whole heads of cabbage ...

To cure your own cabbage leaves, select small, firm cabbages. Allow 2 teaspoons of salt for each pound of cabbage. You will need a large 4-gallon crock or glass or ceramic container to hold the cabbages and a 10-pound weight. Follow the directions for making sauerkraut on page 67. Once the cabbage heads are cured, separate the leaves and store as directed for the sauerkraut.

Sauerkraut Holubtsi

Another version of *holubtsi* adds sauerkraut. Follow the standard recipe (pages 97–98) using fresh cabbage leaves wrapped around your favorite filling. When making the layers, in place of the salt, top each layer of the *holubtsi* with ½ cup drained sauerkraut. Use some of the sauerkraut brine as part of the liquid. Follow the remaining directions and the finished dish will have a delicate sauerkraut flavor. Delicious!

Beet Leaf Holubtsi (Beet Leaf Rolls)

The first tender beet greens of spring are usually used for this Old World specialty. The traditional fillings of choice for these *holubtsi* are buckwheat (page 102), rice (page 101), or yeast-raised dough (see separate recipe next page), and the liquid of choice is melted bacon drippings or butter and a splash of apple cider vinegar.

To make: Dip the beet leaves in boiling salted water just long enough to wilt them for easier handling. Prepare your filling of choice. If the beet leaves are small, use 2 or 3 for each roll. Follow the standard recipe for making *holubtsi* (pages 97–98) but sprinkle each layer with melted bacon drippings (or melted butter or oil) and a drizzle apple cider vinegar (this will not only impart tartness, but will keep the rolls firm). Beet leaf *holubtsi* take less time to bake, about 1 hour. Serve with tart sour cream sauce (page 80) or mushroom sauce (page 80).

Beef Leaf Holubtsi with Bread Dough Filling

In the region of the Carpathian Mountains, Bukovyna and western Ukraine in general, beet leaf *holubtsi* are filled with raised bread dough and served with a different kind of sour cream sauce. Depending on how much you want to make, you will need more than one Dutch oven, covered casserole, or roaster pan, allowing enough room for the yeast dough to raise and bake.

1 batch of your favorite bread dough recipe (enough for 2 loaves)

beet leaves, blanched in boiling water

2 cups finely chopped fresh dill

2 cups finely chopped scallions including green tops

bacon drippings or oil

salt

pepper

SOUR CREAM SAUCE:

1 quart light cream

1 cup sour cream

Preheat oven to 350°F. To assemble, simply take a piece of dough about the size of a golf ball and stretch it out over a beet leaf. Sprinkle some dill and scallions on top of the dough and roll up the dough and leaf together. Line your pan with some extra beet leaves, and then place the rolls side-by-side making up the first layer. Sprinkle with some melted bacon drippings, salt, and black pepper. Make a second layer in the same way. Cover the top with extra beet leaves and put the pan in a warm place to rise for about 1 hour. Continue making the *holubtsi* in two layers per pan until all ingredients are used up. Bake the risen *holubtsi*, uncovered, for 1 hour.

To make the sauce, bring the light cream to a boil over medium heat in a medium saucepan. Add remaining dill, scallions, salt, and black pepper to taste. Reduce the heat to medium-low and let cook for 30 minutes, stirring occasionally to prevent burning. Take the pan off the heat and slowly whisk in the sour cream until thick and creamy. Taste and adjust seasonings if necessary.

When the *holubtsi* are baked, let cool slightly, then pull apart and put into shallow serving dishes. Pour the sauce over top, just enough to cover, and serve.

Rice Filling for Holubtsi

Nachynka na holubtsi z ryzhu

Makes about 6 cups

This everyday filling lends itself well to innumerable variations. I like to cook rice filling in milk rather than water which gives the end result so much more flavor—and momentarily stepping away from my culinary region, I have even used soy milk which produces a deliciously moist filling. A rich soup stock or tomato juice can also be used in place of water.

- 4 cups milk or water
- 2 cups medium-grain white rice
- 4 to 5 tablespoons unsalted butter or any other fat
- 1½ teaspoons salt
- ½ teaspoon freshly ground black pepper
- 1 onion, finely chopped

Pour the milk into a large saucepan and bring to a boil over medium heat, stirring frequently to prevent scorching. Add the rice, reduce the heat to low, and cook about 20 minutes or until tender.

Fluff the rice with a fork and put into a large bowl. Add 2 tablespoons butter, salt, and black pepper and toss gently until the rice is well-coated, adding another tablespoon of butter if needed.

Meanwhile, melt the remaining 1 or 2 tablespoon(s) of butter in a medium skillet over medium heat. Add the onion and sauté until softened, about 5 minutes. Mix the onion with the rice and taste. Adjust the seasonings if necessary. Let the mixture cool before using as a filling for *holubtsi* (see recipes on pages 97–99)

NOTE: *The key to a good rice filling is to make sure it is well-seasoned because your "wrappers," be it cabbage, sorrel, or beet leaves will also absorb flavors. Adding some sort of fat to the filling is therefore essential. Butter, bacon drippings, salted pork fat, rendered goose or duck fat all work well, resulting in a superior filling with which to make* holubtsi.

VARIATION: *Add one or a combination of any of the following to rice filling: finely chopped fresh dill, cooked mushrooms, chopped smoked ham, ground meat.*

Buckwheat Filling for Holubtsi

Nachynka na holubtsi
z hechanoyi kasha

Makes about 6 cups

Of all the grains, buckwheat, with its nutty flavor and excellent nutritional value warrants great respect and acceptance in the Ukrainian diet.

2 cups fine or medium buckwheat groats

1 extra-large egg, slightly beaten

4 tablespoons unsalted butter or any other fat

1½ teaspoons salt

½ teaspoon freshly ground black pepper

4 cups meat or vegetable stock or water

Put the buckwheat in a large saucepan and mix in the egg with a fork. Dry the mixture over medium heat until lightly browned. Add the butter, salt, black pepper, and stock and bring to a boil. Cover, reduce the heat to low and cook about 20 minutes, or until all the liquid is absorbed and the buckwheat groats are tender. Taste and adjust the seasonings if necessary. Let cool completely before using as a filling for *holubtsi* (see recipes on pages 97–99).

VARIATION: *Add chopped fresh dill, parsley, or summer savory.*

Millet and Salt Pork Filling for Holubtsi

Nachynka na holubtsi z prosa i sala   Makes about 6 cups

Millet contains more protein and iron than any other grain, cooks quickly, and makes a delicious *holubtsi* filling. Sorrel leaves are good "wrappers" for millet filling and the pairing is especially popular in western Ukraine; or I would suggest using this filling with Beet Leaf Holubtsi.

2 cups millet

2 tablespoons sunflower oil

1 large onion, finely chopped

4 ounces salt pork, finely chopped

¼ teaspoon freshly ground black pepper

1 tablespoon unbleached all-purpose flour

½ cup sour cream, plus additional for serving

Toast the millet in a large skillet over medium-high heat for about 4 minutes, until it begins to smell roasted and some of the grains start to pop. Remove the pan from the heat and turn the millet out onto a plate.

Warm the oil in a medium saucepan over medium heat. Add the onion and sauté until softened, about 5 minutes. Add the salt pork and continue cooking another 3 minutes. Add the toasted millet, 3 cups of water, and black pepper and bring to a boil. Cover, reduce the heat to low, and cook for 15 to 20 minutes, or until all the water is absorbed and the millet is tender. Remove the pan from the heat and let the mixture cool.

Whisk the flour into the sour cream and lightly stir into the millet using a fork. Taste and adjust the seasonings if necessary. Use as the filling for *Beet Leaf Holubtsi* (page 99), substituting sorrel leaves for beet leaves if desired. Serve with extra sour cream.

Ritual Wheat Berry Dish

Kutia

Makes about 10 servings

Healthy grain dishes play an essential role in Ukrainian cuisine. *Kutia* is a ritual dish in which wheat berries, poppy seeds, and honey are essential ingredients. It is the most sacred of all Ukrainian ritual dishes. Because it is a Lenten dish, you usually do not use milk in the preparation. However, if you want a creamier *kutia*, and you are not observing Lent, by all means use it. *Kutia* can be eaten warm from the oven or served chilled as a breakfast cereal or dessert. The following is my favorite version.

2 cups wheat berries, soaked in warm water to cover for 24 hours, then drained

¼ cup poppy seeds

½ cup sultana raisins

¼ cup honey

½ cup chopped pecans

1 teaspoon salt

In a large heavy pot, cover the drained wheat berries with 6 cups of fresh water. Bring to a boil, cover, reduce the heat to low and gently simmer for 3 hours or more, until the wheat berries burst open and white appears. Add more water as needed, keeping the wheat berries covered at all times.

In a small saucepan, bring ½ cup of water to a boil and add the poppy seeds. Reduce the heat to medium and simmer for 3 minutes. Drain the poppy seeds and let cool slightly. Grind the poppy seeds very finely in a food processor and set aside.

Meanwhile, soak the raisins in about ½ cup of warm water for about 30 minutes to soften and plump them, then chop.

Preheat the oven to 350°F.

When the wheat berries are tender and cooked, drain off the water reserving about ½ cup and pour this water into a medium bowl. Stir the honey into the reserved water, along with the poppy seeds, raisins, pecans, and salt. Put the wheat berries into a large casserole dish and pour the honey mixture over top and mix well with a fork. Bake the *kutia* for about 15 minutes and serve.

VARIATIONS: *If you like, walnuts, almonds, or hazelnuts can be substituted for the pecans, and dried apricots, apples, cranberries, or peaches for the sultana raisins.*

Buckwheat Kasha

Hrechana kasha

In Ukraine, any grain cooked like porridge is referred to as *kasha*. Of all the cereal grains, buckwheat holds a foremost place in the diets of the Ukrainian people. Buckwheat kasha is often a substitute for potatoes or is served in combination with meat or fish. Buckwheat kasha combined with *lokshyna* (homemade egg noodles, page 202) is a popular vegetarian main course. Buckwheat kasha is also served for breakfast, as a stuffing for meat or *holubtsi* (pages 97), as an accompaniment to clear meat and vegetable broths, or baked in casseroles with seasonal vegetables. Using meat or mushroom broth in place of water yields an even richer-tasting kasha.

2 cups whole buckwheat groats

½ teaspoon salt

¼ teaspoon freshly ground black pepper

1 to 2 cloves garlic, crushed (optional)

Melted fat of any kind or oil

The following is a basic recipe for preparing whole buckwheat groats, which can be purchased in any health food store. More conventional cooks may find baking buckwheat kasha more suitable, but I find steaming it produces a nice fluffy dish and is more time-saving. Ukrainian ingenuity never ceases to amaze me, so I have included a number of ways to use up leftovers. Some are traditional ideas and some are contemporary adaptations.

Bring 4 cups of water to a boil in a medium saucepan. Add the buckwheat groats, cover, and reduce the heat to low. Simmer 20 to 30 minutes, or until the buckwheat grains are tender and all the water is absorbed. Stir in the salt, black pepper, and garlic, if using, and drizzle with melted fat to taste. Serve.

Recipes for leftover kasha:

- (traditional) Toss leftover kasha with melted butter or oil, chopped smoked ham, and sliced cooked mushrooms. Put in a casserole dish and place in a 350°F oven until warmed through. Serve hot.
- (traditional) Mix 2 cups cottage cheese with 2 slightly beaten eggs and season to taste with salt and black pepper. In a buttered casserole dish place a layer of kasha, then the cottage cheese mixture, and top with another layer of kasha. Cover and bake in a 350°F oven for 30 minutes. Serve portions hot with a slather of sour cream and sprinkled with chopped green onions or chives.
- (contemporary) Cook about 2 cups sliced carrots in browned butter and add brown sugar and some grainy mustard. In a buttered casserole dish arrange alternate layers of leftover buckwheat kasha and the carrot mixture. Finish with a layer of kasha and sprinkle generously with additional browned butter. Cover and bake in a 350°F oven until warmed through. Serve hot.
- (contemporary) Sauté some red cabbage and Granny Smith apple slices in bacon drippings. In a buttered casserole dish arrange alternate layers of leftover buckwheat kasha and the cabbage mixture. Finish with a layer of kasha. Cover and bake in a 350°F oven for 30 minutes. Serve hot.

Chumak-Style Millet

Proso po-chumats'ky

Makes 4 to 6 servings

Before the time of the railroad in Ukraine, the carters or *chumak* merchants carried on a trade in dried fish and mined salt. These carters made slow and arduous journeys in ox-drawn caravans across the sparsely populated vast steppes of southern Ukraine to the port cities in Crimea. Carters are frequently mentioned in stories and legends and it is said that while stopping to rest their oxen, they prepared meals of millet kasha in iron kettles over open fires—and so the dish bears their name.

Millet is the hardy seed of an annual grass that is cultivated in Ukraine. It has a mild taste, is high in protein, and blends easily with vegetables, meats, and sauces. Millet kasha is served as a side dish with butter or pork cracklings (page 81), or as a dessert with a drizzle of honey and a sprinkle of cinnamon or clove and a dollop of whipped cream. A bowl of millet kasha with a splash of warm milk is also a popular breakfast dish, especially for children.

2½ cups (generous) milk or light cream

1 cup millet

1 to 2 tablespoons unsalted butter, oil, or bacon drippings

½ teaspoon salt

Pour the milk into a heavy, medium saucepan and bring to a boil over medium heat, stirring frequently to prevent scorching. Stir in the remaining ingredients and bring back to a boil over medium heat. Cover tightly, reduce the heat to low, and cook for about 25 to 30 minutes or until the millet is tender. Serve as is or with additional milk or cream.

Millet Kasha with Pumpkin and Honey

Kasha z prosa ta z barbuzom i medom

Makes 4 to 6 servings

T his is a popular millet kasha in Ukraine.

2 tablespoons unsalted butter

1 cup peeled fresh pumpkin cut into small cubes

3 cups milk

1½ cups millet

1 teaspoon salt

3 tablespoons honey

Melted butter and additional honey to serve (optional)

In a deep casserole over medium heat, melt the butter and add the pumpkin. Cover and sauté the pumpkin until fork-tender, about 15 to 20 minutes.

Add the milk and bring to a boil, stirring frequently to prevent scorching. Stir in the millet, salt, and honey. As soon as the honey is dissolved, cover, reduce the heat to low, and cook about 20 minutes, or until the milk is absorbed but the millet is still moist. Meanwhile preheat the oven to 375°F.

Place the covered casserole in the oven and bake for about 30 minutes, or until the millet is dry and the pumpkin is soft and tender. Fluff with a fork and serve in the casserole with melted butter and additional honey if desired.

Rice Pilaf

Plov/Pilav

Plov is basically a rice pilaf that originated in Uzbekistan. It is a dish that is popular in Ukraine and has become part of Ukrainian food culture. It is made with any kind of meat or none at all, as well as with onions, carrots, and rice—which constitutes the very heart of the dish.

This particular regional variation is called *pilav* by Crimean Tatars. It is made with either beef or lamb and when served with a platter of fresh tomato slices, scallions, olives, pickles, and slices of cheese makes for a healthy and nutritious meal. Delicious!

6 tablespoons sunflower or olive oil

A few lamb bones

1 pound lamb shoulder with some fat, cut into 1-inch chunks

10 carrots, peeled and grated

2 large onions, finely chopped

1 tablespoon salt

2 cups medium-grain white rice

Heat 4 tablespoons of the oil in a large casserole over medium heat. When the oil is just starting to smoke, add the lamb bones and let them brown on all sides. Remove and discard the bones.

Turn up the heat to medium-high and add the lamb chunks. Cook, stirring frequently, for about 10 minutes. Add the carrots and onions and the remaining 2 tablespoons of oil and continue cooking another 10 minutes.

Stir in the salt and ½ cup hot water and bring to a boil. Reduce the heat to medium-low, cover, and gently simmer until the meat is tender, about 40 minutes.

Spread the meat mixture with a large kitchen spoon to cover the bottom of the casserole and pour the rice evenly over the meat. Spread the rice to make an even layer. Gently pour 4 cups of hot water over top and turn up the heat to high and bring the mixture to a boil. Reduce the heat to medium-low, cover and cook until all the water is absorbed, about 20 minutes.

Fluff the rice into a mound with a fork, cover, reduce the heat to low and let the rice steam for an additional 10 minutes. Remove the pot from the stove and let stand an additional 10 minutes.

To serve, spread the rice onto a large, warmed serving platter and arrange the meat and vegetables in a mound over top. Serve immediately.

Hutsulian Cornmeal Mush

Kulesha

An ethnographic group of pastoral highlanders known as the Hutsuls occupy the eastern strip of the Carpathian Mountains in Ukraine. The Hutsuls are renowned for their colorful, richly ornamented folk dress and their handicrafts, especially wood carving. Hutsuls are a passionate, freedom-loving people engaged mostly in sheep-herding. Corn is the native grain in the region and a staple of their diet. It is used in the form of hominy and cornmeal.

The following recipe is the Hutsul way of preparing the traditional cornmeal dish called *kulesha*. There is even a special wooden spoon for the purpose of stirring the *kulesha* called a "*kulishyr.*" Hutsul families cut the *kulesha* into servings their own special way using a string-bow cutter (an instrument similar to a cheese cutter). *Kulesha* is traditionally served with *bryndzia* (ewe's milk cheese) or sometimes cottage cheese and a slather of sour cream.

If the cornmeal is prepared with boiling cream or sour cream, this particular dish carries the local name of "*banush.*"

1 teaspoon salt

1 cup stone-ground cornmeal

2 cups cottage cheese to serve

½ cup sour cream to serve

Combine 3 generous cups of water and the salt in a heavy, medium saucepan and bring to a boil. Pour about 3 or 4 tablespoons of cornmeal in a steady stream into the boiling water and whisk until the water returns to a boil. Gradually add the rest of the cornmeal, stirring constantly. Reduce the heat to low and keep stirring until the cornmeal forms a ball. Turn out onto a platter and serve immediately with scoops of cottage cheese and sour cream.

Favorite ways to serve *kulesha:*

* Sprinkle *kulesha* with thinly sliced onions that have been sautéed in butter.
* Sprinkle *kulesha* with grated "*bryndzia*" cheese (a semisoft, somewhat salty, ewe's milk cheese with a fat content of 40 percent).
* Leftover *kulesha* can be sliced and fried in butter and served with bacon.
* Place a slice of smoked ham between two slices of cold, leftover *kulesha*, dip in beaten egg and fry in butter until golden brown.
* Make the *kulesha* with milk or cream sweetened with honey and serve with jam or fruit preserves.

Bukovynian Cornmeal Spoon Bread

Bukovyns'ka kulesha

Makes 6 servings

Bukovyna is an eastern European territory consisting of a segment of the northeastern Carpathian Mountains and the adjoining plain, divided after 1947 between Ukraine and Romania. Ukrainians from this area serve this cornmeal dish, which is more like a soufflé, most often as an accompaniment to meat dishes.

4 tablespoons unsalted butter

1 cup stone-ground cornmeal

3 cups milk

2 extra-large eggs

1 teaspoon salt

¼ teaspoon freshly ground black pepper

½ teaspoon granulated sugar

1 teaspoon baking powder

Preheat the oven to 350°F. Melt the butter in a heavy skillet over medium heat. Mix in the cornmeal and stir constantly until the cornmeal starts to bubble. Take the pan off the heat and set aside.

Bring the milk to a boil in a medium saucepan. Reduce the heat slightly, keeping the milk very hot.

In a medium bowl, beat together the eggs, salt, black pepper, sugar, and baking powder. Gradually stir in the hot milk and then, very quickly but lightly, stir this mixture into the cornmeal just until combined.

Spoon the *kulesha* from the skillet into a buttered casserole dish and bake for 30 minutes. Serve immediately.

Bukovynian Cornmeal Dressing

Bukovyns'ka nachynka

Makes 6 servings

This specialty is usually made in large quantities for festive gatherings or community dinners. It is served as an accompaniment to any meat preparation.

Preheat the oven to 350°F. Fry the bacon in a heavy skillet over medium heat until crisp. Remove from the pan and crumble when cooled.

    Add the onion to the bacon drippings over medium heat, and sauté until softened, about 5 minutes. Mix in the cornmeal, stirring constantly and adding additional fat (butter or oil) if necessary, until the cornmeal starts to bubble. Stir in the salt, black pepper, and sugar, cover, take the pan off the heat and set aside.

    Bring milk to a boil in a medium saucepan over medium heat, stirring frequently to prevent scorching. Gradually pour the hot milk into the cornmeal and stir briskly until smooth and free of lumps. Fold in the beaten eggs and crumbled bacon. Pour the mixture into a buttered casserole dish and bake for 1 hour until crusty and golden brown. Serve hot.

4 thick slices smoky bacon

1 onion, finely chopped

1 cup stone-ground cornmeal

1 to 2 tablespoons butter or sunflower oil (if needed)

¾ teaspoon salt

¼ teaspoon freshly ground black pepper

1 teaspoon granulated sugar or honey

3½ cups milk

3 extra-large eggs, well beaten

Bukovynian Chicken Broth Cornmeal Dressing

Bukovyns'ka nachynka na kuriachomu rosoli

Makes 6 servings

This cornmeal dressing is moist and delicious, flavored by rich chicken broth. There is no added fat in this recipe, so your chicken broth must be well-seasoned.

6 cups richly flavored chicken broth

1 cup stone-ground cornmeal

3 egg yolks, well beaten

Bring the chicken broth to a boil in a medium saucepan. Pour in about 3 or 4 tablespoons cornmeal in a steady stream and whisk until the broth barely returns to a boil. Gradually add the rest of the cornmeal, stirring constantly. Reduce the heat to low and keep stirring until most of the broth is absorbed. This mixture should not be very thick.

    Stir a few tablespoons of the hot cornmeal into the egg yolks to temper, and then stir into the rest of the cornmeal mixture. Continue cooking, gently, over low heat another 5 minutes. Serve hot.

Chapter 5

Meats and Poultry

An extensive collection ...

In Ukraine, pork is the real hero of the feast. Whether draped in the guise of plump sausages, covered in a mantle of garlic-infused jelly, or stuffed or stewed, most Ukrainians will make no bones about the fact that pork reigns supreme as the meat of choice. In culinary circles, Ukraine's pork dishes have been touted as the best in the world and pork cuts, whether large or small, are always beautifully presented. Some are stews and casseroles distinctly endowed with a hearty winter quality and some are crisp crackling roasts. Grilled pork, sometimes marinated first, reveals its sheer genius when laid under a thick fruit sauce and topped with a dollop of rich, melting sour cream. Enough cannot be said about the simplicity of a fresh roast ham or a roast suckling pig, undeniably nourishing and plentiful, yet they are elegant enough to take pride of place at any celebratory table. But slow cooking, as in braising or stewing, is the most popular method of cooking. Organ meats are favored as well and pork is used in numerous kinds of sausages.

Eating pork that is cured and salted is a centuries old tradition that runs deep in the hearts of all Ukrainians. This delicacy is called *salo*, and it has long provided a more conservable alternative to fresh meat. A thin slice of *salo* on rye bread accompanied by some dill pickles is quite tasty and many like a slice with their vodka. It can be substituted judiciously in recipes calling for smoked or cured bacon and for frying. It is not to everyone's taste, but if you have a chance try it. *Salo* can be purchased in Ukrainian and Russian markets and specialty stores.

Beef and veal are eaten with less regularity, but are enjoyed just the same. Beef is usually ground and made into patties or combined with other meats, especially pork. Sometimes beef is cubed, skewered, and charcoal-grilled, but more often than not it is pounded thin and stuffed and served tucked under a rich-tasting sauce. Tender cuts of veal are simply roasted, or ground and baked into a loaf with delicate, fluffy results.

Lamb on the other hand is enjoyed throughout Ukraine, though not nearly as much as pork. Sometimes spit-roasted for special occasions, lamb is more often served as a centerpiece for everyday meals. Prime cuts are grilled or roasted, needing next to no embellishment, while the humbler parts are stewed with the likes of root vegetables, beans, plums, or prunes in robust tomato sauces. So many of these meat dishes take little or no time to prepare, improve with age in your refrigerator, and also freeze well.

Poultry has been appreciated for centuries in Ukraine. Noble barnyard chickens and ducks are absolutely delectable when prepared simply with a few vegetables, such as potatoes, carrots, and parsnips, or stuffed and accented with savory ingredients like sour cream, fruit, honey, or tangy sauces of vinegar and spices. Roast turkey is highly favored in Ukraine, but stuffed roast goose takes center stage on holidays and other important celebratory occasions.

Geese and ducks, both domesticated and wild, possess meat that is darker and more flavorful than chicken or turkey. Sometimes a bit fatty, there is an easy way to degrease the basting liquid when roasting geese and ducks. Just prick the bird's skin all over with a sharp needle, being careful not to pierce the meat. The fat will escape through the skin. After roasting, skim the basting liquid with a spoon to remove the fat on the top. This fat may be discarded, but more often than not it is stored in a jar in the refrigerator for future use. The same is done with chicken fat. Both are excellent for frying and are quite prized in Ukrainian cooking.

But to many Ukrainians, duck and goose livers seem to be more precious than the birds themselves and are delicious in their own right. Most times duck and goose livers are flash fried in a small amount of butter, sliced, and served with a few snipped chives to garnish. Duck and goose skin is also favored and at the end of this chapter I have included a very old but popular method of making goose "cracklings."

Roast Easter Ham

Pechena shynkka na velykden'

Makes 8 servings

In Ukraine, this basic recipe for roast ham rests most comfortably on the Easter table. Serve with traditional accompaniments like mustards, horseradish, crunchy pickles, marinated mushrooms, and plenty of rye bread.

4 cloves garlic, crushed

1 tablespoon coarse salt

½ teaspoon freshly ground black pepper

About ¼ cup pork broth

1 (6-pound) bone-in picnic pork shoulder, trimmed of all but a thin layer of fat

In a small bowl, combine the garlic, salt, black pepper, and pork broth to form a paste. Make small slits all over the roast and insert some of the paste as deep as possible into the meat. Rub the remaining paste all over the roast. Cover and refrigerate for at least 6 hours or overnight.

Preheat the oven to 350°F. Put the roast on a rack in a roasting pan. Add about 2 cups of water to the pan, cover, and roast approximately 3 hours, basting every 30 minutes after the first hour of cooking, and adding more water to the pan as needed.

Remove the roast from the oven and let rest for 20 minutes before carving. Arrange slices of ham on a large warmed platter with some of the pan juices spooned over top. Serve the rest of the juices separately in a sauce boat.

Grilled Pork Tenderloin

Svyniacha poliadvytsia pechena na vubliakh

Makes 6 servings

This is a more contemporary way of preparing pork tenderloin. The flavor of fruit nicely complements all cuts of pork and in this case the sauce, made of fresh plums in combination with red wine, is also suitable spooned over grilled or braised poultry or game meats.

1 (4-pound) boneless pork loin, cut in half lengthwise

2 tablespoons sunflower oil

1 teaspoon coarse salt

½ teaspoon freshly ground black pepper

1½ cups red wine

1 cup apple cider or apple juice

2 tablespoons honey

¼ cup apple cider vinegar

2 cloves garlic, sliced

10 fresh plums, pitted and coarsely chopped

Rub both pieces of pork with the oil and sprinkle with salt and black pepper. Put the meat into a shallow pan or casserole dish and set aside.

In a medium bowl, whisk together the red wine, apple cider, honey, vinegar, and garlic until well blended. Stir in the chopped plums and pour the marinade over the pork. Cover and refrigerate for at least 2 to 3 hours.

Prepare coals for grilling or preheat the broiler. When the coals are hot, remove the pork from the marinade (reserving marinade), pat dry with paper towels, and sear a few inches from the coals on all sides until nicely browned. Adjust the rack on the grill so that it is about 5 inches from the coals and continue to grill the pork for about 20 minutes, turning once, until the meat is done. Remove the pork from the grill and let rest for at least 10 minutes for the juices to settle.

Meanwhile, prepare the sauce by pouring the marinade into a medium saucepan and bringing it to a full boil over high heat. Cover, reduce the heat to medium-low and cook for about 10 minutes or until the plums are tender. Taste and adjust the seasonings if necessary by adding more salt and black pepper and more honey if you like a sweeter sauce.

Slice the pork loin and serve with the hot plum sauce on the side for dipping or lay the pork slices on a large platter, pour a little sauce over top, and serve any extra sauce in a sauce boat on the side.

Ukrainian Pork Basturma

Ukrains'ka basturma

Basturma is a traditional Armenian recipe for cubed beef marinated with onions and basil in red wine vinegar and then threaded on a skewer and grilled. Ukrainians adopted this dish and, like so many dishes, made it uniquely their own by using pork instead of beef. Pork cubes or pork sirloin tips work beautifully in this recipe, but I have opted for a fresh pork steak instead, which is the style one most often finds in the restaurants and cafes of Ukraine.

1 large sweet onion, grated

2 tablespoons chopped fresh dill

½ teaspoon freshly ground black pepper

½ cup red wine vinegar

1 (1½-pound) fresh pork steak

Coarse salt to taste

Shredded scallions, cilantro leaves, and lemon wedges to serve

Put the grated onion and any juices in a small bowl and whisk in the dill, black pepper, and red wine vinegar. Place the pork steak in a large oval dish and pour the marinade over top. Let marinate at room temperature for 5 to 6 hours, turning the steak every 30 minutes to ensure the meat stays coated (see Note).

When ready to cook, remove the pork from the marinade and dry with paper towels. Either grill or cook in preheated broiler, about 6 minutes on each side, until cooked through. Let the steak rest for 5 minutes before slicing. Sprinkle with coarse salt and serve garnished with shredded scallions, cilantro leaves, and lemon wedges.

. . . .

NOTE: *It is traditional to marinate this at room temperature as the vinegar helps keep the meat fresh. I usually do it that way and have never had a problem with it. But if you are more comfortable marinating the meat in the refrigerator that would work fine also.*

Roast Stuffed Suckling Pig

Pechene nachyniuvane porosia

Makes 6 to 8 servings

Roast or stuffed suckling pig is one of the few Old World delicacies still being served in Ukraine today. Its stately appearance inspires an air of festivity and a roast suckling pig often takes center stage as the entrée of choice at weddings, buffets, or gala family occasions. It is delicious hot or cold and very simple to prepare. Here I have paired it with a traditional buckwheat stuffing, but feel free to use your favorite. Presentation can be as simple or as elegant as you choose—offer a selection of simply prepared seasonal vegetables to accompany it or go all out and garnish as elaborately as you wish.

1 (6 to 8 pound) suckling pig

1 tablespoon coarse salt

2 teaspoons freshly ground black pepper

2 tablespoons unsalted butter, softened

1 small potato

BUCKWHEAT STUFFING:

2 tablespoons sunflower oil

2 cups whole buckwheat groats

1 teaspoon salt

½ teaspoon freshly ground black pepper

1 cup chopped onions

1 cup chopped mushrooms

GARNISHES:

1 small red apple

Greens like kale or Swiss chard for platter

Trimmed scallions

Radish roses

Cucumber slices

Sprigs of fresh parsley and dill

A generous side dish of Pickled Horseradish Relish (page 68)

Rinse off the pig inside and out with cold water and pat dry with paper towels. Rub the inside and outside with salt and black pepper and let stand 30 minutes.

Meanwhile, prepare the stuffing: Heat 1 tablespoon of oil in a heavy saucepan over medium heat and add the buckwheat. Stir to coat and then add 4 cups of water and bring to a boil. Add the salt and black pepper, cover, reduce the heat to low and simmer about 20 minutes or until all the water is absorbed. Meanwhile, warm the remaining 1 tablespoon oil in a medium skillet over medium heat and add the onions and mushrooms. Sauté the vegetables until browned and fragrant, about 15 minutes, then add to the buckwheat and mix well. Let cool.

Preheat the oven to 425°F. Stuff the pig's cavity with the buckwheat mixture and sew up or skewer the opening. Rub the pig all over with the softened butter and place it on a rack in a large roasting pan. Wrap the ears and tail in aluminum foil to prevent burning while cooking. Press the forefeet forward and the hind feet backwards and skewer into place if necessary. Put a potato in the pig's mouth to keep it open.

Place the pan in the oven and roast the pig for 20 minutes; then reduce the heat to 325°F and continue cooking until the pig is tender, allowing about 25 minutes per pound. Baste frequently with the pan drippings and remove the foil from the ears and tail the last 30 minutes of roasting in order to brown them. All the skin should be evenly browned and crisp.

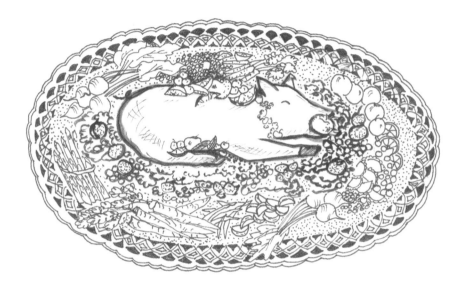

When done, scoop out the stuffing and serve in a dish on the side. Line a large platter with greens and place the pig on top. Remove the potato from its mouth and insert the apple. Garnish the platter with seasonal vegetables and sprigs of parsley and dill. Offer plenty of pickled horseradish relish on the side. To serve, cut the pig lengthwise along the backbone, and then cut each half crosswise between ribs into about 5 or 6 pieces. Enjoy!

Roast Loin of Pork Stuffed with Apples and Cherries

Svyniacha pechenia nachyniuvana yablukamy ta vyshniamy

Makes 8 servings

If tackling a suckling pig recipe seems too daunting, try this simple recipe. Always purchase pastured, free-roaming pork from a local farmer or reputable butcher. Select a boned pork loin with rind which will give you a suitable crackling alternative to roasting an entire suckling pig. Do not baste the last hour and a half of roasting so the crackling (skin) becomes crisp.

This recipe for pork roast is a favorite of mine, and I find it offers a particularly nice change of pace from hearty stews and casseroles in the middle of winter. I have selected a simple, traditional type of bread stuffing adorned with fresh apples and cherries. Serve with any kind of cooked green vegetable, plenty of crusty rolls, and don't forget an assortment of pickles to complete it.

1 (4½-pound) boned loin of pork with rind
1 cup apple cider
2 teaspoons unbleached all-purpose flour
½ cup sour cream
2 teaspoons coarse salt

STUFFING:
2 tablespoons unsalted butter or lard
1 onion, finely chopped
1½ cups fresh white breadcrumbs
2 Granny Smith apples, peeled, cored, and finely chopped
½ cup dried cherries
2 tablespoons dark rum (optional)
Pinch ground cloves
Pinch ground allspice

Preheat the oven to 400°F.

Make the stuffing: melt the butter in a medium skillet over medium heat and add the onion. Sauté until softened, about 5 minutes. Stir in the remaining stuffing ingredients and continue cooking another 2 minutes. Remove the pan from the heat and set aside.

Lay the pork, rind side down on a large cutting board. Make a horizontal cut between the meat and the layer of fat to within one inch of the edges, making a pocket. Push the stuffing into the pocket. Tie the roast in three places with kitchen string to secure. Score the rind at ½-inch intervals with a small paring knife.

Whisk the apple cider in a small bowl with the flour and sour cream. Pour the mixture into a large casserole big enough to fit the pork roast. Add the roast, rind side down, and cook, uncovered, in the hot oven for 30 minutes.

Turn the roast over, baste with the juices and sprinkle the rind with coarse salt. Cook the roast for 1 more hour and then baste. Reduce the oven temperature to 325°F and cook about 1½ hours longer.

Remove from oven and leave the roast stand, uncovered, for at least 20 minutes before carving. Serve slices artfully arranged on a warmed platter.

Stuffed Crown Roast of Pork with Old-Fashioned Liver Stuffing

Svyniacha pechenia reber iz nachynkoyu z pechinky

Makes 8 servings

This is another Old World delicacy still being served in Ukraine today. Only the most dramatic cut of meat, a crown roast of pork, could transform an everyday meal into an elaborate banquet. The substantial liver stuffing I have chosen is my adaptation of an Old World classic that supports the lavishness of this recipe. The stuffing is equally good paired with thick-cut pork chops, a boneless rolled breast of veal, or a pocketed shoulder of lamb.

Make the stuffing:

Bring 4 cups of water to a boil in a large pot. Add the pork heart, reduce the heat to medium and simmer for 10 minutes. Add the pork liver to the pot and simmer another 10 minutes. Drain the meats, cool slightly, and then grind in a food processor. Transfer the meats to a large bowl and gently mix in the ground veal. Set aside.

Meanwhile, soak the bread in the evaporated milk for about 10 minutes. While the bread is soaking, melt the bacon drippings in a large skillet and add the onion and celery leaves. Sauté the vegetables until the onions start to brown, about 12 minutes. Remove from the heat, let cool slightly and then add to the meats, mixing gently.

Remove the bread from the milk and without squeezing it, add it to the meat mixture, along with the egg yolks, salt, and black pepper. Mix well.

Beat the egg whites in a small bowl until they start to foam, then fold into the meat mixture. Cover and refrigerate the stuffing until ready to use.

Prepare the roast:

Preheat the oven to 450°F. Whisk together the oil, brandy, mustard, salt, and black pepper in a small bowl. Place the crown roast in a roasting pan and brush the outside with the mustard mixture. Spoon the stuffing into the center of the roast (you can bake any extra stuffing separately).

LIVER STUFFING:

1 small pork heart

1 pound pork liver

8 ounces ground veal

5 thick slices white bread, crusts removed

½ cup canned evaporated milk

2 tablespoons bacon drippings

1 large onion, finely chopped

½ cup finely chopped celery leaves

3 extra-large eggs, separated

1½ teaspoons salt

½ teaspoon freshly ground black pepper

CROWN ROAST OF PORK:

2 tablespoons sunflower oil

¼ cup brandy

1 tablespoon prepared mustard

1 tablespoon coarse salt

½ teaspoon freshly ground black pepper

1 (8-pound) crown pork roast with 16 ribs

continued on next page ⇨

Cover the stuffing with a piece of buttered aluminum foil and cover each rib individually with a piece of buttered aluminum foil to prevent scorching. Roast the pork for 30 minutes. Reduce the heat to 350°F and continue roasting until the internal temperature of the meat (away from the bone) registers 160°F, about 2 hours.

Transfer the roast to a serving platter. Let stand 15 minutes before removing the foil. Carve and serve with some of the pan drippings drizzled over top.

NOTE: *You will most likely have to pre-order your crown roast from a butcher.*

Stuffed Meat Rolls

Bytky, roughly translated means "rolls." Tender veal, pork, beef, game meats, chicken, or even pieces of turkey are pounded very thin, cut into squares, layered or stuffed, and rolled into packages. These little meat packages are then dipped in beaten egg and breadcrumbs, pan-seared, and then finished off in the oven. Various ground meat and vegetable stuffings are common and seasoned to suit one's individual preferences, but meat rolls stuffed with finely chopped mushrooms are by far one of the most popular variations throughout Ukraine.

One of my favorite versions of *bytky* uses a combination of veal steak and pork tenderloin and a stuffing of sautéed portabella mushrooms. It is a bit time consuming, but really worth the effort. Serve rolls directly from the oven smothered in the sauce, along with steamed or lightly blanched vegetables and pickled red beets (page 66) for a typical Ukrainian meal. Delicious!

1 (1-pound) pork tenderloin, pounded thin

1 (1-pound) veal steak, pounded thin

Salt and freshly ground black pepper to taste

3 tablespoons unsalted butter

4 ounces portabella mushrooms, finely chopped

1 small onion, grated

3 to 4 tablespoons unbleached all-purpose flour seasoned with salt and black pepper

1 extra-large egg, slightly beaten

1 cup dry breadcrumbs seasoned with salt, black pepper, and some finely chopped fresh dill

2 tablespoons heavy cream or sour cream

⅔ cup meat broth or water

Dill or parsley for garnishing

Preheat the oven to 325°F. Cut the pork into 2-inch x 3-inch pieces and season with salt and black pepper. Cut the veal into smaller pieces, about 1-inch x 3-inch pieces and season with salt and black pepper. Place each of the smaller pieces of veal on a larger portion of pork. Set aside.

Prepare the mushroom stuffing: Melt 1 tablespoon of butter in a medium skillet over medium heat. Add the mushrooms and grated onion with any juices and sauté the vegetables until tender and all the liquid has evaporated, about 10 minutes.

Place 1 teaspoon of mushroom stuffing on each square of meat, roll up and secure with kitchen string in 2 places to hold together. Dip the rolls into the seasoned flour, then into the beaten egg, and then into the seasoned breadcrumbs. Melt the remaining 2 tablespoons butter in the same skillet over medium heat and brown the rolls, turning once. Remove the rolls to a baking dish.

Mix any remaining seasoned flour into the fat left in the skillet and stir in the cream and meat broth. Bring the mixture to a boil over medium-high heat, stirring constantly until thickened. Pour the sauce over the rolls, cover with aluminum foil and bake for 45 minutes or until the meat is tender.

Using kitchen tongs or a large slotted spoon, carefully remove the rolls to a warmed serving platter and remove the strings. Pour the pan sauce over top and garnish with sprigs of fresh dill or parsley. Serve immediately.

Kovbasa

Kovbasa is the name for Ukrainian sausage made with pork and beef. Traditionally seasoned with allspice and *peperivka* (spiced whiskey), *kovbasa* is usually served as an entrée with mashed potatoes, or is often part of the *zakusky* spread, sliced and served with a variety of mustards or pickled horseradish relish (page 68). *Kovbasa* is available for purchase at Ukrainian markets and is sometimes smoked, but it is very easy to make at home, can be made several days in advance, and keeps well refrigerated.

NOTE: Mine is a casing-less sausage, so you will need some cheesecloth and kitchen string to make this recipe.

1 pound coarsely ground pork shoulder

1 (½-pound) beef chuck steak, cut into ¼-inch cubes

¼ pound pork back fat, cut into ¼-inch cubes

2 extra-large eggs, beaten

½ teaspoon salt

¼ teaspoon ground allspice

3 cloves garlic, crushed

1 tablespoon *peperivka* (see Note below)

About 4 cups meat broth

1 to 2 tablespoons sunflower oil

Chopped fresh parsley to garnish

Mix the pork, beef, pork fat, eggs, salt, allspice, garlic, and *peperivka* together in a large bowl. In a small skillet over medium heat, fry about 1 teaspoon of the mixture and then taste. Adjust the seasonings if needed to suit your taste by adding more salt or *peperivka* to the meat in the bowl. Form the meat mixture into two 8-inch-long cylinders and wrap each in double cheesecloth and tie securely with kitchen string in three places.

Bring the meat broth to a boil in a large skillet and add the wrapped sausages. Reduce the heat to medium-low and gently simmer about 30 minutes, or until the sausage juices run clear when pricked with a fine skewer. Remove the pan from the stove, but leave the sausages in the broth for an additional 30 minutes before removing.

When cool enough to handle, remove the strings and cheesecloth. Warm the sunflower oil in a large skillet over medium heat. Brown the *kovbasa* in the oil on all sides. Serve garnished with chopped fresh parsley.

....

NOTE: Peperivka *is an age-old Ukrainian liqueur, traditionally made by soaking cayenne peppers that have been pricked with a fine needle in whiskey, bourbon, or brandy for at least 48 hours before serving. I have provided my family's recipe on page 255.*

Pounded Steak

Bytky

This is another classic homestyle dish. Most Ukrainian cooks will choose a beef round steak to make *bytky*, although using a veal steak is not unheard of. Recipes vary only slightly from family to family—usually in embellishments. Adding bits of sweet bell pepper, mushrooms, or fresh herbs makes *bytky* a versatile dish, especially when served with the staple buckwheat kasha (page 105).

½ cup unbleached all-purpose flour

1 (1-pound) beef round steak

2 tablespoons unsalted butter

1 onion, chopped

1 rib celery, chopped

2 cloves garlic, crushed

½ teaspoon salt

½ teaspoon freshly ground black pepper

½ cup (generous) sour cream

2 tablespoons chopped fresh parsley

Preheat the oven to 350°F. Sprinkle half of the flour onto a cutting board. Place the steak on top and cover with the remaining flour. Pound the steak with a kitchen mallet, turning it over and over until the flour melts into the meat on both sides (the steak should be close to ¼ inch thick when finished). Cut the steak into 4 portions.

Melt the butter in a medium casserole over medium heat and add the onion, celery, and garlic. Sauté the vegetables until softened, about 5 minutes. Remove the vegetables from the pan and set aside.

Brown the meat in the same pan over medium heat for about 2 minutes on each side. Add the sautéed vegetables, salt, pepper, and 1½ cups of hot water and bring to a boil. Cover and bake in the oven for about 15 minutes. Remove the casserole from the oven and gradually stir in the sour cream. Put the casserole back in the oven and bake for an additional 10 minutes.

Remove the casserole and thin the sauce with a little boiling water if it is too thick. Serve immediately with a scattering of fresh parsley.

Ukrainian Beef Brisket

Yalovycha hrudynka

Boiled meats are as popular today in Ukraine as they were hundreds of years ago. Serve this dish with sliced cooked beets, plenty of pickled horseradish relish (page 68), mayonnaise, and a variety of mustards.

1 tablespoon coarse salt

1 (3-pound) first-cut beef brisket

4 cloves garlic, sliced

2 bay leaves

10 black peppercorns

4 large sprigs parsley

1 large onion, chopped

4 carrots, peeled and chopped

2 ribs celery, chopped

2 large turnips, peeled and cut into chunks

1 medium rutabaga, peeled and cut into chunks

1 parsley root, peeled and chopped

1 large sweet or red onion, thinly sliced for garnishing

Additional coarse salt and freshly ground black pepper to taste for serving

Rub the salt into the brisket and set aside for 30 minutes.

Put the brisket into a large soup pot and cover with about 8 cups of cold water. Bring to a boil and discard any foam that rises to the top. Add the garlic, bay leaves, black peppercorns, and sprigs of parsley. Cover, reduce the heat to low, and let the meat cook for 1½ hours.

Add the onion, carrots, celery, turnips, rutabaga, and parsley root. Cover and continue cooking another hour or until the meat is very tender.

Remove the brisket and allow it to cool for at least 5 minutes before slicing. Remove the vegetables with a slotted spoon (discard the bay leaf, black peppercorns, and parsley sprigs) and place on a large serving platter. Slice the brisket against the grain and artfully arrange among the vegetables. Spoon some of the broth over top of the meat and vegetables and sprinkle with coarse salt and black pepper. Pour the rest of the broth in a sauce boat to serve on the side. Garnish the platter with the slices of onion and serve.

Homemade Mustard Recipe

Ukrainians are quite fond of mustard and making it from scratch is simple. No matter how old the mustard gets it will not develop bacteria, though its flavor will fade. Once a jar is opened, refrigerate any extra. A portion of mustard can be scooped from a finished jar (one that has rested for at least two weeks) and embellished with a drizzle of honey, chopped fresh herbs, pureed fruit, or a few drops of cognac or brandy and these go well with a quite a number of foods, especially Ukrainian meat dishes.

¼ cup yellow mustard seeds
1½ tablespoons mustard powder
1 teaspoon salt
1 teaspoon granulated sugar
3 tablespoons white vinegar
2 tablespoons sunflower oil

Coarsely grind the mustard seeds using a mortar and pestle or a coffee grinder you keep for spices. Put the ground seeds in a small bowl, add just enough cold water to moisten (about 2 tablespoons) and leave sit for 10 minutes.

Add the remaining ingredients and mix thoroughly. Spoon the mustard into a small jar or mustard pot, cover tightly, set in a cool place, and let the flavors develop for 2 weeks before opening the jar.

Mustard variations:

Dill Mustard—pairs well with fish dishes, smoked fish, and potatoes

Mint Mustard—pairs well with lamb dishes, beef, pork meatballs, and potatoes

Cherry Mustard—pairs well with all smoked meats, game meats, pork, duck, and goose

Ginger Mustard—pairs well with herring dishes and pork dishes

Cognac mustard—pairs well with pork, beef, game meats, salmon, and strongly flavored vegetables like cabbage, broccoli, cauliflower, turnips, or kohlrabi

Beef Patties or Meatballs

Sichenyky abo Zrazy z yalovychyny

Sichenyky (patties) and *zrazy* (meatballs) are typical everyday fare in Ukraine. Crispy on the outside and moist on the inside, this recipe is a basic one used to make either dish, or even a meatloaf—another Ukrainian favorite!

1 cup dry breadcrumbs

1 cup canned evaporated milk

1½ pounds ground beef

½ pound ground veal

1 sweet onion, grated

1 extra-large egg, slightly beaten

1 teaspoon salt

½ teaspoon freshly ground black pepper

1 tablespoon unsalted butter or oil

Preheat the oven to 350°F. Measure out ⅔ cup of the breadcrumbs and place in a large bowl. Add the milk and let the mixture stand for at least 15 minutes.

Add the beef, veal, onion, egg, salt, and black pepper and mix gently but thoroughly. Shape into six flat patties. Pour the remaining ⅓ cup breadcrumbs on a plate and coat each patty on both sides with the breadcrumbs. Cut an "X" on one side of each patty.

Melt the butter in a large skillet and brown the patties about 2 minutes on each side. Transfer the patties to a casserole dish, cover, and bake for about 20 minutes. Serve immediately.

....

NOTE: *Sichenyky and zrazy can also be stuffed with fillings such as buttery fried mushrooms, a combination of sweet grated beets and bits of apple, beans laced with fragrant herbs, chopped pickles, or even mashed anchovies. Any kind of filling is acceptable as long as you like it and recipes such as these reflect the nuance that is purely the cook's own.*

Crimean Tatar Beef with Beans

Yalovychyna z fasoleyu po-tatars'ky   Makes 4 to 6 servings

Crimean Tatars who live in the steppe region of Ukraine eat more meat than those living on the southern coast. Mutton and beef are widely used. The slaughtering of animals in Crimean Tatar culture is carried out by a special method and if there is any deviation from the religious directions then believers will not eat the meat.

This is a light meat and bean dish. I like this dish on the spicy side, so feel free to adjust the heat to your taste. Any kind of meat can be used and I have opted for ground beef for convenience sake as it cooks quickly. Canned beans are also time-saving and work well in this dish. Serve with a plate of fresh vegetables and plenty of bread to sop up all the juices.

1 pound lean ground beef

1 large onion, chopped

1 teaspoon salt

2 cups cooked white beans, drained

1 tablespoon tomato paste

¼ teaspoon ground dried hot pepper or ground cayenne pepper

2 tablespoons unsalted butter

Chopped fresh parsley to taste

In a large skillet over medium heat, brown the beef with the onions until onions are soft, about 5 minutes. Add the salt and ½ cup of water and simmer for 15 minutes.

Add the beans, tomato paste, and red pepper and continue cooking another 10 minutes. Stir in the butter and ladle into shallow bowls with some of the broth. Sprinkle with chopped fresh parsley and serve hot.

Braised Beef Tongue

Tushkovanyi lyzen' z yalovychyny

Makes 6 servings

B eef tongue makes a delicious cold dish and is usually served as an appetizer in Ukraine. Boiling is the traditional method of cooking beef tongue, but I prefer to bake it at a very low temperature for several hours. The result is moist and tender, and the tongue makes its own gravy while it cooks. Since this way takes eight hours to cook and 30 minutes more "resting" time, make sure you allow enough time or cook it the day before you plan on serving it.

Beef tongue, as well as veal, pork, or lamb's tongue, can be purchased fresh, smoked, corned, or pickled and all can be prepared in this manner.

1 (2½-pound) fresh beef tongue

2 teaspoons salt

½ teaspoon freshly ground black pepper

1 tablespoon apple cider vinegar

1 onion, quartered

3 cloves garlic, sliced

2 carrots, peeled and coarsely chopped

2 parsnips, peeled and coarsely chopped

2 ribs celery, coarsely chopped

1 turnip, peeled and coarsely chopped

1 kohlrabi, peeled and coarsely chopped

¼ cup chopped fresh parsley

Freshly grated horseradish for serving (optional)

Preheat the oven to 200°F. Rinse the tongue under cold running water and pat dry. Season the tongue with salt and black pepper and place in a deep casserole dish. Add the vinegar and ½ cup of water. Cover tightly and place the casserole in the oven. Cook for 5 hours.

Add all the vegetables except the parsley and horseradish to the casserole. Cover tightly again and put back into the oven and bake for another 2½ hours, or until the tongue is tender. Remove the pan from the oven and let sit for about 30 minutes.

Remove the tongue from the casserole. Peel off the skin and cut off any gristle or connective tissue. Slice and place on a large serving platter along with the vegetables. Garnish with chopped fresh parsley and some freshly grated horseradish if desired. Serve the pan juices in a sauce boat on the side.

....

NOTE: *If using a smoked, corned, or pickled tongue, omit the salt or reduce it by half. Any sort of seasonal vegetables can be used to flavor tongue.*

....

VARIATION: *If you prefer to boil the beef tongue, season with salt and black pepper, cover with water and simmer on low heat with the vegetables for 3 hours (2 hours for pork or lamb's tongue). If using a pressure cooker, follow the manufacturer's instructions regarding length of cooking time.*

Shish Kebabs

Shashlyky

Shashlyky (barbecued skewered meat) is a staple throughout Ukraine and possesses ancient roots. Originally, chunks of meat were barbecued over open flames on the tip of a sword by the nomads of the Caucasus. Today, *shashlyky* are grilled on long metal skewers over a charcoal fire or broiled indoors. Either way it is a featured dish at family picnics as well as a symbol of Ukrainian cuisine.

The following is a standard way of preparing *shashlyky*. Any type of meat can be used: beef, pork, and lamb are the usual choices, but chunks of turkey, chicken, or even a sturdy fish are additional choices. Many people combine one or two of the meats or prefer a meat-and-fish combination, creating a type of "surf and turf" style of *shashlyky*. I personally like lamb kebabs.

Serve *shashlyky* on a plate of greens if you like, garnished with lemon wedges and trimmed scallions, or on a bed of steamed rice with a scattering of finely chopped fresh herbs like dill or finely chopped red onion.

½ cup sunflower oil or olive oil

½ cup red wine vinegar

½ cup dry red wine

1 onion, grated

2 cloves garlic, crushed

2 tablespoons freshly grated horseradish (optional)

1 bay leaf

1 teaspoon coarse salt

½ teaspoon freshly ground black pepper

2½ pounds boneless leg of lamb, cut into 2-inch chunks

1 tablespoon granulated sugar (optional)

Skewers

In a large bowl, combine the sunflower oil, vinegar, red wine, onion, garlic, horseradish, bay leaf, salt, and black pepper. Add the chunks of lamb and toss to coat evenly. Cover and refrigerate for at least 6 hours or overnight.

Bring the meat to room temperature before grilling. Prepare the coals for grilling or preheat the broiler. Drain the meat (reserving the marinade) and pat dry with paper towels. Pour the marinade into a medium saucepan and bring to a boil. Boil 5 minutes, uncovered, reducing it somewhat, and then turn the heat to low. Taste and adjust the seasonings, adding some sugar if desired. Let the marinade simmer on low and use to baste the meat while grilling.

Skewer the chunks of meat and grill or broil about 4 inches away from the heat, turning frequently and basting with the hot marinade. Total cooking time is about 12 minutes.

To serve, wrap a cloth napkin around the hot end of each skewer and serve, or slip the meat off the hot skewers and onto a plate. Serve immediately.

Ukrainian Meat-on-a-Stick

Patychky

Makes 20 to 24 skewers

This is another wonderfully aromatic, yet straightforward recipe for skewered meat. *Patychky* is an Old Country specialty, a popular wedding dish, and one that is served during the holidays or at functions catering to a large number of guests. It is a substantial nibble and a perfect choice for *zakusky* hour.

My version uses pork tenderloin, but cubed beef in combination with pork is also popular. I like to serve *patychky* with a side of buttered noodles with some of the stewed onions scooped on top.

6 pounds pork tenderloin, cut into 2-inch cubes

Short (6-inch) sturdy wooden skewers

2 cups fine dry breadcrumbs

1 teaspoon crushed dry marjoram

½ teaspoon salt

½ teaspoon freshly ground black pepper

2 extra-large eggs, beaten

2 large onions, thinly sliced

1 tablespoon unsalted butter, softened

4 large ribs celery, sliced in half lengthwise (optional)

About 1 cup (generous) sunflower oil for frying

MARINADE:

1½ cups dry sherry or white wine

3 cloves garlic, crushed

2 teaspoons salt

½ teaspoon freshly ground black pepper

Make the marinade: Pour the sherry into a large bowl and whisk in the garlic, salt, and black pepper. Add the chunks of pork and toss to coat evenly. Cover and refrigerate overnight.

Bring the pork to room temperature before using. Remove the pork from the marinade and discard the marinade. Pat pork dry with paper towels. Skewer the pork, about 4 chunks per skewer, pushing them close together.

Pour the breadcrumbs onto a large plate and toss with the marjoram, salt, and black pepper. Put the eggs in a shallow dish. Roll a skewer of meat in the breadcrumbs, then into the beaten eggs, and then back into the breadcrumbs. Repeat this process with all the skewers.

Preheat the oven to 350°F. Toss the onions with the softened butter and place in a large casserole or roasting pan. Lay the pieces of celery over top of the onions with the rounded side of the celery pointed upward as to not collect any of the pan juices. Set the pan aside.

Heat the sunflower oil in a deep, heavy skillet and when a drop of water flicked into it sputters, the oil is at the right temperature to fry. Brown each skewer of meat in the hot oil, about 2 minutes on each side. Place these first browned skewers horizontally over top of the celery sticks. This will keep the meat from getting soggy. Lay the second layer of skewers in the opposite direction from the first. Make a third layer if need be.

Bake the *patychky*, uncovered, about 45 minutes, or until the meat is tender. Before serving, discard the celery, but scoop the onions into a small decorative bowl. Serve the *patychky* on a large serving platter with the onions on the side.

....

NOTE: *Short (6 inch) wooden skewers can be purchased in any Ukrainian, Russian, or Polish market. Just ask for "patychky sticks."*

Roast Leg of Lamb

Pechena yahniatyna

Makes 10 servings

I love leg of lamb and my family always served it with red beans and turnips on a bed of greens—simple and elegant. A Ukrainian favorite, small glasses of warm plum brandy to drink will bring complexity and charm to this already earthy dish. Ah, the pleasures of rustic life!

1 (7-pound) leg of lamb with shank bone

5 cloves garlic, slivered

1 tablespoon unsalted butter, softened

1 tablespoon coarse salt

1 teaspoon freshly ground black pepper

1 pound dry red kidney beans, soaked in cold water overnight

20 small turnips (about 5 pounds), peeled

2 bay leaves

½ cup fruity red wine

Additional butter, coarse salt, and black pepper for serving

Watercress or lettuce for lining platter

Preheat the oven to 425°F. Cut small slits all over the leg of lamb and insert the pieces of garlic. Rub the roast all over with softened butter and sprinkle with coarse salt and black pepper. Place the lamb on a rack in a shallow roasting pan. Pour 2 cups of water into the bottom of the pan and put into the oven. Roast for 20 minutes, then reduce the heat to 350°F and continue roasting about 2 hours longer for medium-rare meat.

While the meat is roasting, drain the beans and put into a large pot. Add the turnips, bay leaves, and fresh cold water to cover and bring to a boil. Reduce the heat to medium and simmer about 20 minutes, or until the turnips are tender. Remove the turnips from the pot and set aside. Continue to simmer the beans for an additional 40 minutes, or until the beans are tender. Remove pot from heat and add turnips back to pot. Cover and set aside until ready to serve.

Transfer the leg of lamb to a large plate and cover with aluminum foil until ready to serve. Put the roasting pan directly over a burner, skim the fat off the top and add the red wine. Bring to a full boil, scraping the bottom of the pan to remove and dissolve all the browned bits. Cook about 5 minutes, strain, and pour into a warmed sauce boat. Drain the warm beans and turnips, toss with additional butter if you like and sprinkle with coarse salt and black pepper.

To serve, place the leg of lamb on a large watercress-lined platter and surround with beans and turnips. Serve with the pan juices on the side.

Chicken Kyiv

Kuriachi kotlety po-Kyievs'ky   Makes 12 rolls or 6 to 12 servings

This is probably the best-known Ukrainian classic. How the noble city of Kyiv came to lend its name to the dish is not clear. In traditionally prepared Chicken Kyiv, a boned chicken breast (with the wing attached) is stuffed with butter, dredged in coarse breadcrumbs, pan-fried, and then served immediately so the butter spurts out as the meat is cut. It is a preparation that bears witness to the humble chicken's almost cult status in Ukraine.

Ask your butcher to special cut and debone your chicken breasts while leaving the wing attached, or if you fancy, use boneless, skinless chicken breasts. This is my preferred version. Use the freshest sweet cream butter you can find and finely chopped fresh dill. Potato pancakes (*deruny*, page 84) or small slices of fresh rye bread browned in butter are traditional accompaniments.

12 tablespoons unsalted butter, softened

¼ cup finely chopped fresh dill

Pinch of freshly ground black pepper

12 boneless, skinless chicken breast halves

1 tablespoon coarse salt

About 3 cups sunflower oil for deep frying

1 cup unbleached all-purpose flour

2 extra-large eggs, beaten

1½ cups unflavored coarse dry breadcrumbs

In a small bowl, blend the softened butter with the fresh dill and pinch of black pepper. On a plate covered in waxed paper, shape the butter into twelve logs, about 1½-inches long by ½-inch wide. Wrap each log in clean pieces of waxed paper and refrigerate until firm, about 3 to 4 hours.

Put a chicken breast half on a board and pound with a kitchen mallet until thin. Sprinkle with coarse salt and place a butter "log" lengthwise on it. Tuck in both ends of the chicken breast over the butter and then roll up. Secure with toothpicks making sure there are no tears or openings (so the butter has no way of running out). Repeat with remaining chicken breasts. Place all the chicken rolls on a large plate and refrigerate for 30 minutes.

Preheat the oven to 250°F. Heat the sunflower oil to 350°F in a large skillet. Retrieve the chicken rolls from the refrigerator. Put the flour, eggs, and breadcrumbs each on a separate large plate. Dip each chicken roll into the flour, then into the beaten eggs, and then roll in the coarse breadcrumbs, making sure the rolls are completely coated.

Drop the rolls, about 2 to 3 at a time into the hot oil (do not crowd). Fry the rolls until they are golden brown and float, about 6 minutes. Carefully drain on paper towels and keep the rolls warm in the oven until all are fried. Serve immediately.

Chicken Pies

Kuriachi sichenyky

My "pies" are beautifully moist on the inside and crispy on the outside, quick and easy to make, and unfailingly delicious. Normally a combination of chicken breast and leg meat would be ground together, however, I find ground chicken thigh meat works just as well and is readily available. Use whatever cooked vegetables are leftover in your refrigerator in the stuffing—cooked carrots, mushrooms, chopped green beans, corn, or any combination of vegetables.

Sichenyky are served plain, smothered in your favorite sauce (see pages 80–81), or topped with a dollop of herbed mayonnaise for a true and authentic Ukrainian meal.

3 slices stale bread (about 1½ cups torn)

½ cup canned evaporated milk

2 pounds ground chicken thigh meat

1 extra-large egg, beaten

1 teaspoon salt

½ teaspoon freshly ground black pepper

About 1½ cups cooked mixed vegetables, finely chopped into small pieces

½ cup unflavored dry breadcrumbs

2 tablespoons unsalted butter or sunflower oil

Tear the bread into pieces and put into a large bowl. Add the milk and let the bread soak for 15 minutes. Add the ground chicken, egg, salt, and black pepper. Mix gently but thoroughly and form into 6 balls.

Make an indentation in each ball and fill with about 2 tablespoons chopped vegetables. Cover the filling with ground chicken and gently flatten into a plump patty. Coat each patty with breadcrumbs and lay on some waxed paper.

Melt the butter in a large skillet over medium heat and fry each patty about 4 to 5 minutes on each side, until the juices run clear when pierced with the tip of a small knife. Serve while hot.

· ·

NOTE: *Ground beef, pork, lamb, veal, or turkey can be substituted for the ground chicken in this recipe with great success.*

Poached Chicken with Walnut Sauce

Tushkovana kurka z horikhovoyu pidlyvoyu Makes 6 to 8 servings / 1½ cups walnut sauce

Poached chicken is another important Ukrainian stand-by dish. It is served hot or cold with mustard, mayonnaise, sour cream, or fresh lemon juice as part of *zakusky* hour, or as a first course or light dinner. It provides Ukrainian cooks with plenty of other options for casseroles and soups, or when combined with any cooked kasha and vegetables makes another nutritious meal.

Nuts are a home product of Ukraine, Crimea in particular. Walnuts are available all year long and used in savory as well as sweet dishes. Almonds and hazelnuts also hold a prominent place in Ukrainian cookery and can be used in place of walnuts in many recipes. Both work well in this accompanying sauce. Walnut sauce is also good served over *varenyky* (dumplings, page 192) or over *lokshyna* (homemade noodles, page 202), thus making a nutritious side dish or vegetarian main course.

Poach chicken:

Put the chicken pieces in a large pot and cover with cold water. Bring to barely a boil over high heat and discard any foam that rises to the top. At the boiling point, stir in the salt, reduce the heat to low, cover, and simmer about 1 hour, or until the chicken is tender.

Make the walnut sauce:

Put the walnuts, garlic, and parsley in a food processor and pulse just until the walnuts are finely ground. Transfer the mixture to a medium bowl and stir in very hot broth, lemon juice, coriander, and ground red pepper. Taste and add salt to your liking. Cover and let the sauce stand for a few minutes before serving.

POACHED CHICKEN:

2 chickens (about 3 pounds each), quartered

1 tablespoon plus 1 teaspoon coarse salt

Freshly ground black pepper to taste

Sweet Hungarian paprika to taste

Cucumber and tomato slices for garnish (optional)

WALNUT SAUCE:

1½ cups toasted walnuts, coarsely chopped

2 cloves garlic, coarsely chopped

¼ cup chopped fresh parsley or cilantro

1 cup hot meat or vegetable broth

2 tablespoons fresh lemon juice

¼ teaspoon ground coriander

Pinch of ground red pepper or pepper flakes

Salt to taste

When the chicken is cooked, remove with a slotted spoon and let cool. (Reserve the broth for other recipes.) Remove the skin and bones and discard, leaving the meat in large pieces. Arrange the chicken meat on a large serving platter and sprinkle with coarse salt, black pepper, and sweet paprika. Garnish with cucumber and tomato slices and serve with Walnut Sauce.

Poached Chicken with Onion-Honey Sauce

Tushkovana kurka z tsybuliano-medovoyu pidlyvoyu

Makes 6 to 8 servings / 1½ cups sauce

This is another delicious use for poached chicken. Sauces concocted from a particular vegetable or fruit, made sweet and sour with the addition of vinegar and honey, are an ancient Ukrainian specialty. This is my version of onion and honey sauce. It is a sauce that pairs well with all meats, but is especially good with poultry.

Poach chicken:

Put the chicken pieces in a large pot and cover with cold water. Bring to barely a boil over high heat and discard any foam that rises to the top. At the boiling point, stir in the salt, reduce the heat to low, cover, and simmer about 1 hour or until the chicken is tender.

Make the onion-honey sauce:

Warm the oil in a large skillet over medium heat and add the onions. Reduce the heat to low and gently sauté the onions until very soft and fragrant (not browned), about 20 minutes, stirring occasionally. Add the broth, increase the heat to high and cook uncovered until the liquid is reduced by half, about 5 minutes. Stir in the honey and vinegar, reduce the heat to low and continue cooking another 10 minutes. Taste and add salt and black pepper to taste.

POACHED CHICKEN:

2 chickens (about 3 pounds each), quartered

1 tablespoon plus 1 teaspoon coarse salt

Freshly ground black pepper to taste

Sweet Hungarian paprika to taste

Cucumber and tomato slices to garnish (optional)

ONION-HONEY SAUCE:

3 tablespoons sunflower oil

2 sweet onions, quartered and thinly sliced

1 cup meat or vegetable broth

2 tablespoons honey

2 tablespoons apple cider vinegar or more to taste

Salt and freshly ground black pepper to taste

When the chicken is cooked, remove with a slotted spoon and let cool. (Reserve the broth for other recipes.) Remove the skin and bones and discard, leaving the meat in large pieces. Arrange the chicken meat on a large serving platter and sprinkle with coarse salt, black pepper, and sweet paprika. Garnish with cucumber and tomato slices and serve with the Onion-Honey Sauce.

Baked Chicken with Champignons and Sour Cream

Pechena kurka z hrybamy ta smetanoyu Makes 4 to 6 servings

Ukrainians, as do most Slavs, have a special reverence and possess a certain flair for creating sauces with sour cream and mushrooms. Perhaps it is similar to the way the French combine wine and shallots in so many of their sauces. In this dish the chicken is baked with a good deal of ordinary white mushrooms, permeating the meat with flavor. You may use a cut-up whole chicken or an assortment of legs and breasts, or whichever parts you prefer.

It is not unusual that some Hungarian staples have found their way across the Carpathian Mountains throughout the centuries, bringing with them a satisfying bite and piquancy to Ukrainian foods. In this case it is caraway seeds which impart a slightly sweet, almost aniseed finish to the dish. As far as I am concerned there is only one accompaniment to this chicken dish—*buckwheat kasha* (page 105), which beautifully absorbs all the delicious juices of the chicken and mushrooms.

3 pounds chicken leg quarters (split if desired)

1 tablespoon salt

½ teaspoon freshly ground black pepper or more to taste

2 tablespoons lard or sunflower oil

1 large onion, quartered and sliced

1 carrot, peeled and grated

1 rib celery, finely chopped

1½ pounds champignons or button mushrooms, sliced

½ cup chopped fresh parsley

1 tablespoon caraway seeds, bruised

1 cup sour cream

Sweet Hungarian paprika to taste

Preheat the oven to 325°F. Rub all of the chicken pieces generously with salt and black pepper. Melt the lard in a large casserole over medium-high heat. Add the chicken pieces and brown on all sides. Remove the chicken pieces from the pan with kitchen tongs and put on a platter.

Reduce the heat to medium and add the onion. Sauté the onion for about 8 minutes or until nicely browned. Add the carrot, celery, and mushrooms, and continue sautéing another 5 minutes. Put the chicken pieces back into the pan and add 1 cup of water and the parsley and caraway seeds. Bring the mixture barely to a boil over high heat. Cover and bake in the oven for about 1 hour, basting with the cooking juices after 30 minutes. If necessary, add more water if the liquid dries out.

When the chicken is cooked and the skin crisps a bit, remove from the pan and put on a warmed serving platter. Put the casserole pan directly on a burner over medium heat. Add a bit more water, enough to make 2 cups liquid. If the sour cream is not at room temperature, add a few tablespoons of the hot liquid to temper it, and then add to the pan, stirring to combine. Blend the mixture well for about 2 minutes with a whisk, and then pour over the chicken pieces. Sprinkle with sweet paprika and serve immediately.

Breaded Turkey Cutlets

Obkacheni kotlety z indyka

Another name for meat that has been pounded thin is *kotlety* or cutlets. This dish is a family favorite and features fresh lemon juice and capers—two Ukrainian favorites for seasoning meats.

1½-pound turkey breast tenderloin, cut into 4 pieces

Juice and grated zest of 1 large lemon

½ cup fine dry breadcrumbs

1 extra-large egg, slightly beaten with 2 tablespoons water

4 tablespoons sunflower oil

1 tablespoon small capers, rinsed and drained

2 tablespoons finely chopped fresh parsley or dill

Salt and freshly ground black pepper to taste

Lemon wedges and sprigs of parsley to garnish

Place the turkey tenderloins on a board and pound thin with a kitchen mallet. Put the flattened turkey cutlets into a shallow baking dish. Sprinkle the lemon zest over top and drizzle with the lemon juice. Turn to coat both sides of the cutlets and let stand at room temperature for 30 minutes.

Put the breadcrumbs and the egg mixture in separate shallow dishes. Dip each cutlet into the breadcrumbs, coating both sides, then into the egg mixture, then into the breadcrumbs again.

In a heavy skillet over medium heat, warm 2 tablespoons of the sunflower oil until hot. Add the cutlets and cook for 2 to 3 minutes, turning once, until golden brown and tender. Transfer to a warmed plate.

Wipe out the skillet and add the remaining 2 tablespoons sunflower oil, capers, and parsley and heat through. Spoon a little of the sauce over the turkey cutlets and sprinkle with salt and black pepper. Serve garnished with lemon wedges and sprigs of fresh parsley.

Roast Turkey Breast with Spinach-Sorrel Sauce

Pechena hrudynka indyka iz shpinatovo-shchavlevoyu pidlyvoyu

Makes 6 servings

Roasting the turkey breast covered in aluminum foil keeps the meat particularly moist and tender. This creamy, almost lemony-flavored sauce is always poured under the slices of carved meat in order to keep the fine white color of the turkey breast meat, or better still, serve the sauce in a warmed separate gravy boat.

To risk departure from my culinary region, I admit to substituting condensed skim milk for traditional heavy cream in this sauce. I have tried this recipe all sorts of ways and I like the lighter version best. Feel free to experiment with it though.

Spinach-sorrel sauce is equally good with roast veal, chicken, or fish such as haddock, cod, or flounder.

ROAST TURKEY BREAST:

2 tablespoons sunflower oil

3½-pound turkey breast

1 tablespoon coarse salt

1 teaspoon freshly ground black pepper

½ teaspoon freshly grated nutmeg

1 onion, coarsely chopped

1 small knob celery root, peeled and coarsely chopped

1 small parsley root, peeled and coarsely chopped

¼ cup brandy or white wine

SPINACH-SORREL SAUCE:

2 cups tightly packed cleaned fresh spinach leaves, shredded

2 cups tightly packed cleaned fresh sorrel leaves, shredded

2 cups boiling water flavored with ½ teaspoon salt

Bowl filled with 6 cups ice water

½ cup white wine

2 cups unsweetened condensed skim milk

2 tablespoons very cold unsalted butter, cut into small pieces

Salt and freshly ground black pepper to taste

Roast turkey breast:

Preheat the oven to 325°F. Gently rub sunflower oil all over the turkey breast, then gently lift the skin and rub some oil directly on the breast meat. Season the entire breast with salt, black pepper, and nutmeg. Transfer the turkey breast to a roasting pan, breast-side up and scatter onions, celery root, and parsley root all around the turkey breast. Pour the brandy and 1 cup of water around the turkey breast and cover the entire pan with buttered aluminum foil. Roast for 1½ hours, opening the foil and basting the turkey breast every 30 minutes.

Make the spinach-sorrel sauce:

Blanch the spinach and sorrel leaves in the salted boiling water for about 45 seconds, then immediately plunge into the ice water. Drain and completely squeeze dry. Put the leaves and the wine into a food processor or blender and puree until smooth. Pour the condensed milk into a medium saucepan and bring to a boil over medium heat, stirring constantly to prevent scorching. Cook the milk, stirring constantly, for 3 minutes to reduce by a third. Stir in the spinach-sorrel mixture and heat again to boiling over medium heat, stirring the entire time. Remove the pan from the heat and whisk in the butter a piece at a time until thoroughly incorporated. Taste and adjust the seasonings by adding salt and black pepper to your liking. Serve hot.

When the turkey juices run clear after being pricked with a skewer, remove from oven and remove the vegetables with a slotted spoon and place on a warmed serving platter (any extra pan juices may be used in other recipes). Let the turkey breast rest for 10 minutes. To serve, carefully remove the breast meat from the bone and slice. Spoon some of the sauce onto the platter, and then lay slices of meat over top. Pour any extra sauce into a warmed gravy boat and place next to the platter. Serve immediately.

The noble barnyard chicken ... duck ... goose

If you ask inhabitants of Ukraine why poultry enjoys such a second-rate reputation in the United States, they would probably attribute it to factory farming. Every self-respecting Ukrainian, they would say, not only buys directly from the farmer or private market, but buys at the very least, according to strict family recommendations or from the likes of a good and trusted friend. It is not unusual for one to make a detailed inquiry about what the diet and lifestyle was like of the prospective purchase. There is a great respect for these noble farm animals—an admirable Ukrainian trait. Then and only then, will one obtain the healthiest birds and in return the most lean and flavorful meat.

Ukrainian Roast Duck

Pechena kachka

Makes 2 servings

Ducks are plentiful in Ukraine. In this recipe, the initial slow cooking and pricking of the skin helps to draw out any extra fat. The finish of blackberry brandy crisps the skin and is just delectable. A four-pound duck after roasting will feed only two people, so plan accordingly.

1 (4-pound) duck

1 tablespoon coarse salt

½ teaspoon freshly ground black pepper

½ cup granulated sugar

¼ cup apple cider vinegar

⅓ cup blackberry brandy

Preheat the oven to 300°F. Trim all the excess fat and excess skin from the duck and prick the skin all over with a sharp needle or skewer, being careful not to pierce the meat. Season the duck all over with salt and black pepper. Tie the legs together with kitchen string. Place the duck on a rack in a roasting pan, cover tightly with aluminum foil, and roast in the oven for about 2½ hours.

Meanwhile, put the sugar and vinegar in a medium, heavy (non-reactive) saucepan and stir to dissolve the sugar. Bring to a boil over high heat, without stirring, until the mixture is caramel in color. Remove the pan from the heat and carefully add the blackberry brandy, pouring it down the side of the pan. Swirl the pan to blend it and then place the pan over medium heat and simmer for 3 minutes.

Remove the duck from the oven and take off the foil. Pour off all the fat in the pan and reserve for future use if desired. Raise the oven temperature to 400°F and return the duck to the oven, uncovered. Roast for another 30 minutes, basting the duck often with the brandy mixture until glazed and golden. Remove the duck from the pan and place on a board. Let rest, uncovered, for at least 10 minutes before carving.

Pour the remaining roasting juices into the saucepan, skim off the fat and discard, and bring juices to a boil over medium heat. Reduce the heat to low and simmer for 5 minutes, stirring frequently. Carve the duck and serve with the sauce in a warmed gravy boat on the side.

Podillia Stuffing

Podil's'ka nachynka

This old-fashioned poultry stuffing originated in the central region of Ukraine known as Podillia and is still popular today. Delicious served with roasted poultry, it contains both ground beef and giblets and is usually made with homemade bread, but use whatever you have on hand. This is my adapted version.

4 cups cubed toasted bread

1 cup Rich Ukrainian Chicken Broth (page 44)

½ pound ground sirloin

Chicken gizzard and heart, cooked and finely chopped

2 tablespoons unsalted butter, melted

1 extra-large egg, slightly beaten

½ teaspoon salt

½ teaspoon freshly ground black pepper

Preheat the oven to 350°F. Put the toasted bread in a large bowl and soften with the chicken broth, using just enough to moisten—the bread should be crumbly, not soggy. Add the rest of the ingredients and mix gently, but well.

Spoon the mixture into a buttered casserole dish and bake about 45 to 60 minutes, or until firm with a golden brown crust. This dish is most often served with meat preparations such as roast suckling pig, beef brisket, roast leg of lamb, beef or pork sausages, or roast chicken, duck, or goose.

Holiday Stuffed Roast Goose

Nachyniuvana pechena huska na sviato   Makes 6 to 8 servings

The sight of a crisp, golden roast goose on a holiday table is truly beautiful. Their meat is darker and more flavorful. It should be noted that while geese (and ducks) are notorious for the amount of fat rendered during cooking, the meat itself is actually lean, for the fat is just under the skin. For this reason alone a goose should be stuffed, for the stuffing does not absorb the fat.

Any type of traditional stuffing will suit a goose. The one I give here is a modern-day favorite and is proudly served not only during the holidays, but on other special occasions as well. It features raisins, prunes, and wild mushrooms, bound together with rice instead of bread or breadcrumbs. If the liver is provided with the goose, simply sauté it in butter, then mash it into the stuffing. I like to garnish roast goose with apples roasted with and basted with the pan drippings—they are always a hit!

And lastly, goose fat is highly prized in many food cultures, and Ukrainian cuisine is no exception. While the more "figure-conscious" may choose not to indulge, I thought it only fair to include directions on how to make goose cracklings—for the "purists" or "farmhouse cooks." I think most would agree the best way to serve goose cracklings is scattered over hot mashed potatoes!

GOOSE:
1 (8 to 10 pound) goose
2 large cloves garlic, cut in half
2 tablespoons coarse salt
1 teaspoon freshly ground black pepper

RAISIN, PRUNE AND WILD MUSHROOM STUFFING:
½ cup raisins
8 ounces dried pitted prunes
½ cup cognac or brandy
⅔ cup dried wild mushrooms or about 4 ounces fresh wild mushrooms
2 thick slices smoky bacon, cut into small chunks
1 onion, finely chopped
½ cup celery pieces, finely chopped
2 cups cooked long-grain or wild rice
3 tablespoons unsalted butter, melted
½ teaspoon ground allspice
¼ teaspoon ground cloves
2 extra-large eggs, lightly beaten
1 teaspoon salt
½ teaspoon freshly ground black pepper

GARNISHES:
4 large Granny Smith apples, halved and cored

Prepare stuffing ingredients:
Put the raisins and prunes in a small bowl. Bring 1 cup of water to a boil and add the cognac. Remove the pan from the heat, let cool slightly, and then pour over the fruit. Let the fruit soak a few hours. Drain, reserving the liquid, and chop the fruit into small pieces. Set aside.

Put the dried mushrooms in a medium bowl. Bring 1 cup of water to a boil and pour over the mushrooms. Let the mushrooms soak for 30 minutes, and then drain and strain the liquid and reserve. Finely chop the mushrooms and set aside.

Prepare goose:
Preheat the oven to 425°F. Wash and dry the goose. Cut off all excess fat from the breast, drumsticks, and all other parts of the goose. Cut this fat into long pieces and place in a covered bowl; refrigerate until ready to render (optional).

Rub the goose with the garlic halves (then save the garlic for use in the stuffing). Season the goose inside and outside with salt and black pepper. Prick the skin all over with a needle or skewer to release the fat during cooking, being careful not to pierce the meat.

Make stuffing:

In a medium skillet over medium heat, fry the bacon until almost crisp. Add the onion and sauté until golden, about 5 minutes. Chop up the garlic cloves used to season the goose and add to the skillet, along with the celery and soaked mushrooms. Continue cooking another 5 minutes. Transfer the mixture to a large bowl and add the soaked raisins and prunes, rice, melted butter, allspice, and cloves. Stir to combine. Add the beaten eggs and season with salt and black pepper. Loosely stuff the goose and skewer the opening closed. Put any remaining stuffing in a buttered casserole dish. Cover the pan with aluminum foil and bake separately during the last hour of roasting the goose.

Roast goose:

Put the stuffed goose, breast-side up on a broiling rack in a roasting pan (make sure goose will be above any juices collecting in the pan). Pour the reserved soaking liquids from the raisin/prune mixture and the mushrooms into the pan, and then place it in the oven. After roasting for 20 minutes, baste the bird with the drippings and turn the temperature down to 325°F. Continue roasting the goose for 3 hours, basting occasionally. Remove all but 3 tablespoons of the accumulated drippings from the pan. Place the halved apples around the goose and drizzle with some of the drippings in the pan. Continue roasting, basting the apples once or twice, for about 30 minutes longer, or until the juices run clear when the fleshiest part of the thigh of the goose is pricked with a skewer and the apples are soft.

Serve:

Remove the apples and place on a warmed serving platter. Transfer the goose to a carving board and remove the skewers from the stuffing cavity. Cover the bird loosely with aluminum foil and let sit for 20 minutes before carving. Remove the stuffing from the bird and place on the serving platter (any extra can be served on the side). Cut off the wings, legs, and thighs and place over the stuffing. Remove the breast meat from the bone, slice and lie on top of the other parts on the platter and serve immediately. The drippings left from roasting can also be served on the side.

Goose Cracklings

Husiachi shkvarky

Retrieve the reserved goose fat from the refrigerator and put in a large skillet with barely enough water to cover. Bring to a boil, cover the pan, and reduce the heat to medium-high. Continue to cook, stirring occasionally, until nearly all the water has evaporated and the crackling rises to the surface of the fat. Take the lid off and continue frying until the fat becomes clear—almost transparent. Remove the pan from the heat, shake a few drops of water on it and quickly put the lid back on—this will make the cracklings crisp. Strain off the fat before it cools, sprinkle the cracklings with some coarse salt, and serve.

Chapter 6

Fish and Game

Adventures in hook and hunt ...

There is a noble tradition of fish cookery in Ukraine and even though the supply is ample, grabbing a rod and hook and going fishing is considered a most rewarding pastime. Fabulously rich in natural reservoirs, Ukraine's rivers and lakes teem with dozens of varieties of fish, such as carp, pike, perch, tench, bream, shad, eel, barbell, carp-bream, trout (introduced), catfish, Carpathian lamprey, small spiny crawfish referred to as "lobsters," and many others with no English equivalent. The Crimean coastline offers an abundance of plump herring and the smaller version known as sprats, as well as skate, salmon, anchovies, tuna, mackerel, grey mullet, and several whitefish varieties. When one thinks of Ukrainian fish cookery, shellfish does not often come to mind, but various types, especially shrimp and mussels, abound in the coastline waters of southern Ukraine, and in beach resort towns like Yalta vendors sell cooked shellfish on the streets.

All of these specimens, along with many months of Lenten days, combine to make Ukrainian fish cuisine one of the most interesting. Most are very easy to prepare with lots of room for variation and experimentation. While so many traditional fish dishes feature carp (small young carp of 3 to 4 pounds are best), many are just as good made with pike, trout, catfish, pickerel, or bass. As a rule, if the specified fish is not available or does not seem fresh, do not hesitate to use another with the same characteristics. Fish cook and taste differently, depending on if they come from fresh or salt water or are farmed, whether the flesh is light or dark in color, or whether the meat flakes in large pieces after cooking or is dense. As you become more familiar with different species, it is easier to pick up family resemblances.

Ukrainians have long had a passion for the hunt and the profusion of game meats has always been highly prized. Mother Nature is generous to Ukraine and today the woods, forests, and mountains still yield an abundance of deer called "roe," wild boar, brown bear, and moose (more often referred to as "elks"). Further south, between more forests and steppes, there are several more types of deer, wild hare, and countless feathered game such as pheasant, quail, partridge, wild geese, woodcocks, and wild ducks, especially mallards. I offer only a few game dishes mainly because the meat is hard to come by unless you are a hunter or have access to farmed sources.

Pike Fillets Baked in Sour Cream

File shchuky zapechene v smetani

Makes 6 servings

This is a Ukrainian favorite. It can be made with almost any kind of fish fillets or steaks. The sour cream helps to keep the fish nice and moist. Serve with potatoes and a cooked green vegetable or salad and plenty of crusty bread.

3 pounds pike fillets

Salt and freshly ground black pepper to taste

1 tablespoon unsalted butter or sunflower oil

1 onion, coarsely chopped

1 large carrot, peeled and coarsely chopped

1 rib celery, coarsely chopped

½ cup fish broth or chicken broth

2 tablespoons unbleached all-purpose flour

1 cup sour cream

Chopped fresh parsley or dill to garnish

Preheat the oven to 400°F. Sprinkle the pike fillets with salt and black pepper and place in a large, shallow baking dish in a single layer. Let stand while preparing the vegetables.

Melt the butter in a medium skillet over medium heat and add the onion. Sauté for about 1 minute, and then add the carrot, celery, and fish broth. Reduce the heat to medium-low, cover, and cook the vegetables until tender, about 12 minutes. Remove the pan from the heat and let cool slightly.

Whisk the flour into the sour cream and spread over the pike fillets. Spoon the vegetables and their juices all around the fish. Cover with aluminum foil and bake 15 to 20 minutes.

To serve, spoon portions of fish and some of the vegetables onto warmed dinner plates, drizzle with some of the sauce, and garnish with a sprinkling of chopped fresh parsley or dill.

Roast Pickerel with Lemon Butter and Horseradish

*Pechena moloda shchuka v
tsytrynovomu masli ta z khronom*

Makes 4 servings

Pickerel is a very fine tasting freshwater fish. Roasting the fish whole with its head makes for a pretty dish (place a thin slice of radish over the eye before serving). I use fresh dill to flavor this dish, though scallions or chives would also be good. This fish could also be stuffed if you like. Serve with roasted red potatoes and some fresh peas or asparagus for a light and refreshing meal.

4 whole pickerel (about 1½ pounds each)

Coarse salt and freshly ground black pepper to taste

Juice of 2 lemons

1½ tablespoons freshly grated lemon zest

4 tablespoons unsalted butter, softened

1 tablespoon pickled horseradish relish (page 68) or more to taste

2 tablespoons chopped fresh dill

Melted butter flavored with lemon juice (optional)

Preheat the oven to 400°F. Clean and gut the fish, then rinse with cold water and pat dry with paper towels. Season the fish with salt and black pepper and place in a buttered baking dish in a single layer.

Drizzle about 2 tablespoons of fresh lemon juice over the fish and sprinkle with the lemon zest. Dot the fish with butter and some horseradish relish and sprinkle with fresh dill.

Roast the fish in the oven for about 20 minutes or until tender. Serve immediately with additional melted butter flavored with lemon juice if desired.

Poached Carp Fillets with Yogurt-Scallion Sauce

Tushkovani file koropa z pidlyvoyu iz yogurtu ta tsybul'ky

Makes 4 servings

Nutritionists recommend eating more seafood of all types, but if you would like to get maximum benefit per mouthful, know that carp—probably the most popular fish used in Ukrainian cooking—is an omega-3 treasure chest. The yogurt sauce is equally as healthy and is also good served with other fish such as sole, catfish, or trout.

2 cups fish broth, chicken broth, or water

½ teaspoon freshly grated nutmeg

1 tablespoon honey

4 carp fillets (6 ounces each)

Snipped chives for garnishing

YOGURT-SCALLION SAUCE:

1 cup plain yogurt, drained for at least 2 hours

2 teaspoons honey

¼ teaspoon ground ginger

½ cup chopped scallions, including some green tops

Make the yogurt-scallion sauce:

Combine all ingredients in a small bowl. Cover and let sit for at least 1 hour for the flavors to marry. This sauce can be served chilled or at room temperature.

Prepare fish:

In a large skillet, combine the fish stock, nutmeg, and honey. Bring the mixture to a boil over medium-high heat. Gently lay the carp fillets in the liquid, return to a simmer over medium heat and poach the fish for about 6 minutes. Carefully spoon the fillets onto a warmed serving platter and garnish the fillets with a generous sprinkling of snipped fresh chives. Serve the Yogurt-Scallion Sauce on the side.

Grilled Bacon-Wrapped Trout

Smazhenyi forel', zavynenyi v solonynu

Makes 2 to 3 servings

Stuffed with porcini mushrooms and wrapped in smoky pieces of bacon, this is a delightful way of preparing the day's catch. My grilling choice is trout, but carp or pike are just as tasty. Serve with a variety of pickles, sliced garden tomatoes, and perhaps a good Ukrainian beer.

1 whole (3-pound) trout

Salt and freshly ground black pepper to taste

2 tablespoons unsalted butter

10 ounces fresh porcini mushrooms, chopped

1 tablespoon finely chopped fresh dill

4 thick slices smoky bacon

Lemon wedges to serve

Clean and gut the fish, then rinse under cold water and pat dry with paper towels. Season the fish inside and outside with salt and black pepper and set aside.

Melt the butter in a large skillet over medium heat and add the mushrooms. Cook the mushrooms until they give off their liquid and the liquid has evaporated, about 10 minutes. Stir in the dill, season with salt and black pepper, and remove the pan from the heat. Let the mushrooms cool slightly.

Stuff the cavity of the trout with the cooled mushrooms and wrap the body of the fish with the 4 slices of bacon, securing with small skewers.

Grill the fish about 3 inches above hot coals, about 4 to 5 minutes per side, or until the flesh of the trout is white and the bacon is crisp. Remove the fish from the grill and place on a warmed platter. Remove the skewers and serve immediately garnished with lemon wedges.

Grilled Salmon Steaks with Tomato Dressing

Pecheni na vuhliakh steiky lososia z pomidorovoyu polyvoyu

Makes 4 servings

Ukrainians love nature and going for a barbecue (*na shashlyky*) is a much-favored activity. Whether it is a picnic in the countryside or in the back yard of someone's *dacha* (country home), selecting fish steaks that have a natural affinity for smoky flavors for the entrée is the perfect choice. The finish of sour cream completes the recipe with just the right amount of contrast and an emphatically Ukrainian flavor.

2 large tomatoes, peeled, seeded, and chopped

1 cup Marinated Mushrooms (page 18), sliced, plus 2 tablespoons of the marinade

1 small red onion, finely chopped

1 clove garlic, crushed

2 tablespoons chopped fresh parsley

2 tablespoons chopped fresh chives

1 tablespoon honey

2 tablespoons sunflower oil

2 tablespoons unsalted butter

¼ cup finely chopped fresh dill

4 (6-ounce) salmon steaks

Coarse salt and freshly ground black pepper to taste

½ cup sour cream, room temperature

In a medium bowl, mix together the tomatoes, mushrooms and their marinade, red onion, garlic, parsley, chives, and honey. Stir in the oil and let the mixture rest for 1 hour. Meanwhile, prepare the charcoal grill.

Melt the butter in a small saucepan and stir in the dill. Remove the pan from the heat and brush both sides of the salmon steaks with the dill butter. Sprinkle salmon steaks with some salt and pepper. Grill about 3 inches above hot coals, about 4 to 5 minutes per side or until nicely browned.

While the salmon steaks are grilling, pour the tomato mixture into a medium saucepan and bring to a boil. Reduce the heat to low and simmer 5 minutes. Stir in the sour cream and continue cooking 1 more minute.

Put the salmon steaks on a warmed serving platter and spoon some of the tomato dressing over top. Serve immediately with the rest of the dressing in a separate bowl on the side.

....

VARIATION: *Sturgeon (see sidebar), swordfish, shark, halibut, or tuna steaks can all be used in this recipe instead of salmon.*

Is the sturgeon endangered?

As of the printing of this book, the answer to this question is yes, some species are endangered—the Beluga sturgeon of the Caspian Sea, prized not only for its flesh but also its eggs (better known as caviar), is not only endangered, but critically endangered.

There is a population of sturgeon here in North America and the fish is still found in abundance in the waters from Ensenada, Mexico, to the Gulf of Alaska. The sturgeon enjoys iconic status in the state of Wisconsin, where locals gather at the banks of waterways like the Wolf River each spring to catch sight of the huge ancient species as they spawn.

Baked Stuffed Salmon

Pechenyi nachyniuvanyi losos' – okremi portsiyi

Makes 4 servings

When one thinks of Ukrainian fish cuisine, sturgeon and salmon are usually the fish that come to mind. The salmon's elegant appearance, brilliant color, and superior taste is why it is so often served as a centerpiece for a special occasion or stately buffets. While I do not want to discourage anyone from working with a whole fish, I do think some home cooks find it a daunting task and too labor-intensive to prepare such a dish on a regular basis. So I wanted to devise a recipe for stuffed salmon that was just as dramatic as the fish in its full glory yet was quick and easy to prepare. I started to experiment, first with the stuffing and then with presentation. I thought about traditional Ukrainian ingredients and bound together a mixture of hearty fresh rye breadcrumbs, lush tomatoes, fresh dill, and a signature crunch of sweet pickles. I then placed individual salmon fillets, skin-side-up over mounds of the stuffing. This proved in the end to be just as opulent in presentation as any whole stuffed fish. In a pinch, rockfish or sturgeon fillets will work if salmon is not available and impart just as much oomph as salmon—ever adding to one's Ukrainian culinary repertoire!

4 thick salmon fillets (6 ounces each)

2 tablespoons sunflower oil

Coarse salt and freshly ground black pepper

STUFFING:

2 tablespoons unsalted butter

½ cup finely chopped scallions including green tops

¼ cup finely chopped celery

6 cups fresh light rye breadcrumbs

¼ cup finely chopped sweet pickles

2 tablespoons finely chopped fresh dill

1 teaspoon salt

¼ teaspoon freshly ground black pepper

2 small tomatoes, seeded and finely chopped

2 egg yolks

Preheat the oven to 400°F. Brush each salmon fillet with sunflower oil and season with salt and black pepper. Set aside.

Make the stuffing: In a medium skillet over medium heat, melt the butter and add the scallions and celery. Sauté the vegetables for 5 minutes. Meanwhile, put the breadcrumbs, pickles, dill, salt, and black pepper in a large mixing bowl. When the scallions and celery are soft, add the tomatoes, coating evenly with the scallions and celery. Remove from the heat and add to the breadcrumb mixture. Stir well to combine and let the mixture sit for 10 minutes. Bind the stuffing together with the egg yolks.

Arrange 4 heaping portions of stuffing on a well-greased baking tray, leaving room between each portion. Bake the stuffing for 20 minutes.

Place a salmon fillet, skin-side-up, over each portion of stuffing in a tilted fashion, and bake for 10 to 12 minutes or until the salmon is cooked and the skin is lightly browned. Remove each portion with a large, greased spatula and place on individual dinner plates. Serve at once.

Ukrainian Kulebiak

Kulebiak po-ukrains'ky

Ukrainian cuisine throughout history has adopted recipes and techniques from other regions of the world. This oblong-shaped savory fish pie was created in the late 1800s in Russia. A true multilayered *kulebyaka* of that time was filled with choice fish, dilled rice, wild mushrooms, thin crepes, and the dried spine marrow of sturgeon. Unfortunately this version is but a memory and lives on only in the pages of Russian literature. In Ukraine today, *kulebiak* is the generic name for an oblong savory pie filled with meat or cabbage. In the West it is known by its French variation—salmon in puff pastry.

Ukrainian cookery offers a variety of savory pies and this one in particular is usually suited to festive occasions. Modified to more contemporary and Ukrainian tastes, my version forgoes the crepes and unavailable sturgeon marrow and uses moist canned salmon, buttery-flavored buckwheat kasha instead of rice, and is adorned with layers of silky, sautéed mushrooms and hard-cooked eggs, all of which are encased in crisp puff pastry. I think my version provides a happy compromise and is very easy to make. I have served it to my family many times and at countless celebratory gatherings for many years with great success.

- 3 tablespoons unsalted butter
- 1 small onion, finely chopped
- 10 ounces fresh portabella mushrooms, sliced
- 1 cup cooked buckwheat kasha (page 105)
- 2 tablespoons finely chopped fresh dill
- 1 tablespoon fresh lemon juice
- Salt and freshly ground black pepper to taste
- 1 pound puff pastry, defrosted if frozen
- 16 ounces canned salmon, drained
- 3 hard-cooked extra-large eggs, chopped
- 1 extra-large egg, beaten
- Sprigs of parsley to garnish

Preheat the oven to 400°F. Melt the butter in a large skillet over medium heat and add the onion. Gently sauté for 5 minutes. Add the mushrooms and continue cooking another 10 minutes, or until the mushrooms give off their liquid and it has evaporated. Set the mixture aside to cool. In a small bowl, combine the buckwheat kasha with the dill and lemon juice and season the mixture to taste with salt and black pepper.

Roll out the pastry on a lightly floured board or counter to a 12-inch square. Spoon the kasha mixture over half the pastry, leaving a ½-inch border around the edges. Spread the mushroom mixture over top of the kasha. Flake the salmon with a fork and arrange on top of the mushrooms. Scatter the hard-cooked eggs among and over top of the salmon. Sprinkle with salt and black pepper to taste.

Brush the edges of the pastry with the beaten egg and fold the other half of the pastry over the filling to make a rectangle, pressing the edges firmly together to seal. Carefully lift the pastry onto a lightly oiled baking sheet. Using a pastry brush, glaze the entire pastry with beaten egg, and then make 3 evenly spaced slits in the top with a sharp knife to let steam escape.

Bake on the middle rack of the oven for 15 minutes, then reduce the oven temperature to 350°F and bake until golden brown, another 20 to 25 minutes. Allow the pie to cool slightly before slicing using a serrated knife. Serve slices garnished with sprigs of fresh parsley.

NOTE: *If you prefer to use fresh salmon, cut 1 pound of skinned salmon fillet into 1-inch pieces and proceed with the recipe. If you have leftover scraps of puff pastry, roll the dough thin and cut out decorative fish shapes. Brush the decorations with beaten egg and arrange on the top crust. Press gently to adhere and brush with a little more beaten egg. Bake as directed.*

Pisni oseledtsi z hrybamy

Makes 4 servings

Plump herring hold a special place in the hearts of Ukrainians. This fish is often teamed with Ukrainian favorites such as sour cream, wild mushrooms, pickles, and robust sauces and is prepared in many ways all year long.

Combined with mushrooms, this herring dish, although good on any day, often appears on the Christmas Eve table—where the cream is omitted and oil replaces the butter. It is delicious served with sauerkraut *varenyky* (page 193) or buckwheat kasha *holubtsi* (page 102).

1½ pounds salt (*schmaltz*) herring fillets

1 cup milk

3 tablespoons unsalted butter

1 small onion, finely chopped

8 ounces mushrooms, sliced

2 tablespoons unbleached all-purpose flour

½ cup sour cream

Soak the herring in the milk, covered, in the refrigerator for 2 hours. Drain the herring (discard the milk) and rinse, pat dry with paper towels, and cut into 1-inch pieces.

Melt 2 tablespoons of butter in a medium skillet over medium heat. Add the onion and sauté until soft, about 5 minutes. Add the mushrooms and continue cooking another 10 minutes, or until the mushrooms give off their liquid and it has evaporated. Set aside.

In a large skillet over medium heat, melt the remaining 1 tablespoon of butter and stir in the flour making a paste. Cook for 2 minutes, and then stir in 1 cup of water. Keep stirring until the mixture boils. Slowly stir in the sour cream, mushrooms, and herring. Reduce the heat to medium-low and simmer gently, stirring frequently, for 10 minutes to blend the flavors. Serve hot.

Ukrainian Gefilte Fish

Ryba po-yevreis'ky

Gefilte fish is a Jewish dish, but regional. In Ukraine, finely chopped carrots and parsnips are often added to the ground fish mixture that is used to make gefilte fish. I like to leave the onions whole and unpeeled because I like a darker broth in which to poach the fish patties. Sugar is another point of contention. Some people add sugar while others do not (I do not). Most gefilte fish recipes are very personal and most Ukrainian cooks have strong opinions conforming to their own family traditions.

This is a basic recipe that I think is quite tasty. Let your fishmonger grind the fish for you. Ask him or her to save all the bones, skin, trimmings, tails, and heads to make the fish broth.

7 to 8 pounds fresh roe carp, whitefish, and/or pike, filleted and ground (bones, skin, trimmings, tails, and heads reserved)

4 teaspoons salt

3 whole onions, unpeeled

4 carrots, peeled

2 teaspoons granulated sugar or more to taste (optional)

2 parsnips, peeled and finely chopped

4 extra-large eggs

Freshly ground black pepper to taste

⅓ cup matzo meal

Sprigs of watercress or parsley to serve

Pickled Horseradish Relish (page 68) to serve

Put the reserved fish bones, skin, trimmings, and all but 1 head in a large pot. Pour in about 16 cups of cold water and bring to a boil. Skim off any foam that rises to the top and discard. Add 3 teaspoons salt, the whole onions, 2 of the carrots, and sugar (if using) and bring back to a boil. Cover, reduce the heat to medium-low, and simmer for 30 minutes.

Meanwhile, put the ground fish into a large bowl. Finely chop the remaining 2 carrots and add them along with the parsnips to the fish and mix gently. Add the eggs one at a time, remaining 1 teaspoon salt, and black pepper and mix gently but thoroughly. Stir the matzo meal into the fish mixture, adding a little cold water if necessary. At this point, remove a tablespoon of the mixture, poach, and taste. Adjust seasonings as needed. Shape the fish mixture into 6 oval patties about 3-inches long, and stuff the cavity of the 1 reserved fish head with any remaining fish mixture.

Strain the fish broth, saving only the cooked carrots. Return the stock to the rinsed out pot and bring to a simmer over medium heat. Gently place the fish patties and stuffed fish head in the simmering stock. Partially cover, and simmer on medium-low heat for about 20 to 25 minutes.

When the fish patties are cooked, remove carefully with a slotted spoon and arrange on a serving platter along with the fish head. Strain some stock and pour about ½ cup over the fish patties. Let the fish cool for about 15 minutes.

Slice the 2 cooked carrots into rounds and place on top of each gefilte fish patty and put a slice of carrot over the fish eye on the head. Refrigerate for at least 6 hours. Serve garnished with sprigs of watercress or parsley with some pickled horseradish relish on the side to accompany.

Ukrainian Fish Babka

Babka z ryby

Makes 6 servings

Fish *babka* is a traditional Jewish dish from Ukraine. It is a "fish pudding" of sorts, lightened with whipped egg whites, giving the final product a more soufflé-like texture—but it is much more stable than a soufflé and can be turned out and cut into wedges to serve. This makes a nice brunch dish served with a fresh green salad.

1 pound whitefish fillets, skinned and cut into 1-inch cubes

2 cups fresh white bread cubes

1 cup milk

1 tablespoon unsalted butter or sunflower oil

1 small onion, finely chopped

3 extra-large eggs, separated

¼ teaspoon grated nutmeg

2 tablespoons finely chopped fresh tarragon

½ teaspoon salt

½ teaspoon freshly ground black pepper

Sprigs of tarragon to garnish

Preheat the oven to 350°F. Butter a 6-inch by 9-inch rectangular baking dish. Put the fish cubes in a large bowl, add the bread cubes and pour the milk over top. Set aside to soak while you cook the onions.

Melt the butter in a small skillet over medium heat and add the onion. Reduce the heat to medium-low and sauté until very soft and fragrant, but not browned, about 10 to 15 minutes. Let the onions cool for a few minutes, and then toss with the fish mixture. Whisk the egg yolks and add to the fish mixture, along with the nutmeg, tarragon, salt, and black pepper. Mix well.

Put the egg whites in a large bowl and whisk until stiff. Gently fold them into the fish mixture.

Spoon the fish mixture into the baking dish and cover with a piece of buttered or oiled aluminum foil. Bake 45 minutes or until the *babka* is set. Remove the pan from the oven and allow the *babka* to rest for 10 minutes. Loosen the edges with a knife, invert onto a large serving platter, cut into wedges. Serve garnished with sprigs of tarragon.

Boiled Crawfish

Vareni richkovi raky

Freshwater crawfish (or crayfish) are probably the most popular crustacean in Ukraine. Crawfish has always been popular and dishes using them were especially elaborate during the nineteenth century, most often in combination with game meats and caviar. Today, however, crawfish are usually boiled whole in beef stock and served with lots of beer to drink!

3 quarts (12 cups) beef stock
1 large unpeeled onion, quartered
2 tablespoons salt
10 black peppercorns
2 tablespoons dill seeds
10 whole cloves
1 bunch fresh dill
2½ to 3 pounds live crawfish (see Note)

In a large kettle, bring the beef stock to a boil over medium-high heat. Add the onion, salt, black peppercorns, dill seeds, cloves, and fresh dill. Reduce the heat slightly and simmer uncovered for about 20 minutes.

Bring the stock back up to a boil and add half the crawfish. Cook until the shells turn red, about 5 minutes. Remove the cooked crawfish with a slotted spoon to a large serving platter and cover loosely with aluminum foil. Cook the remaining crawfish. Serve hot.

....

NOTE: *Whole crawfish range in size from 3½ inches to 8 inches and once cooked take some time to clean. It takes about 7 pounds of crawfish to equal 1 pound of cleaned meat. As far as a serving size, market form generally recommends: tail meat equals about ⅓ pound per person; whole crawfish equal about 6 to 12 per person; so plan accordingly.*

Fried Tench Strips with Creamy Mustard Sauce

Smazheni smyzhky lynu iz
smetankovo-hirchychnoyu prypravoyu

Makes 4 to 6 servings /
¾ cup of sauce

Freshwater tench is the smallest member of the carp family. It has a sweet, firm flesh and few bones. In this recipe the tench fillets are sliced into strips and skillet-fried until crisp and golden. It is an excellent dish served as a snack with beer. Carp fillets can also be used in this recipe, as well as catfish fillets or whole fresh smelts. Sometimes fried fish is simply served with a splash of vinegar, which is certainly a traditional option, but I wanted to include yet another sauce which I think is just delectable with fried fish—Creamy Mustard Sauce .

1½ pounds tench fillets

3 tablespoons unbleached all-purpose flour, seasoned with salt and freshly ground black pepper

1 extra-large egg, beaten

1 cup fresh white breadcrumbs

1 cup (generous) sunflower oil

Vinegar on the side to serve (optional)

CREAMY MUSTARD SAUCE:

1 cup light cream

2 tablespoons Homemade Mustard (page 127)

2 tablespoons chopped fresh chives

2 hard-cooked eggs, finely chopped

Make the creamy mustard sauce:

Pour the cream into a medium saucepan and whisk in the mustard. Bring the mixture to a boil over medium heat, stirring frequently to prevent scorching. Reduce the heat to medium-low and cook for 2 minutes. Stir in the chives and eggs and take the pan off the heat. Let the sauce rest for a few minutes, and then pour into a decorative bowl to serve.

Prepare fish:

Preheat the oven to 200°F. Cut the tench into thin strips, about 2½-inches long by about ½-inch wide. Dip the fish into the seasoned flour, then into the beaten egg, and finally into the breadcrumbs.

Heat the oil in a heavy skillet (there should be about ½ inch of oil). The oil is hot enough for frying when a drop of water flicked into it sputters. Working in batches, fry the fish for about 3 minutes, flipping them over until golden-brown. Drain on paper towels and keep warm in the oven until all the fish is fried. Serve drizzled with vinegar or with the Creamy Mustard Sauce.

Lake Trout Pickle

Marynovanyi ozernyi forel'

Makes 4 to 5 servings

Some Ukrainians call this dish "sour fish." It can be eaten cold as a relish or as an entrée.

2 whole small trout (about 1 pound each)

Salt and freshly ground black pepper to taste

2 cups dry white wine or water

1 small onion, very thinly sliced

1 small green bell pepper, seeded and very thinly sliced

½ cup fish broth

¼ cup champagne vinegar or white wine vinegar

1 teaspoon mixed pickling spice or 1 fresh bay leaf

1 teaspoon salt

6 black peppercorns

2 tablespoons sunflower oil or olive oil

Salt and pepper the trout. In a large skillet, bring the white wine to a boil over medium-high heat. Gently lay the fish in the liquid, return to a simmer over medium-low heat, cover and gently poach the fish for about 6 minutes.

While the fish are poaching, put half the onion and bell pepper slices in a shallow, oblong casserole. When the fish are tender, carefully remove with a slotted spoon and lay on top of the onion and pepper slices. Let cool for about 20 minutes and then cover the fish with the remaining onion and bell pepper slices.

Pour the fish broth and vinegar into a medium bowl and add the pickling spice, salt, and black peppercorns. Mix thoroughly and let stand for a few minutes.

Drizzle the oil into the marinade and whisk until well-blended. Pour over the fish, then flip them over, making sure all the fish and vegetables are coated with marinade. Cover and refrigerate at least 24 hours before serving, turning the fish occasionally. The marinated fish will keep for 1 week in your refrigerator. Let the pickled trout sit at room temperature for about 10 minutes before serving.

NOTE: *Poached filleted fish (haddock, carp, flounder, salmon, etc.) can also be prepared in this manner.*

Venison Sirloin with Cherry Mustard Butter

Steiky z olenyny iz chereshnevo-hirchychnym maslom

Makes 4 servings

Choice cuts of venison should be cooked pink in the center—although this particular game meat when cooked well done is still quite tasty. If venison is difficult to come by, use beef tenderloin.

Ukrainians like foods with a tangy "bite." In this game dish, the finish of cherry-mustard butter starts with the recipe for Homemade Mustard, to which a few tablespoons of finely chopped cherries has been added and then combined with softened butter, overall nicely compliments the venison.

- 4 (6 ounces each) venison sirloin steaks
- 1 clove garlic, crushed
- 1 teaspoon cracked black peppercorns
- 1/3 cup (generous) brandy
- 4 tablespoons unsalted butter, softened
- 2 tablespoons Homemade Mustard (page 127)
- 2 tablespoons finely chopped cherries
- 2 teaspoons coarse salt

Lay the steaks side by side in a large casserole dish. Mix the garlic and cracked black peppercorns into the brandy and pour over the venison, flipping the steaks over to coat evenly. Cover and refrigerate for at least 4 hours.

Meanwhile, in a small bowl, mix together 3 tablespoons of the softened butter, mustard, and cherries until well blended. Shape into a log, wrap in plastic, and refrigerate until needed.

Retrieve the steaks from the refrigerator, drain, reserving the marinade, and pat dry with paper towels. Melt the remaining 1 tablespoon of butter in a large skillet over medium-high heat and sear the steaks for 2 minutes on each side, turning only once. The meat will be springy to the touch for medium-rare or firmer for well-done. Transfer the steaks to a warmed serving platter.

Add the reserved marinade to the skillet and bring to a full boil. Boil for 1 minute, scraping up any bits on the bottom of the pan. Pour the sauce evenly over the steaks and top each steak with a slice or two of the cherry-mustard butter. Sprinkle to taste with coarse salt and serve immediately.

Braised Rabbit with Red Wine and Capers

Tushkovanyi zayats' abo krilyk u chervonomu vyni z kaparamy

Makes 3 to 4 servings

Wild rabbit and hare are enjoyed frequently in Ukraine, usually with sharp or piquant sauces. Here the combination of red wine, garlic, and capers is ideal to serve with the rich rabbit meat.

This recipe is made with domesticated rabbit. If you are unaccustomed to rabbit, have the butcher or farmer portion it for you: chop the saddle in half and separate the back legs into two pieces each; leave the front legs whole.

1 (3½-pound) rabbit, cut into serving pieces

1 tablespoon salt

½ teaspoon freshly ground black pepper

½ cup unbleached all-purpose flour

3 tablespoons (generous) lard or unsalted butter

1 large onion, quartered and thinly sliced

2 cloves garlic, sliced

½ cup chopped fresh parsley

1 cup fruity red wine

About 1½ cups Rich Ukrainian Chicken Broth (page 44)

2 tablespoons capers, rinsed and drained

Honey to taste (optional)

Chopped scallions for garnishing

Season the rabbit pieces with salt and black pepper. Put the flour in a plastic bag and drop the pieces of rabbit into it, one at a time; shake them to coat evenly, tap off any excess flour and put on a large plate.

Melt the lard in a large, heavy skillet over medium heat. When the lard is very hot and bubbly, add as many pieces of the rabbit that will fit without overcrowding the pan. Brown the rabbit pieces on all sides using kitchen tongs to turn to help color evenly. Remove the pieces of rabbit as they brown and put on another large plate.

Reduce the heat to medium and add the onion, garlic, and parsley and sauté for about 3 minutes. Add the wine and bring to a boil over medium-high heat, scraping up the browned bits on the bottom of the pan. Add the pieces of rabbit and enough chicken broth to cover the meat. Partially cover skillet, reduce heat to low, and simmer gently for 1 to 1½ hours, or until the rabbit is tender and the juices run clear when the thickest part is pricked with a skewer.

Stir in the capers and continue cooking, uncovered, for another 5 minutes. Taste and adjust the seasonings if necessary. The dish may need some salt and if the pan juices are a bit sour-tasting for you, add some honey, 1 tablespoon at a time, until you reach your desired sweetness. Serve each portion in a shallow bowl with some sauce ladled over top and garnished with chopped scallions. Delicious!

Roast Wild Duck with Juniper Berries

Pechena dyka kachka z yahodamy yalivtsiu

Makes 4 servings

Wild duck (preferably a mallard) should be served slightly underdone or the meat will be tough. There is little meat on the leg, so one duck will only serve two people. If you like, freeze the legs of wild ducks until you have enough to make soup or stew and use the carcasses to make duck broth for use in other game dishes.

There are notable French influences in many Ukrainian dishes and particularly in this one (although there was a time when many Slavophiles frowned upon advocating French cuisine). The high art of *cotelettes de volailles*, the preparation of dishes using choice breast meat, migrated from France in the nineteenth century, but was quickly reinvented and interpreted by Ukrainians in their own distinctive way.

Serve this delicious dish with thick slices of homemade bread, grated boiled beets, and a simple green salad.

- 2 wild ducks (about 4 pounds each)
- 2 tablespoons freshly grated orange zest
- 3 tablespoons unsalted butter, softened
- 2 teaspoons coarse salt
- ½ teaspoon freshly ground black pepper
- 1 tablespoon dried juniper berries, crushed
- 3 tablespoons vodka
- 1 cup duck or chicken broth
- ⅓ cup heavy cream
- Fresh sprigs of parsley for garnishing

Preheat the oven to 425°F. Remove any excess fat from each of the ducks and tie the legs of each duck together with kitchen string. Prick the skin all over with a sharp needle or skewer to release the fat during cooking, being careful not to pierce the meat.

In a small bowl, mix 1 tablespoon of orange zest with the butter and spread over both ducks. Sprinkle the ducks with salt and black pepper, and then press the crushed juniper berries into the skin of the ducks. Put the ducks on a broiling rack in a shallow pan.

Roast the ducks 45 to 60 minutes, basting occasionally. When the juices run slightly pink when the thigh is pierced with a skewer, carefully pick the ducks up and pour any juices from the cavities into the roasting pan, and then transfer both ducks to a cutting board. Cover loosely with aluminum foil and let stand 20 minutes.

Skim as much fat as possible from the roasting pan. Place the pan directly over medium-high heat and stir in the vodka. Cook until most of the liquid evaporates, leaving about 3 tablespoons. Add the stock and boil over medium-high heat until reduced by half. Slowly pour in the cream and continue cooking, stirring frequently, until the sauce thickens slightly. Remove the pan from the heat and strain the sauce into a small saucepan and place over low heat.

Carve the legs from the ducks. Remove the breast meat and arrange the pieces on a warmed serving platter. Pour the sauce over top and sprinkle with the remaining 1 tablespoon orange zest. Garnish with sprigs of fresh parsley and serve immediately.

NOTE: *This recipe will work just as well with domesticated duck—cooking time will be approximately 1½ to 2 hours for a domesticated duck weighing 4 pounds.*

Wild Boar and Sausages with Sauerkraut

Bigos iz dykym kabanom ta kovbasamy Makes 8 servings

This specialty shows the kinship between Ukrainian fare and the foods of the Germanic and Northern Slavic peoples—sauerkraut is stewed with the likes of wild boar and sausages made of venison and wild boar. This is a great dish for a very special occasion and a hungry meat-eating crowd. Serve with plenty of boiled potatoes, pickled horseradish relish (page 68), a green vegetable or salad, and plenty of crusty bread or rolls.

1 teaspoon salt

Freshly ground black pepper to taste

1 (3-pound) wild boar shoulder roast (see Note)

1 tablespoon sunflower oil

1 large onion, sliced

2 thick slices smoky bacon, chopped into small pieces

2 pounds sauerkraut, drained

1 Granny Smith apple, peeled, cored, and sliced

2 bay leaves

1 teaspoon dried thyme

4 juniper berries

1 cup white wine

½ cup apple cider or water

4 (6 ounces each) venison sausages

2 (6 ounces each) smoked wild boar sausages

Additional salt and freshly ground black pepper to taste

Preheat the oven to 300°F. Salt the wild boar roast and sprinkle with black pepper. Set aside.

In a large, flameproof casserole, warm the oil over medium heat. Add the onion and chopped bacon and cook, stirring occasionally, for 5 minutes. Tilt the pan and spoon off the fat. Stir in the sauerkraut, apple, bay leaves, thyme, and juniper berries. Place the roast on top of the mixture and pour the wine and apple cider over top. Cover and bake in the oven for approximately 2½ to 3 hours, or until the meat is very tender.

Remove the roast from the pan and place on a carving board. When cool enough to handle, shred the meat and put it back into the pot, along with the venison and wild boar sausages, pushing all of the meat down into the sauerkraut mixture. Cover and place the casserole back into the oven and cook 30 more minutes. Taste and adjust the seasonings, adding more salt and black pepper if needed. Serve.

NOTE: *Broken Arrow Ranch is an artisanal producer of high-quality, free-range wild boar, venison, and antelope meats, partnering with ranchers in central and southern Texas. As of the printing of this cookbook, online purchases can be made at* **www.brokenarrowranch.com** *for in home preparation. It is a great sustainable way to try game meats that are safe and nutritious.*

Crispy Fried Quail with Orange Zest and Honey

Prysmazhena perepilka iz tertoyu lushpynkoyu pomaranchi ta medom

Makes 2 servings

If quail are hard to find, use domesticated Cornish game hens and adjust the cooking time to about 10 to 12 minutes per side. Serve the quail on a bed of buttered noodles with a lightly cooked green vegetable on the side.

4 quail (about ¾ pound each)

Salt and freshly ground black pepper to taste

3 tablespoons unsalted butter

1 tablespoon sunflower oil

2 tablespoons fresh orange juice

2 tablespoons grated orange zest

¼ cup light-flavored honey (orange blossom, clover, or wildflower)

Sprigs of parsley to garnish

With a small sharp knife, split open or butterfly each quail and remove the breast bones. Cover each bird with waxed paper and gently pound with a kitchen mallet until flattened. Sprinkle both sides of each bird with salt and black pepper.

Heat the butter and sunflower oil in a large heavy skillet over medium heat and when bubbly, place the birds skin-side down in the skillet. Cover the birds with something flat such as an ovenproof plate, and then place a heavy object (such as a brick or can) on top so the quail are firmly pressed down. Cook until the skin is deep golden and crispy, about 5 minutes. Turn the birds over, re-weight, and cook the other sides for another 5 minutes. Pierce a thigh and if the juices run clear, the quail are cooked.

Mix the orange juice, orange zest, and honey together in a small bowl. Generously brush the mixture over the top of each quail, flip them over and let cook for about 1 minute. Brush the tops with more of the orange-honey mixture and flip over to sear the other side for about 1 minute. Immediately remove the quail to a warmed serving platter and garnish with sprigs of parsley. Serve the extra orange-honey mixture on the side.

Chapter 7

Breads, Buns and Rolls

"the Breadbasket of Europe ..."

Ukraine has been a formidable producer of grains such as wheat, rye, millet, oats, and the staple buckwheat since time immemorial, so it is no wonder that bread is an ancient symbol of Ukrainian hospitality. In fact, bread plays an integral role in so many holidays, rituals, and celebrations, that a home without it would just be unthinkable. As a result, breadmaking has risen to an art form in Ukraine, revealing an amazing range of shapes, textures, and tastes. Bread is the holiest of all foods to Ukrainians and nary a crumb is wasted.

Several types of Ukrainian breads have their own essential features and symbolic meanings. For instance, on one's wedding day, the bride and groom are blessed by parents with a gift called *kolach*, a braided ring-shaped bread symbolizing prosperity, good luck, and eternity. This bread also has the same ritual meaning at a memorial service for the deceased. Three loaves of *kolach* graduated in size and stacked on top of one another with a candle inserted in the top loaf (symbolizing the sun) are featured at the holy Christmas Eve supper known as *Svyata Vechera*, and are a traditional Christmas table decoration. *Korovai* is another type of celebration bread that symbolizes family and community and is baked for weddings and anniversaries.

Paska is a round bubble-bread baked for Easter celebration and is decorated with dough ornaments and often a cross motif. It is much richer than ordinary bread. *Paska* is prepared with love and attention because it is taken to church along with small amounts of other foods in a decorated basket, to be blessed in a lovely ceremony on Easter morning. *Babka* is another Easter favorite, but is also enjoyed throughout the year and is one of the most distinctive of Ukrainian breads. *Babka* is a rich, yeast-raised cake-bread of extraordinary quality traditionally baked in a fluted pan, but more often in a tall, cylindrical pan. Numerous recipes include nuts or dried fruit, and sometimes rum, brandy, lemon, or even pumpkin. Some *babkas* are served plain, but more often they are decorated with glazes and baker's confetti, with some finishing touches more elaborate than others.

It should be noted, however, that the grind and quality of flour and the bread ovens used in Ukraine are somewhat different than those in North America. This makes exact replication difficult, but do not let this stop you from trying the recipes given here. I think organic flours work best and come very close to authenticity, and are better-tasting and kinder to the environment. I have also found that active dry yeast, made especially for whole grains and whole flours, works well in my recipes.

Ukraine's reputation as "the breadbasket of Europe" is quite evident in the number of bread recipes there are and here I offer a mere drop in the ocean of recipes that make up Ukraine's baking repertoire. The following are family favorites and are no more difficult to make than a cake. Besides, nothing guarantees your reputation as a good Ukrainian cook more quickly than making your own bread, buns, and rolls, and I think people find it particularly satisfying to be able to offer friends and family their own home-baked creations.

"The importance of bread and salt ..."

In Ukraine there is a custom of greeting guests with bread and salt. The host or hostess would greet the guest at the door with the usual salutations, carrying a platter with a loaf of bread and a shaped mound of salt on it. It was the belief that while a household may (or may not) have lavish foods to offer, the guest was always welcome to share the bread and salt. This was considered an expression of hospitality and sincerity. Charming as it is, this custom is still very much alive throughout Ukraine today.

Sour Rye Bread with Caraway Seeds

Zhytnyi khlib z kmynom

Traditionally, this rye bread would be made with a "starter," which is usually a little bit of dough left over from the previous baking session. The starter is what gives the bread its delicious flavor and speaks to the characteristic Ukrainian preference for all things sour. For this particular recipe, the first step is to make this sourdough starter.

I like to add ground caraway seeds to the dough and dust the loaves with extra rye flour. There are no hard and fast rules when it comes to topping individual loaves of this type—just use what you like. Sour rye bread keeps fresh for one week, but I am willing to bet the loaves will be consumed in just one sitting!

4 cups unbleached bread flour

4 cups whole rye flour plus extra for dusting

2 teaspoons salt

1 tablespoon ground caraway seeds

2½ teaspoons active dry yeast for whole grains

2 tablespoons unsalted butter, softened

2½ cups warm water (about 110°F)

Parchment paper

2 tablespoons cornmeal

SOURDOUGH STARTER:

4 tablespoons whole rye flour

3 tablespoons warm raw (unpasteurized) milk

Make the starter:

Mix the rye flour and warm milk together in a small glass or ceramic bowl that has been warmed with hot water. Cover with plastic wrap and pierce the plastic with a fork to release any gases. Put the bowl in a very warm, draft-free place (about 85°F) for 2 to 3 days, or until the mixture smells pleasantly sour. (To increase the amount of starter for later use and storage tips, see Note.)

Make the sour rye bread loaves:

Sift the bread and rye flours together and put in a large bowl. Add the salt and ground caraway seeds. Stir in the yeast. Make a well in the center and add the butter, warm water, and sourdough starter. Mix well until the dough starts to pull away from the edges of the bowl. Turn the dough out onto a lightly floured board or counter and knead the dough for 10 minutes, until elastic and smooth. Place the dough in another large bowl, cover with a kitchen towel, and leave in a warm, draft-free place to rise for about 1 hour or until doubled in volume.

Remove the dough from the bowl and knead for 1 minute. Divide the dough in half. Shape each piece into a round loaf. Cover 2 baking sheets with parchment paper and

continued on next page ⇨

sprinkle with cornmeal. Place 1 loaf on each sheet, cover with kitchen towels and let rise for another 30 minutes. Preheat the oven to 400°F.

Brush the loaves with some water and sprinkle with rye flour. Bake about 35 minutes or until the loaves are browned and fragrant. The loaves are done when they sound hollow when tapped on the bottom. Let the loaves cool completely on a wire rack before slicing.

NOTE: *This sour rye bread can be made without yeast, yielding much denser but tasty loaves.*

NOTE: *You may increase the amount of starter so you have some in reserve by adding more flour and milk, in the proportion of 1 cup of milk to 1 heaping cup flour and then let it stand in a warm place for 2 to 3 days. (Make sure your bowl or container is large enough for the starter to expand slightly. Any lumps that form will disappear as it sits.) When the mixture smells pleasantly sour, whip the starter with a whisk to incorporate oxygen. Cover loosely with a fresh piece of plastic wrap that has been pierced with a fork to release any gases. Store in the refrigerator. The starter will stay "active" for about 1 month without attention. If you have not used it within a month, "feed" it by whisking it well and then discarding about half of it and replacing the discarded amount with the same amount of the flour and milk mixture. After whisking it all together, let the starter sit, loosely covered, for a few hours at room temperature and then cover and refrigerate.*

When you want to bake, allow the starter to come to room temperature and whisk it well. Remove what you need and immediately replenish the same amount, let it sit for a few hours once again, then loosely cover and refrigerate. Always maintain a large enough starter so that you have at least 1 to 2 cups more than you will ever need at one time.

Ukrainian Black Bread

Chornyi khlib

Makes 2 loaves

Dark, dense breads such as this one are pretty standard across Ukraine. The deep color is due to rich, syrupy blackstrap molasses and brewed coffee. Black bread needs steam to bake well so you use a "moist" oven. You do so by filling a jelly roll pan with boiling water and placing it on the bottom rack of your oven; you then use the middle rack to bake the bread. This same recipe can be used to make rolls (see variation next page).

1 cup warm water (about 110°F)

⅓ cup blackstrap molasses

2½ teaspoons active dry yeast for whole grains

⅔ cup strong-brewed coffee, cooled

1½ teaspoons salt

1 tablespoon caraway seeds

2 cups whole rye flour

2 cups buckwheat flour

1 cup unbleached all-purpose flour

Parchment paper

2 to 3 tablespoons cornmeal

Pour 1 cup of warm water into a medium bowl and stir in the molasses until dissolved. Add the yeast and stir to dissolve. Cover the bowl with a kitchen towel and put in a warm place for about 10 minutes or until foamy. Uncover and stir in the coffee, salt, and caraway seeds.

Combine the three flours in a large mixing bowl and add the yeast mixture. Mix well and turn out onto a lightly floured board or counter. Knead the dough by hand for 10 minutes, or use a dough hook on an electric mixer for about 5 minutes.

Lightly grease a large bowl with sunflower oil. Shape the dough into a ball and put into the bowl, turning it until it is completely coated with oil. Cover the bowl with a kitchen towel and let the dough rise in a warm, draft-free place until doubled in volume, about 2 to 3 hours.

Turn the dough out and knead again by hand for 5 minutes. Return the dough to the large bowl, cover and let rise again until doubled in volume, about 1 hour.

Cover a baking sheet with parchment paper and sprinkle with cornmeal. Divide the dough into two pieces. Shape each piece into a rectangular loaf about 2 to 3 inches high and place apart on the baking sheet. Cover the loaves with a kitchen towel and let rise in a warm place for another hour. Preheat the oven to 375°F.

Cut a few slits about ¼-inch deep diagonally across each loaf. Place a jelly roll pan on the bottom rack of the oven and fill with boiling water. Place the baking sheet with the bread on the middle rack and bake the loaves for about 30 to 40 minutes. The loaves are done when they sound hollow when tapped on the bottom. Place the loaves on a

continued on next page ⇨

wire rack and cover with a clean kitchen towel to keep the crust soft. Let the bread cool completely before slicing.

··

VARIATION:

Black Bread Rolls

After letting the dough rise twice, turn it out onto a lightly floured board or counter. Roll out the dough to about ¼-inch thickness and cut 2 dozen 3-inch squares. Roll each square into a neat, log-shaped roll. Place the rolls on a sheet of parchment paper sprinkled with cornmeal, cover and let rise 1 hour. Brush the rolls with sunflower oil and sprinkle with coarse salt and bake in a 350°F "moist" oven for about 20 minutes, until browned and fragrant. Place the rolls on a wire rack to cool and cover with a clean kitchen towel to keep the crust soft, or serve warm if desired. These rolls are a wonderful accompaniment to steaming hot bowls of borshch or with a plate of cold cuts and cheese.

Hutsul Corn Bread

Malai

This is my contemporary version of the native Hutsulian corn bread called *malai*. Corn and maize flours are used extensively in regions of the Carpathian Mountains and southwestern Ukraine, adding rich color and flavor to many local dishes. There has always been a very flexible give-and-take between the different cultures of people there, ranging from subtle shadings to lavish ambitions. Traditionally, this bread is served with either fried meat or a thick slice of cheese, or smeared with a thick layer of cream or sour cream.

Malai is very simple to prepare and while older recipes call for yeast as leavening, I have found that a combination of buttermilk and baking soda works just fine. I have taken a few more liberties and added a crust of melted goat's milk feta cheese. Garnished with a scattering of finely chopped sweet bell peppers, I think my version provides a happy compromise and is particularly good with slices of a Ukrainian sausage called *kovbasa* (page 124) and a light vegetable salad.

½ cup sour cream

2 extra-large eggs, lightly beaten

⅔ cup buttermilk

2 tablespoons unsalted butter, melted and cooled slightly

1 cup yellow cornmeal

1 cup sifted unbleached all-purpose flour

½ teaspoon salt

½ teaspoon baking soda

1½ cups crumbled goat's milk feta cheese

½ cup seeded and finely chopped sweet bell peppers (in any color combination)

Preheat the oven to 350°F. Grease the sides and bottom of an 8-inch or 9-inch cast-iron skillet with sunflower oil and set aside.

In a large bowl, mix together the sour cream, eggs, buttermilk, and melted butter. Mix in the cornmeal, flour, salt, and baking soda. Blend well and then let the batter sit for 15 minutes.

Place the oiled skillet over medium-high heat. When a drop of water flicked into it sizzles, pour the batter into the pan and immediately remove it from the burner. Place the pan in the oven and bake the corn bread for about 20 minutes, or until it is golden-brown and firm to the touch.

Remove the pan from the oven and sprinkle the cheese over top. Return the pan to the oven and bake until the cheese is bubbly, about 4 minutes. Serve the *malai* warm by the wedge with a sprinkling of sweet bell peppers.

Kolach

The Ukrainian bread *kolach* is served at Christmas feasts (beginning on Christmas day) and other family celebrations. It is shaped in a circle or "*kolo*," hence its name. This recipe makes one large traditional circular loaf, but the dough can be divided into three pieces and braided into one loaf as it is often done in today's households. The choice is certainly yours.

To make a traditional three-tier or three-bread *kolach*, triple the recipe, divide the risen dough into three pieces and shape each loaf separately. Bake in two or three batches and cool completely before stacking. It is best to bake the loaves the day before you plan on assembling the *kolach*.

3 teaspoons active dry yeast

1 cup warm water (about 110°F)

2 teaspoons granulated sugar

1⅓ cups warm milk

6 tablespoons unsalted butter, melted

2 extra-large eggs, beaten

2 teaspoons salt

6½ cups (generous) unbleached all-purpose flour

Egg wash: 1 egg beaten with 2 tablespoons water

GLAZE:

2 tablespoons evaporated milk

1 tablespoon confectioners' or granulated sugar

In a small bowl, dissolve the yeast in warm water and add 2 teaspoons of sugar. Stir well and let the mixture sit in a warm place until frothy, about 10 minutes.

Pour the warm milk into a large bowl and stir in the melted butter, beaten eggs, and salt. Add the yeast mixture and stir well. Add the flour, 1 cup at a time, stirring to incorporate after each addition. When the dough begins to pull away from the sides of the bowl, turn it out onto a lightly floured board or counter and knead for 5 minutes, or until the dough is smooth, firm, and elastic. Place the dough in another large bowl, cover with a kitchen towel, and let rise in a warm, draft-free place until double in volume, about 2 hours.

Pull the dough away from the sides of the bowl deflating it, turn it over, cover again, and let rise for 1 hour or until again doubled in volume.

Grease a 10-inch cake pan with butter. Turn the dough out onto a lightly floured board or counter and cut in half. Cut each half of dough into 3 pieces, totaling 6 pieces all together. Cover 4 pieces of dough with a kitchen towel and set aside. Roll the remaining 2 pieces into 2 long ropes each about 36 inches in length. Lay 1 rope diagonally across the other to form an "X." Working from the center, twine the ropes around each other towards each end to make one long coiled rope. Bend the rope into a circle, pressing the ends neatly together and place in the greased cake pan.

Roll out the remaining dough into 4 ropes each approximately 24 inches in length. Follow the above twining directions and make 2 more coiled ropes. Take these 2 coiled ropes and coil them around each other to make a double coil. Lay this coil inside of the one in the cake pan, pinching the ends neatly together to make a joint, trimming the dough if necessary. There should be a gap in the center of the bread. Place a tightly rolled kitchen towel in this gap to prevent the dough from filling in the hole when rising (later a cross or candle may be placed there). Cover the pan with a clean kitchen towel and let dough rise 1 hour.

Preheat the oven to 400°F. Remove the rolled up kitchen towel from the pan. Brush the top of the dough with the egg wash. Bake the bread for 15 minutes. Then reduce the heat to 350°F and bake an additional 30 minutes.

Meanwhile, make the glaze by mixing the 2 tablespoons evaporated milk with 1 tablespoon sugar in a small bowl.

The *kolach* is done when it sounds hollow when removed from the pan and tapped on the bottom. Immediately upon removing the *kolach* from the oven, brush it with the glaze. Carefully remove the *kolach* from the pan and let cool on a towel-covered rack.

Korovai

Korovai is the traditional Ukrainian celebration bread baked for weddings and anniversaries. It symbolizes family and community and there are many varieties based upon regions. *Korovai* is often adorned with dough ornaments such as doves, pine cones, braids, swirls, the moon, and the sun. Other trinkets such as actual coins, leaves, berries, branches, ribbons, and flowers are popular additions. Red, gold, and silver are the colors most associated with and seen on *korovai*. Two dough birds or doves represent the couple and the rest of the ornaments represent family and friends. The entire *korovai* is surrounded by a wreath of green periwinkle, an evergreen symbolizing eternal love, future prosperity, and good luck.

Babka

Makes 2 10-inch fluted breads or 1 10-inch fluted bread and 4 small cylindrical loaves

"**B**aba" is the colloquial Ukrainian word for woman or grandma. "*Babka*" is the diminutive of that word but is more commonly used as the name of the yeast-raised breads served at Easter. *Babka* is usually a tall, cylindrical bread similar to Italian pantone, but it can also be baked in a fluted tube pan. Folktales revolve around two explanations of how this bread got its name. One explanation is that the shape of the loaf represents a statuesque matron or even a phallic symbol. And the other is that when the *babka* is baked in a fluted pan, does the bread not resemble the flared skirt of a peasant woman or grandmother? In truth, the true meaning is not known, but it is fascinating just the same. One thing is for certain though, and that is that *babka* is delicious and is enjoyed not only at Easter, but any time of year.

If *babka* is baked in a cylindrical pan, it is customary to slice the bread in rounds across the loaf. The very bottom of the crust is not eaten, but is used as a protective cover to help keep the loaf from drying out. Usually 2-pound coffee cans will work as cake pans for this, but if you want even taller *babkas*, use large empty juice cans. (Make sure the rough rim is removed from the tops of the cans, otherwise the edges will make the removal of your bread difficult.) Always generously grease the cans and sprinkle with fine, dry breadcrumbs or grease and line with parchment paper which will help keep the bread from sticking to the can.

This is a very old family recipe and yields at least two loaves. I always make one fluted *babka* and some tall ones using coffee cans. To do the same, you will need one 10-inch fluted tube pan and four small (1 pound) coffee cans. I have included two simple glazes. To decorate my *babkas*, sometimes I use baker's confetti, sometimes dried fruit and nuts, and yet other times, candied fruit.

⅓ cup fine dry breadcrumbs
1 cup warm water (about 110°F)
2½ tablespoons active dry yeast
1 cup plus 2 tablespoons granulated sugar
8 to 9 cups unbleached all-purpose flour
1½ cups milk
1 cup (2 sticks) unsalted butter
¼ cup rum
¾ cup raisins
7 extra-large egg yolks
2 teaspoons pure vanilla extract
2 teaspoons salt
Grated zest of 1 lemon
2 extra-large egg whites, beaten

LEMON GLAZE:
2 extra-large egg whites
1 cup confectioners' sugar
1 tablespoon fresh lemon juice
Baker's confetti for decoration

ORANGE GLAZE:
1 cup confectioners' sugar
2 to 3 tablespoons freshly squeezed orange juice
1 tablespoon freshly grated orange zest
Candied orange peel (or slivered toasted almonds and dried cherries) for decoration

Generously grease 1 10-inch tube pan and 4 small (1 pound) coffee cans with butter and sprinkle the insides with the dry breadcrumbs. Set aside.

Pour the warm water into a medium glass bowl, stir in the yeast and 2 tablespoons of granulated sugar. Let stand in a warm place until frothy, about 10 minutes. Whisk in ½ cup of the flour, cover the bowl with plastic wrap, and let stand in a warm, draft-free place until the mixture doubles in volume, about 10 to 15 minutes.

Meanwhile, put the milk and butter in a medium saucepan over medium heat and stir just until the butter has melted. Remove from heat and let the mixture cool slightly.

Pour the rum into a small saucepan, add the raisins and bring to a boil over medium heat. Remove the pan from the stove and set aside to cool slightly.

In a large mixing bowl, beat together the egg yolks and the 1 cup of granulated sugar until thick and lemon-colored, about 5 minutes. Beat in the yeast mixture, milk mixture, raisin mixture, vanilla extract, salt, and lemon zest. Gradually beat in 6 cups of flour, and then stir in enough of the remaining flour to make a soft dough.

Turn the dough out onto a lightly floured board or counter and gently knead for about 3 minutes, until the dough is smooth and satiny, making sure the raisins are distributed evenly throughout. Divide the dough in half. Arrange half of the dough in the bottom of the tube pan. Divide the other half of dough into 4 pieces, form into small balls and place 1 in each coffee can, filling only about ⅓ full (if needed, add a fifth coffee can—remember the dough will rise when proofing and even more when baked). Cover the pan and coffee cans with kitchen towels and let the dough rise in a warm, draft-free place until doubled in size, about 1½ hours.

Preheat the oven to 375°F. When the dough has risen, beat the 2 egg whites with 1 tablespoon of water and brush the tops of the dough. Bake the *babkas* on the bottom rack of the oven for 10 minutes; then reduce the temperature to 325°F and continue baking about 35 minutes more for the coffee cans and about 50 to 60 minutes more for the fluted pan. If necessary, cover the tops of the *babkas* with aluminum foil to prevent scorching.

Remove the *babkas* from the oven and let rest 5 minutes before removing from the fluted pan and coffee cans, tipping each loaf from its pan gently and very carefully. Place the hot *babkas* on a flat, cloth-covered pillow—do not cool the *babkas* on a hard surface. Baked *babka* is touchy and careless handling could cause it to fall or settle. As the *babkas* are cooling, change their positions frequently to help prevent settling. Meanwhile, make the glazes and then drizzle over the cooled *babkas*.

Make lemon glaze:

Place the egg whites in a large mixing bowl and beat until frothy. Gradually add the confectioners' sugar and continue beating until the mixture is very glossy, about 10 minutes. Beat in the lemon juice. Drizzle over top of the 10-inch cooled fluted *babka* and sprinkle with baker's confetti if desired.

Make orange glaze:

Sift the confectioners' sugar into a medium bowl and beat in the orange juice a little at a time. Continue beating until mixture is thick. Quickly stir in the orange zest. Immediately ice the tops of the 4 cooled tall *babkas* and sprinkle with candied orange peel if desired.

Paska Bread

Makes 1 large round loaf

Paska bread is a work of art baked especially for the blessing of foods at church on Easter morning. Much richer than ordinary bread, it is flavored with plenty of eggs and rich melted butter. This makes a lovely round loaf of bread traditionally decorated with dough ornaments such as crosses, rosettes, swirls, and twists, and sometimes even more elaborate pieces such as pine cones and small birds! A little beaten egg is brushed on the loaf prior to baking and the result is a stunning golden brown gloss over the entire bread.

I decorate my *paska* with a cross and swirls. I often keep one piece of dough to make three or four *paska* doves (see sidebar) which I bake separately. You may find it unusual that I use a Dutch oven pot to make my bread—but this is what my Baba (grandmother) used and the end result was always this big beautiful bubble bread! A flameproof, round oven casserole pan that is at least 4 inches deep or a 10-inch cake pan will also work just fine.

¼ cup fine dry breadcrumbs

3 teaspoons active dry yeast

3½ cups warm water (about 110°F)

¼ cup plus 1 tablespoon granulated sugar

8 extra-large eggs, beaten

⅔ cup melted unsalted butter

2 teaspoons salt

9 to 10 cups unbleached all-purpose flour

Egg wash: 1 egg beaten with 2 tablespoons water

Generously grease a 4-quart Dutch oven (not the lid) with butter and sprinkle with the dry breadcrumbs. Set aside.

In a small bowl, dissolve the yeast in ½ cup of the warm water and stir in 1 tablespoon of sugar. Mix well and let the mixture stand in a warm place until frothy, about 10 minutes.

Put the remaining 3 cups of warm water, ¼ cup sugar, eggs, melted butter, salt, and the yeast mixture in a large bowl and mix well. Gradually add the flour and when the dough starts to pull away from the sides of the bowl, turn it out onto a lightly floured board or counter and knead by hand for 10 minutes, or use a dough hook on an electric mixer for about 5 minutes. The dough should be smooth and elastic and just a little stiffer than for bread.

Put the dough in a large bowl, cover with a kitchen towel and let rise in a warm, draft-free place until doubled in volume, about 1½ hours. Then punch the dough down, knead in the bowl for a few minutes, cover and let rise again until doubled in volume, about 1 hour.

Remove the dough from the bowl and divide into 3 pieces. Cover 1 piece with a clean kitchen towel and set aside. Make a round 1-inch thick base with the first piece of dough and cover the bottom of the greased pan. Divide the second piece of dough into 2 pieces and roll out into 2 long ropes, each approximately 24 inches in length. Lay 1 rope diagonally across the other to form an "X." Working from the center, twine the ropes around each other towards the end to make 1 long coiled rope. Starting at the center lay this coiled rope on the dough base in a coiled circle all the way to the edge.

Divide the third piece of dough into 4 equal pieces and roll into 4 ropes, each approximately 12 inches in length; follow the above directions and make two coiled ropes. Lay these ropes across the base in opposite directions to make a cross—curling each end neatly along the base. Cover the dough with a kitchen towel and let rise in a warm, draft-free place for about 1 hour. *Do not let the dough rise too long at this point, or the ornamental finish may lose its shape.*

Meanwhile, preheat the oven to 400°F. When the bread is risen, brush the top of the loaf with the egg wash. Bake bread 10 minutes; then reduce the heat to 350°F and continue baking another 35 to 40 minutes. The top of the loaf may brown quickly—if so, cover with aluminum foil to avoid scorching.

Remove the loaf from the oven and let cool for 5 minutes. Gently remove the bread from the pan and cool on a soft surface—a few layered kitchen towels work well. Gently change position of the loaf a few times so it will cool evenly. When completely cooled, slice the *paska* from the bottom in rounds across the loaf. Save the sliced bottom crust and use it as a protective cover to keep the rest of the loaf from drying out.

Paska Doves

In days gone by, the return of birds in the spring was celebrated with special spring songs. Dough shaped like birds were baked representing larks who were returning from their northern migration. Today, these "doves" are still made from dough for Easter.

To make "*paska* doves," use the same dough as for *paska*. Roll out a small section of dough twice the thickness of a pencil and cut into 5-inch lengths. Tie each small strip into a knot. Flatten half to make a tail and round the other half to shape the head. Make two slits for eyes. Cover with a kitchen towel and let rise in a warm, draft-free place for about 2 hours. Insert a whole clove in each slit to make eyes, brush with an egg wash of 1 beaten egg mixed with 2 tablespoons water, and bake for 20 minutes at 350°F. *Paska* doves look stunning in one's Easter basket next to *pysanky* (inedible batik-decorated Easter eggs) and *krashanky* (edible hard-cooked, solid-colored eggs).

Jam-Filled Ukrainian Doughnuts

Pampushky

Makes 2 dozen

Without a doubt there is a national love in Ukraine for these small, round, rich-tasting pastries called *pampushky*. Coined "Ukrainian doughnuts," they are, however, more similar to Italian *zeppole* than our American doughnuts.

Pampushky can be served plain or filled with fresh berries, jam, fruit pulp called *povydlo* (page 71), pitted stewed prunes, fruit preserves, or a sweet poppy seed filling, and are dusted with either confectioners' sugar or granulated sugar and cinnamon. *Pampushky* are highly portable and sold at kiosks on the streets or at bakeries throughout the country. Those filled with rose petal preserves (page 75) are a holiday favorite among Ukrainians.

Savory renditions are usually made at home from a combination of buckwheat and whole wheat flours and served with a drizzle of sunflower oil, a smattering of crushed garlic, and a sprinkle of coarse salt. Savory *pampushky* are more like small buns, baked and served with hot borshch, bouillon, and meat or fish soup. The savory baked *pampushky* (*pamPUshky*) are pronounced slightly different from the sweet deep-fried *pampushky* (*pampushKY*).

I have included two recipes. The first features a basic sweet dough that will be used and referred to again and again throughout this book. This recipe will make 24 *pampushky*, enough dough for one pie, filled rolls, or one loaf of sweet braided bread (recipe follows on page 185). The second recipe for *pampushky* is a quicker version that also produces light and puffy results.

About 2 cups jam of your choice

3 to 4 cups lard or sunflower oil for deep frying

Confectioners' sugar for dusting

BASIC SWEET DOUGH:

2½ teaspoons active dry yeast

1 cup warm milk (about 110°F)

¼ cup plus 1 teaspoon granulated sugar

3 extra-large egg yolks

1 tablespoon brandy or rum (optional)

5 tablespoons unsalted butter, melted

1 tablespoon freshly grated lemon zest

¼ teaspoon salt

3½ cups (generous) unbleached all-purpose flour

Make the sweet dough:

In a small bowl, dissolve the yeast in the warm milk and stir in the 1 teaspoon sugar. Mix well and let the mixture stand in a warm place until frothy, about 10 minutes.

Put the ¼ cup sugar, egg yolks, brandy, and 4 tablespoons of the melted butter into a large mixing bowl and combine well. Stir in the yeast mixture, lemon zest, and salt. Gradually add the flour, 1 cup at a time, and when the dough starts to pull away from the sides of the bowl, turn it out onto a lightly floured board or counter. Knead the dough until smooth, about 7 to 10 minutes by hand or using the dough hook of an electric mixer for about 5 minutes, adding just enough flour to prevent sticking.

Transfer the dough to another large bowl, drizzle with the remaining 1 tablespoon of melted butter and turn the dough over making sure it is completely coated. Cover the bowl with a kitchen towel and let dough rise in a warm, draft-free place until doubled in volume, about 1½ hours. The dough is now ready to use or you can keep it covered in the refrigerator for up to 24 hours.

Make jam-filled *pampushky*:

After the dough has risen, punch it down, remove from the bowl, and divide it into 2 equal pieces. Cover 1 piece with a kitchen towel, and roll out the other half on a lightly floured board or counter to a thickness of ¼ inch. Cut into 3-inch circles and transfer to greased baking sheets. Place 1 teaspoon of jam on half of the circles of dough; cover each with another circle of dough, seal the edges together and roll gently between the palms of your hands to give them a round shape. Repeat with the other half of dough. Leave the *pampushky* to rise in a warm, draft-free place, UNCOVERED (see note), until doubled in size, about 1 hour.

In a deep fryer or skillet, heat the lard to 375°F. Fry the *pampushky* a few at a time until golden brown, about 6 minutes, turning them over midway to brown evenly. Drain the *pampushky* on a wire rack and when dried sprinkle with plenty of confectioners' sugar. Serve warm or at room temperature.

....

NOTE: *Leaving the filled* pampushky *uncovered to form a crust during the second proof helps them to absorb less fat when frying.*

Buckwheat Doughnuts

Hrechani pampushky

Makes about 2 dozen pampushky

My favorite way to eat these *pampushky* is with a little melted butter and a generous sprinkling of crusty brown sugar.

- 8 tablespoons unsalted butter
- ½ teaspoon salt
- 2 cups (generous) buckwheat flour
- 4 extra-large eggs
- 2 to 3 cups lard or sunflower oil for deep frying
- 2 tablespoons melted unsalted butter and crusty brown sugar for serving

Pour 1 cup of water into a medium saucepan and add the butter and salt. Bring the mixture just to a boil and then add the flour, stirring briskly to incorporate, until the batter starts to leave the sides of the saucepan. Remove the pan from the heat and let dough cool for 5 minutes. Briskly beat in the eggs one at a time. Let the mixture rest again until thickened, about 20 minutes.

Heat the oil in a deep fryer or skillet to 375°F. Drop the batter by teaspoonfuls into the hot fat and gently fry until golden brown, turning over to brown evenly, about 2 to 3 minutes. Drain the *pampushky* on paper towels and serve while still hot, piled high on a platter and drizzled with melted butter and a sprinkling of crusty brown sugar.

"Who wants to go to the "*rynok*"?

Ukrainians cannot imagine food shopping without a trip to the *rynok*. Comparable to our American farmer's markets, the *rynok* is the best place to buy fresh fruits, vegetables, cottage cheese, salo, sour cream, pickles, organic eggs, honey, and sauerkraut, just to name a few items that can be found there. Since the Chornobyl disaster, all fresh produce is checked for radiation and certified. Everything is safe to eat. The markets are always an explosion of colors and sounds and aromas. Expect some free samples—slices of cheese, smoked ham, or almost any kind of pickled vegetable— and it is entirely respectable to haggle over the prices!

Sweet Braided Bread

Pleten'

This is a typical Ukrainian sweet loaf bread with poppy seeds.

1 recipe Basic Sweet Dough (page 182)

1 egg yolk

3 tablespoons poppy seeds

Turn out the dough onto a lightly floured board or counter and divide into 3 balls of equal size. Roll out each ball into a rope approximately 12 inches in length. Braid the 3 ropes together, tucking the ends underneath the loaf. Place the loaf on a greased baking sheet, cover with a kitchen towel and let rise in a warm, draft-free place until doubled in size, about 1 hour.

Preheat the oven to 375°F. Mix the egg yolk with 1 tablespoon of water in a small bowl and brush across the top of the loaf. Sprinkle with poppy seeds. Bake about 35 minutes or until the top is nicely browned. Cool on a wire rack.

VARIATION: *To make sweet buns or rolls: cut the 3 ropes of dough into 2-inch pieces and let rise until doubled in size, about 1 hour. Glaze the buns with the egg wash and sprinkle with your favorite topping (poppy seeds, crushed nuts, sesame seeds, etc.). Bake at 375°F for about 25 minutes or until nicely browned. Serve warm or room temperature.*

Whole Wheat Bublyky with Poppy Seeds

Razovi bublyky z makom

Makes about 8

Bublyky are rings of dough similar to bagels, but with a chewier texture and a wider hole. They are often hung on a string by the dozen at the *rynok* (market), in bakeries, or at county fairs. A pleasant teatime or after-school sweet or savory snack, *bublyky* are usually eaten as a pastry rather than a bread, dipped into tea, coffee, milk, or hot chocolate. Another way to eat *bublyky* is to break them into pieces to scoop up dips, sour cream, or jam.

Bublyky are made from dough that is boiled before baking. This is my more contemporary version in that I put poppy seeds both in the dough and on top. Coarse salt, sesame seeds, or vanilla sugar are other popular toppings.

1 cup warm milk (about 110°F)

3 teaspoons active dry yeast for whole grains

2 tablespoons honey

2 extra-large egg whites

4 tablespoons unsalted butter, melted

2 teaspoons salt

3 tablespoons poppy seeds

4½ cups whole wheat flour

1 tablespoon granulated sugar

3 tablespoons cornmeal

1 extra-large egg, beaten

Pour the warm milk into a small bowl and add the yeast. Stir in the honey, mix well, and let the mixture stand in a warm place until frothy, about 10 minutes.

Put the egg whites, melted butter, salt, and 2 tablespoons of the poppy seeds into a large bowl and mix well. Stir in the yeast mixture. Gradually add the flour, 1 cup at a time, and when the dough starts to pull away from the sides of the bowl, turn it out onto a lightly floured board or counter. Knead the dough by hand for 10 minutes, or with the dough hook of an electric mixer for about 5 minutes, until smooth and elastic. Transfer the dough to another large bowl, cover with a kitchen towel, and let rise in a warm, draft-free place until doubled in volume, about 1 hour.

Remove the dough from the bowl and cut into 8 pieces. Roll each piece into a rope about 1 inch thick and 8 inches long. Twist each rope a few times, shape into a ring, and join the ends. Make sure the rings are uniform in size. Cover the rings with a kitchen towel and let proof another 15 minutes.

Preheat the oven to 375°F. Fill a large pot with about 16 cups of water; add the sugar and bring to a brisk boil. Reduce the heat to medium and when the water is simmering, carefully add the dough rings, a few at a time, and cook for 3 minutes. Flip the rings over and cook another 3 minutes. Drain well and place on parchment paper until ready to bake.

Grease a large baking sheet with butter and sprinkle with the cornmeal. Place the rings on the baking sheet and brush with some of the beaten egg. Sprinkle with the remaining 1 tablespoon of poppy seeds and bake 30 minutes or until the *bublyky* are golden brown. Cool on a wire rack.

NOTE: *The rings are somewhat delicate after rising. Be careful when picking up the rings just before boiling, as not to "deflate" them.*

Zhytni bulky z syrom

Makes 2 dozen rolls

These rolls are made using a mixture of rye and whole-wheat pastry flours, since rye flour alone does not contain the gluten necessary for the bread to rise. The recipe yields excellent plain rye rolls that make a great addition to any meal. However, I like to add a slice of Swiss cheese to each roll before baking which elevates them to quintessential cocktail fare.

24 thin deli slices of Swiss cheese, cut into 3-inch squares

3 tablespoons unsalted butter, melted

1 extra-large egg, beaten

1 tablespoon milk

RYE YEAST DOUGH

½ cup warm milk (about 110°F)

1¼ teaspoons active dry yeast

1½ teaspoons granulated sugar

1 extra-large egg, well beaten

2 tablespoons unsalted butter, melted

½ teaspoon salt

1⅛ cups whole grain rye flour

1⅛ cups whole wheat pastry flour

Make the dough:

Pour the warm milk into a small bowl and add the yeast. Stir in the sugar, mix well and let sit until frothy, about 10 minutes.

Put the egg, melted butter, and salt in a large bowl and mix well. Stir in the yeast mixture. Add the flours ½ cup at a time, stirring well after each addition. Turn out the dough onto a lightly floured board or counter and knead for about 10 minutes, or use the dough hook on an electric mixer for about 5 minutes, until smooth and elastic.

Lightly coat another bowl with butter or oil and put the dough in it, turning it over to coat evenly. Cover the bowl with a kitchen towel and put in a warm, draft-free place until the dough is doubled in volume, about 1½ hours.

Make the rolls:

Preheat the oven to 350°F. Punch the dough down in the bowl and turn it out onto a lightly floured board or counter and knead for about 30 seconds. With a floured rolling pin, roll it out to a large rectangle. With a small knife, cut the dough into 24 3-inch squares. Place a slice of cheese on each square of dough, drizzle with a little melted butter, and roll each square jelly-roll fashion into a neat roll. Grease 2 baking sheets with butter. Arrange the rolls seam-side-down on the baking sheets. Mix the beaten egg with the milk in a small bowl and brush across the top of each roll. Bake 35 to 40 minutes or until the rolls are golden brown. Serve warm.

VARIATION: *Sprinkle the rolls with some caraway seeds before baking.*

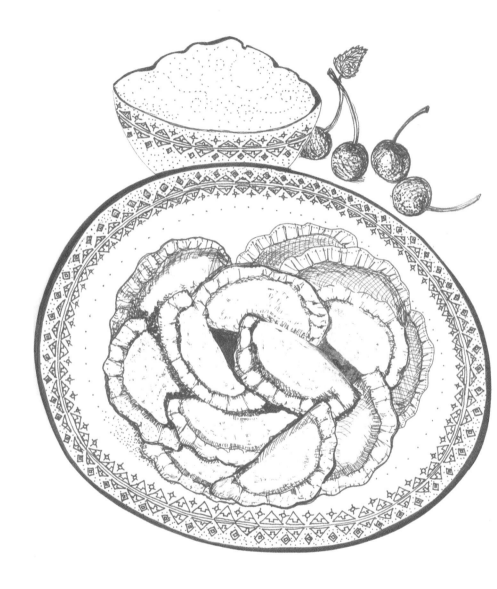

Chapter 8

Dumplings, Noodles, and Griddlecakes

Ceaseless versatility ...

Large parts of the world clearly love the intensity of flavors that come wrapped in compact, edible packages and Ukraine is no exception. Plump filled dumplings called *varenyky* are a Ukrainian staple and there must be as many different kinds as there are stars in the sky. Similar to the Polish "pierogi," *varenyky* are half-moon shaped versions of ravioli with the most popular savory fillings being potato, cabbage, and cheese. Sweet filling favorites include sweetened sour cherries, strawberries, and blueberries. *Varenyky* are traditionally boiled, but they can also be fried in unsalted butter or oil. Usually two or more toppings are suggested for variety: sour cream, buttery fried onions, or pork or bacon cracklings. If *varenyky* have a sweet filling, serve sour cream sweetened with a drizzle of honey on the side, or a dollop of whipped cream on top. A splash of cream or fruit juice and a dusting of confectioners' sugar are quite delicious and acceptable, too.

Homemade egg noodles called *lokshyna* are made in every shape and size in Ukraine and small "drop" dumplings called *halushky* are added to soups, stews, and casseroles to help absorb all the good juices. *Halushkas* (plural for *halushky*) can be made with or without fillings and are flavored with poppy seeds, crushed nuts, or even chopped pork fat—a traditional Ukrainian favorite. The variations are as numerous as the names by which they are known: *bootziki*, *shulyky*, *halushki*—all original, silly nonsense diminutives for which there is no English equivalent.

Small, thick griddlecakes called *mlyntsi* are marvelously adaptable, as both the batter and toppings are infinitely variable. Despite being considered a cheap and homey food in Ukraine, these pancakes can also incorporate other rather formal ingredients like caviar, smoked fish, grated fresh vegetables, or even fresh fruit. This type of adornment elevates the simple pancake to a refined dish.

Another variation of griddlecakes are thin, lacy pancakes rolled around fillings. They are called *nalysnyky*—French crepes being similar. If stuffed with meat, *nalysnyky* are served hot for lunch or as a light supper. If stuffed with fruit or slathered with thick fruit preserves, *nalysnyky* are usually served warm or room temperature with a dusting of confectioners' sugar and a dollop of sour cream on the side.

Varenyky

Even though many of the world's "stuffed dumplings" resemble one another, Ukrainian *varenyky* are in a class all their own—how the dough is made, the shape, and the filling make all the difference in the world.

Pyrohy (plural) is another name for *varenyky*, used particularly in western Ukraine more than anywhere else in the country.

First of all, it is not only wheat flour that is used to make *varenyky*. Corn, barley, rye, buckwheat, or any grain that can produce flour is all one needs to make them. In Zakarpattya oblast, *varenyky* called "*terchani pyrohy*" are made from grated potatoes rather than flour.

Second, the dough must be kneaded quickly but well to make it springy and soft. The addition of egg yolks yields a richer-tasting and nutritious dough and sour cream, melted butter, or oil will insure tenderness.

While the dough is the skin that holds it together, the filling is the soul of the *varenyky!*

Third is the all important filling. What is chosen to be a filling depends on the time of year, local traditions, and personal tastes. More exotic choices are mashed beans, dried pears, poppy seeds, and boiled buckwheat. Mashed potatoes flavored with bits of sautéed onions; fresh or cured cabbage; mushrooms; mashed potato and cheddar cheese seem to be the most popular fillings here in the United States. However, in Ukraine proper, all kinds of meats, liver, and small pieces of salted pork fat or salo (cured pork belly bacon) are also very high on the priority list—as are lighter choices such as sautéed nettles, chopped fresh dill, beet greens, or spinach. "*Maslyana*" or Mardi Gras season sees *varenyky* stuffed with cottage cheese on every table in the countryside. And in the summertime, pitted sour cherries rise to the top of the filling list. I think Ukrainians all over the world will tell you there is nothing else like the taste of dumplings stuffed with fresh sour cherries. Strawberries and blueberries quite possibly run a close second and third to cherries—all of them are delicious! Homemade jams and fruit preserves also make their way into *varenyky*.

Some Ukrainians say that without a dressing, *varenyky* are like a church without a cross above it.

And last, enhancing the flavor of *varenyky* with a dressing is almost as important as the filling. Chopped fresh dill, parsley, pieces of salted pig fat, buttery fried onions, and crushed garlic are the most popular, but "*smetana*" or sour cream is the queen of them all! Sweetened with a drizzle of honey, *smetana* is also served with fruit-filled *varenyky*, along with some of the fruit juices. Delicious!

Varenyky are generally made in large quantities and brought to the table in a "*makitra*"—a traditional, brightly-painted earthen pot, vessel, or bowl.

In the land of Hutsulshchyna, in the area of the Carpathian Mountains in western Ukraine, special "wedding *varenyky*" are given to the parents of the bride by the groom's mother, filled with clay, sand, and other inedibles—a tradition that brings joy and merriment to the occasion!

Titso na varenyky

Makes about 5 to 6 servings as an entrée or about 36 to 40 varenyky

This is the basic recipe for making *varenyky*. First choose and make one of the many fillings on the following pages and then follow these instructions for making the dough and assembling and cooking the *varenyky*.

2 cups unbleached all-purpose flour

2 teaspoons salt

2 extra-large egg yolks

1 tablespoon sunflower oil or melted unsalted butter plus additional for sprinkling

Filling of choice (pages 193–197)

Make dough:

Put the flour and 1 teaspoon salt into a food processor and mix together. With the motor running, add the egg yolks and oil through the feeding tube. Then add 7 to 8 tablespoons of cool water a few tablespoons at a time in a slow and steady stream. When the dough clumps together around the blade, remove it and place on a lightly floured board or counter. Knead the dough just until smooth, about 3 minutes. Cover with a kitchen towel and let rest 15 minutes.

Assemble *varenyky*:

Make sure your chosen filling is chilled before using. On a lightly floured board or counter, roll the dough out to about 1/16-inch thick and cut into 4-inch circles. Place 1 tablespoon of your chosen filling on one side of each circle of dough and fold the other half of the circles over it to form half-moons, making sure the edges are free of filling. Crimp the edges with your fingers or the tines of a fork, making sure the dumplings are well-sealed so the filling does not run out when boiling. Cover the filled *varenyky* with a kitchen towel to prevent them from drying out until all the dough is filled.

Cook the *varenyky*:

In a large pot, bring about 8 cups of cold water seasoned with 1 teaspoon of salt to a full, rolling boil. Gently drop the *varenyky* a few at a time into the boiling water. Do not over crowd the pot. Gently stir the water with a wooden spoon to prevent the *varenyky* from sticking to the bottom of the pan. Boil for 3 to 6 minutes (depending on the thickness of the dough and size of dumpling), until the *varenyky* are puffy. Gently remove them with a large slotted spoon and drain thoroughly in a colander. Put the *varenyky* in a large shallow dish and immediately sprinkle with oil or melted butter to prevent them from sticking together. Cover the dish with aluminum foil to keep warm until all are cooked.

Dress and serve the *varenyky*:

Serve *varenyky* in a large dish without crowding them and offer a variety of condiments to accompany, such as sour cream, buttery fried onions, crushed garlic, chopped crisp bacon or pork fat, finely chopped fresh dill or parsley, browned buttered bread crumbs, etc.

Nachynky do varenykiv

Each filling recipe makes enough
to stuff about 36 to 40 varenyky

Potato Filling
Z kartopli

I think Yukon gold potatoes give this filling a superior flavor. Feel free to vary the proportions and seasonings to suit your taste.

In a small skillet over medium heat, sauté the onion in the butter until soft, about 5 minutes. Let the mixture cool and then add to the mashed potatoes along with the salt and white pepper. Mix well. Chill and then use to fill *varenyky* (page 192).

1 small onion, finely
chopped
1 tablespoon unsalted
butter
2½ cups cold mashed
potatoes
½ teaspoon salt
¼ teaspoon freshly ground
white or black pepper

Sauerkraut Filling
Z kvashenoyi kapusty

Homemade fresh sauerkraut makes this an absolutely delicious filling for *varenyky*, and is my personal favorite. However, if fresh sauerkraut is not available, one could use packaged sauerkraut found in most grocery stores. Finely shredded *fresh* green cabbage that has been sautéed in chicken, duck, or goose fat, bacon drippings, pork fat, salo, butter, or any vegetable oil, equivalent to 2½ cups cooked, can also be substituted for the sauerkraut in this filling.

2 tablespoons (generous)
bacon drippings
1 small onion, finely
chopped
2½ cups fresh homemade
sauerkraut (page 67),
well-drained
Salt and freshly ground
black pepper to taste

Melt the bacon drippings in a large skillet over medium heat and add the onion. Sauté until soft, about 5 minutes. Add the sauerkraut and continue cooking, adding more bacon drippings if necessary, for 20 minutes. Cover, reduce the heat to low and gently simmer the mixture for another 20 minutes. Taste and add additional salt and black pepper if necessary. Remove the pan from the heat and let cool completely. Chill and then use to fill *varenyky* (page 192).

Farmer's Cheese Filling
Z biloho syru

I love the combination of farmer's cheese and fresh dill, but feel free to substitute your favorite fresh herb or eliminate it completely.

Combine all the ingredients in a large bowl and mix well. Chill and then use to fill *varenyky* (page 192).

1 pound farmer's cheese
2 extra-large egg yolks
1 to 2 teaspoons sour cream
½ teaspoon salt
¼ teaspoon freshly ground
white or black pepper
1 tablespoon finely chopped
fresh dill (optional)

fillings continued on next page ⇨

Potato and Cheddar Cheese Filling

Iz zhovtoho amerykans'koho syru "cheddar"

Definitely a North American invention from the Canadian prairies, grated cheddar cheese adds a wonderful flavor to a potato filling for *varenyky*. In the Hutsul region of Ukraine, *bryndzia* (an aged ewe's milk cheese) would be substituted for the cheddar cheese.

In a small skillet over medium heat, sauté the onion in the butter until soft, about 5 minutes. Let the onion cool slightly and then mix in the mashed potatoes. Stir in the grated cheese. Taste and add salt and black pepper if needed and mix well. Chill and then use to fill *varenyky* (page 192).

1 small onion, finely chopped

1 tablespoon unsalted butter

2½ cups cold mashed potatoes

1 cup grated cheddar cheese

Salt and freshly ground black pepper to taste

Fish Filling

Z ryby

The addition of a combination of chopped fresh herbs greatly enhances this filling.

In a small skillet over medium heat, sauté the onion in the butter until soft, about 5 minutes. Stir the onion into the chopped fish, along with the herbs, egg yolks, salt, and black pepper. Mix well. Chill and then use to fill *varenyky* (page 192).

1 small onion, finely chopped

1 tablespoon unsalted butter

2½ cups leftover fish (such as carp, haddock, pike, salmon, or cod), finely chopped

2 tablespoons finely chopped fresh herbs such as: dill, parsley, tarragon, basil, thyme, or savory

2 extra-large egg yolks, beaten

½ teaspoon salt

½ teaspoon freshly ground black pepper

Mushroom Filling
Z hrybiv

In a medium skillet over medium heat, sauté the onion in the butter until soft, about 5 minutes. Add the cooked mushrooms, dill, and parsley and cook together for 10 minutes. Taste and add salt and black pepper if needed. Remove the skillet from the stove and beat in the egg yolks. Chill thoroughly and then use to fill *varenyky* (page 192).

1 small onion, finely chopped

1 tablespoon unsalted butter or sunflower oil

2½ cups cooked finely chopped mushrooms

1 tablespoon finely chopped fresh dill

1 tablespoon finely chopped fresh parsley

Salt and freshly ground black pepper to taste

2 extra-large egg yolks

Little Ear Dumplings

"Little ear dumplings" or *vushka* are tiny *varenyky* (you use the same dough recipe, page 192) with the two bottom corners folded over into a triangle and the two corners then attached together giving them the resemblance to tiny little ears. Usually stuffed with mushrooms and served as accompaniments to soups or plain chicken broth, *vushka* are traditionally served in clear *borshch* on Christmas Eve. (When served on Christmas Eve, the filling and dough should be made without animal fat, so omit the butter in both and replace with sunflower or olive oil.) *Vushka* are delicious on their own tossed with chopped fresh herbs like dill or tarragon and a drizzle of browned butter. To make *vushka*, simply cut the *varenyky* dough into 2-inch squares (or even smaller), reduce the amount of filling to 1 teaspoon (or less) per square and proceed with the recipe.

fillings continued on next page ⇨

Sour Cherry Filling

Z vyshen'

Varenyky stuffed with pitted sour cherries is a true Ukrainian specialty! Running a close second is a filling made from wild strawberries—but farmed strawberries are used, too, as well as fresh blueberries or blackberries. Mulberries are a favorite choice in the southern regions of Ukraine. Feel free to substitute any of these for the cherries in this recipe.

....

NOTE: *If fresh sour cherries are not available, jarred cherries can be used. Some jarred sour cherries are pre-sweetened so adjust sugar accordingly.*

8 cups pitted sour cherries or jarred sour cherries, drained (reserve the liquid)

1 cup granulated sugar (or less if using jarred cherries)

¼ teaspoon salt

About ¼ cup unbleached all-purpose flour

2 extra-large egg whites, beaten

Put the fresh or jarred sour cherries in a large bowl and add the sugar and salt. Mix well and let sit for about 3 hours for the fresh (or until they start giving off their juices) or 1 hour for the jarred. Strain the juice and reserve. Dust the well-drained sour cherries with some flour and use to fill *varenyky* (page 192), 3 or 4 cherries per dumpling. Brush the filled dumplings with beaten egg whites just before boiling.

Pour the reserved cherry juice into a saucepan and bring to a boil. Let the liquid reduce by half, and then let it cool to room temperature. Serve over the cooled *varenyky*.

Sweet Cherries and Sour Cherries

Sweet cherries are commonly eaten out of hand as fresh cherries, while sour or tart cherries are used primarily for cooking and baking in Ukrainian cuisine. Sweet cherries simply do not hold up when cooking and lose much of their flavor, while sour cherries stay plump and juicy. Though I personally enjoy eating sour cherries with a sprinkle of crusty brown sugar and a dollop of honey-sweetened sour cream, most of these crimson jewels go into making sour cherry dumplings called "*varenyky z vyshniamy.*"

Sour cherry season is very short in the United States, so take advantage when they are available wherever you live and freeze some for use throughout the year. Pit sour cherries using a small, serrated knife over a bowl to catch all the juices. Once drained, place the cherries on a baking sheet in a single layer (do not overcrowd) and freeze. When the cherries are hard, transfer them to a container or plastic bag and store in the freezer. Be sure to sweeten the leftover drained juice to your liking and drink—sour cherry juice is not only delicious, it is nutritious!

Sweet Poppy Seed Filling

Iz posolodzhenoho maku

I love *varenyky* stuffed with sweetened ground poppy seeds and I only serve them on special occasions. My version is laced with orange blossom honey and mace. To serve, drizzle with a little more orange blossom honey, a scattering of fresh orange zest, and a dusting of confectioners' sugar.

2 cups poppy seeds

½ teaspoon salt

¼ teaspoon ground mace or freshly grated nutmeg

¼ cup orange blossom honey (plus more for serving)

2 tablespoons freshly grated orange zest for serving

Bring 3 cups of water to a boil in a medium saucepan. Stir in the poppy seeds and then remove the pan from the stove. Let the mixture sit for about 20 minutes.

Thoroughly drain the poppy seeds and grind very fine in a food processor. Put the ground poppy seeds in a medium bowl and stir in the salt, mace or nutmeg, and honey, mixing well. Use to fill *varenyky* (page 192).

Bakhchisaray-Style Steamed Dumplings

Manty

Makes about 24 manty

These juicy meat dumplings are comfortably at home in Ukraine's southern regions, but especially in Bakhchisaray, the heartland of the Crimean Tatar people. *Manty* in Crimea are filled with any type of minced meat flavored with only salt and black pepper. The stuffed dumplings are steamed rather than boiled and served with chopped fresh dill and a side of sour cream or yogurt.

I stuff *manty* with finely chopped lamb, preferably from the leg or shoulder. I have the butcher mince it, rather than grinding it, for if the meat is too fine, it will clump together. To steam the dumplings, I use a Chinese multilevel bamboo steamer.

1 recipe dough for *Varenyky* (page 192)

1½ pounds finely chopped leg of lamb

1 onion, finely chopped

½ teaspoon salt

½ teaspoon freshly ground black pepper

½ cup meat broth or water

¼ cup finely chopped fresh dill

Sour cream or plain yogurt to serve

After the dough has rested, divide the dough in half. On a lightly floured board or counter, roll out half of the dough (keep the other half covered with a kitchen towel) to ⅟₁₆-inch thickness and cut into 5-inch squares. Roll out the second half of the dough and cut in the same way.

In a large bowl, combine the lamb, onion, salt, and black pepper and mix thoroughly. Mound 2 teaspoons of the lamb mixture in the center of each dough square, fold up the sides around the filling, wet your fingers with cold water, and pinch the edges together.

Pour about 2 inches of meat broth into the bottom of a bamboo steamer and bring to a boil. Add as many *manty* as will fit, without touching the steamer top. Cover and steam the dumplings about 20 minutes or until the meat is cooked. Remove the *manty* to a decorative serving platter, cover with aluminum foil and keep warm while cooking the remaining dumplings. Sprinkle the fresh dill over the *manty* and serve with sour cream or plain yogurt on the side.

Crimean Meat Pies

Chebureky

Makes 1 dozen

Chebureky are native to Crimea. These little meat pies are a source of passion and pride to the people who live there and they insist *chebureky* should be eaten out of hand rather than with a knife and fork—so the first bite sends a spurt of hot juice right into the mouth!

These days more contemporary versions of *chebureky* are served in cafes and restaurants. Some are stuffed with wild mushrooms, cottage cheese, tomatoes, a mélange of vegetables, or simply plain meat or potato. These versions are fine examples of Tatar tradition meeting the Crimean climate and the ample amount of fresh ingredients available there. Add to that the flair of Ukrainian cooking and, in my opinion, you have some of the best examples of multinational gastronomy, more so here than anywhere else in the country.

1 recipe dough for
    Varenyky (page 192)
6 ounces ground beef
6 ounces ground lamb
1 teaspoon salt
½ teaspoon freshly ground
    black pepper
1 onion, finely chopped
2 cloves garlic, crushed
3 tablespoons unsalted
    butter, melted
6 tablespoons ice water
½ cup sunflower oil for
    frying

After the dough has rested, divide it into 12 equal portions and roll each into a ball. Cover the dough balls with a kitchen towel and let rest another 15 minutes.

Put the ground beef, ground lamb, salt, black pepper, onion, and garlic into a large bowl and gently mix with your hands.

On a lightly floured board or counter with a floured rolling pin, roll out the balls of dough into 3-inch rounds and brush each with some melted butter. Cover lightly with a kitchen towel and let rest another 15 minutes.

Roll out each round some more and gently pull the sides until the circles are about 6 inches in diameter. Mix the ice water into the filling and divide it into 12 portions. Place a portion of filling on one side of each round of dough. Fold the other sides over the filling and press the edges together making half-moons. Seal the edges with the tines of a fork.

Pour the oil into a deep, heavy skillet and warm over medium heat. The oil is hot enough when a drop of water flicked into it sizzles and sputters. Fry the *chebureks* about 4 minutes on each side until golden brown. Drain on paper towels or a wire rack and serve immediately.

NOTE: Yantik *is a* cheburek *that is grilled rather than fried.*

Ukrainian Halushky (Soft Dumplings)

Halushky

Makes 4 servings

Halushky is the Ukrainian name for small pieces of pasta-like dough cooked in boiling water, broth, or milk. Healthy and filling, *halushky* can be made from wheat flour, buckwheat flour, semolina, or potatoes. Easily prepared, they are delicious added to soups, stews, and clear broth or served on their own with traditional toppings like sour cream, chopped fresh herbs, melted butter, salted pork fat, or one's favorite sauce. *Halushky* can also be served as dessert dumplings by adding a ½ cup of granulated sugar to this recipe and simmering in milk. Serve dessert *halushky* with fresh berries, crisp sweet-buttered breadcrumbs, or sweetened sour cream.

As with so many dumpling recipes, Ukrainian cooks have their own family favorites and this is my own adaptation.

2 cups unbleached all-purpose flour

½ teaspoon salt

2 tablespoons unsalted butter, melted

2 extra-large eggs, beaten

6 cups meat broth or water

Crispy bacon bits and chopped fresh parsley to serve

Sift the flour and salt into a large bowl. Make a well in the center, add the butter and eggs and mix to make a dough. Turn the dough out onto a lightly floured board or counter and knead until smooth, about 5 minutes. Wrap the dough in plastic wrap and leave to rest for 20 minutes.

On a lightly floured board or counter, roll out the dough to a ½ inch thickness and using a small sharp knife, cut the dough into 1-inch pieces. Place the pieces of dough on a floured kitchen towel and let dry for 30 minutes.

Pour the broth into a large saucepan and bring to a boil over medium heat. Add the *halushky* and simmer about 10 minutes or until puffy and cooked. Remove with a slotted spoon, drain, and serve in a shallow decorative bowl garnished with crispy bacon bits and chopped fresh parsley.

Cheese Halushky (Soft Dumplings)

Halushky zi syrom

Makes about 6 to 8 servings

In Ukraine, these *halushky* are made with *bryndzia*, a semisoft cheese made from ewe's milk containing 40 percent milk fat. It is favored by the Hutsul people of western Ukraine. Unfortunately this type of cheese can be hard to find in the United States. Risking departure from my culinary region, I have found Welsh Caerphilly cheese comes closest to the taste of real *bryndzia* and can be used with great success in recipes that call for it. Even though Caerphilly cheese is made from raw (unpasteurized) cow's milk, when aged from two to eight weeks, it develops a mild and salty taste, closely resembling the consistency and flavor of real *bryndzia*.

- 2 cups unbleached all-purpose flour
- 2 teaspoons baking powder
- 1¼ teaspoons salt
- 4 tablespoons cold unsalted butter
- ⅔ cup bryndzia or Caerphilly cheese, crumbled
- 2 tablespoons finely chopped fresh dill or parsley
- ¼ teaspoon freshly ground black pepper
- Crispy buttered breadcrumbs or melted butter and finely chopped fresh dill to garnish

Sift the flour, baking powder, and salt together into a large bowl. Rub in the cold butter just until the mixture resembles fine breadcrumbs. Stir in the cheese, dill, and black pepper. Add ½ cup of cold water, and mix into a firm dough. Shape into 24 balls.

In a large pot, bring 12 cups of water seasoned with 1 teaspoon of salt to a boil. Add the dumplings a few at a time, then cover and reduce the heat to medium-low. Simmer the dumplings for about 20 minutes or until light and puffy. Remove the *halushky* with a slotted spoon, drain, and place in a shallow decorative bowl. Serve immediately with a scattering of crispy buttered breadcrumbs and some chopped fresh dill.

Homemade Egg Noodles

Lokshyna

Makes 2 servings

Ukrainians are partial to homemade egg noodles called "*loyshyna*" in Ukrainian. *Lokshyna* are served as an accompaniment to meat roasts, cooked kashas (grains), and vegetable entrees—and occasionally as a dessert. *Lokshyna* are an absolute must with Rich Ukrainian Chicken Broth (page 44) and many enjoy a bowl with a splash of milk and a pat of melting butter. *Lokshyna* are usually made in large quantities, dried, and stored in containers for future use. Increase this basic recipe to suit your needs.

1 cup unbleached all-purpose flour plus more for dusting

¼ teaspoon salt

1 extra-large egg

Mound the flour and salt together on a lightly floured board or counter. Make a well in the center of the flour and add the egg and 1 tablespoon of water. Knead together, adding a little more water if necessary, until the dough is smooth, about 2 to 3 minutes. Cover the dough with plastic wrap and let rest for 30 minutes.

On a lightly floured surface, roll out the dough to ¹⁄₁₆-inch thickness and let dry for about 10 minutes. Turn the dough over to allow the other side of the dough to dry for the same amount of time.

Roll up the dough and slice into three-inch strips. Stack the strips on top of each other and slice crosswise into fine shreds. Spread the *lokshyna* out to dry or cook at once in salted boiling water. The cooking time will depend on the size of the noodles. Drain and serve at once or if using in another recipe, toss with a light coating of sunflower oil to prevent sticking until ready to use.

Other serving suggestions for *lokshyna*:
- Toss buttered *lokshyna* with fresh cottage cheese and top with bits of crispy bacon
- Toss *lokshyna* with 2 tablespoons heavy cream, cooked mushrooms, and chopped cooked ham
- Toss buttered *lokshyna* with cooked buckwheat kasha (page 105)
- Toss *lokshyna* with sunflower oil, cooked shredded cabbage, sauerkraut, or any cooked vegetable or greens and top with chopped fresh herbs

"Maqarne and Suzme"

Starchy foods made of flour pastes are popular all over Ukraine, but *maqarne* and *suzme* are two popular noodle dishes served in the Crimean peninsula and are worth mentioning, once again dispelling the myth that all Ukrainian food is rich and fattening.

Maqarne is prepared the same way as *lokshyna* (page 202), but the dough is cut into 3x3-inch squares and twisted in the center, making a bowtie-shape. The noodles are boiled, then drained and mixed with a little melted butter and topped with a generous helping of crushed nuts—walnuts, hazelnuts, or almonds—making for nutritious and delicious eating!

Suzme is also prepared like *lokshyna*, but the noodle is broader and about 2 inches in length. After boiling and draining, the noodles are tossed with cooked beans and a little melted butter, and served with a healthy sprinkling of chopped fresh dill. Fabulous!

Griddlecakes

Mlyntsi

Mlyntsi is the Ukrainian word for griddlecakes or pancakes. Whether thick or thin, yeast-raised or not, griddlecakes are one of the most ancient of Slavic foods, dating back to the pre-Christian era. *Mlyntsi* are always served warm, usually as an appetizer, but sometimes they are served as an entrée garnished with a variety of toppings such as dabs of caviar, bits of herring or sprats mixed with sour cream, or a mélange of lightly cooked vegetables—additions that take this dish from homey to refined. Sweet toppings include fresh fruit or fruit preserves.

2 extra-large eggs, separated

2 tablespoons granulated sugar

1 teaspoon salt

4 cups milk

2 tablespoons unsalted butter, melted

3 cups unbleached all-purpose flour

2 tablespoons (generous) lard, unsalted butter, or sunflower oil

Preheat the oven to 200°F. In a large mixing bowl, whisk together the egg yolks, sugar, and salt. Add the milk and melted butter and mix thoroughly.

Put the flour in another large bowl and add the liquid mixture, beating thoroughly to crush any lumps that form. In a small bowl, whisk the egg whites until frothy, then fold them into the batter.

Melt the lard on a large griddle over medium-heat. Drop some batter by the tablespoonful onto the griddle, spacing the griddlecakes about 1 inch apart. Cook until golden underneath, and then flip with a spatula to cook the other side, about 1 to 2 minutes. Transfer the *mlyntsi* to a heatproof dish and keep warm in the oven until ready to serve. Repeat the process with the remaining batter, melting more lard on the griddle to prevent sticking, if needed, between batches. Serve hot with toppings.

Buckwheat Griddlecakes

Hrechanyky

These buckwheat griddlecakes have yeast in the batter, giving the end result a nice, almost brioche-like texture. *Hrechanyky* are always served the week before Lent in Ukraine with plenty of butter, thick sour cream, or honey. If you are pressed for time, the yeast batter can be mixed the day ahead and left to rise overnight in the refrigerator.

1½ cups warm milk (about 110°F)

2½ teaspoons active dry yeast

2 tablespoons granulated sugar

1 cup buckwheat flour

½ cup unbleached all-purpose flour

½ teaspoon salt

4 tablespoons unsalted butter, melted and slightly cooled

3 extra-large egg yolks

Pour the warm milk into a large mixing bowl and stir in the yeast and sugar. Let the mixture stand until frothy, about 10 minutes.

Whisk in the flours, salt, 2 tablespoons melted butter, and egg yolks, and mix until the batter is smooth. Cover the bowl with a kitchen cloth and put in a warm place until doubled in volume, about 1½ hours.

Preheat the oven to 200°F. Place a large griddle over medium-high heat. Brush the griddle with some melted butter. For each griddlecake, ladle onto the griddle about ¼ cup batter, keeping them about 2 inches apart. Cook until golden underneath, and then flip with a spatula to cook the other side, about 2 to 3 minutes. Transfer the *hrechanyky* to a heatproof dish and keep warm in the oven until ready to serve. Repeat the process with the remaining batter, brushing the griddle with more butter as needed to prevent sticking between batches. Serve hot with toppings.

Ukrainian Crepes

Nalysnyky

Makes about 12 crepes

Nalysnyky are yet another type of griddlecake. While *mlyntsi* (page 204) are small and thick, *nalysnyky* are very thin, lacy griddlecakes, most often rolled around a sweet or savory filling—much like French crepes. Filling possibilities are infinite and every household has their favorites.

I like to serve savory renditions stuffed with ground meat fillings or sautéed vegetables blanketed under a creamy sauce (see sauces on pages 80–81). But more often than not, I slather *nalysnyky* with homemade fruit preserves or jam, roll them up tightly, pile them high on a platter and give them a liberal dusting of confectioners' sugar. Such a versatile dish, *nalysnyky* is a much loved Ukrainian favorite.

4 extra-large eggs

1 cup milk

2 cups unbleached all-purpose flour

½ teaspoon salt

2 tablespoons melted unsalted butter or sunflower oil plus extra for frying

Sour cream for serving

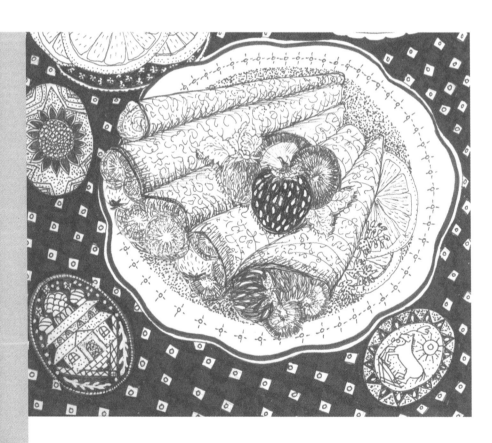

In a large bowl, beat together the eggs, milk, and 1 cup of water. Sift the flour with the salt and gradually add it to the liquid mixture, beating continually to prevent lumps from forming. When the batter is smooth, stir in 2 tablespoons of melted butter and set aside for 10 minutes.

Brush the inside of an 8-inch crepe pan or small skillet with some melted butter. Set the pan over medium-high heat. When a drop of water sizzles and sputters when flicked into the pan, lift the pan from the heat and pour about 2 to 3 tablespoons of batter into it, tipping the pan as you pour it in so that the batter runs all over the bottom. Return to the heat and when the top is set (about 15 to 30 seconds), flip the *nalysnyky* over with a spatula to cook on the other side. Remove to a warmed plate and cover with a kitchen towel. Continue in this manner until all the batter is used up, lightly buttering the pan each time to prevent sticking.

If serving immediately, *nalysnyky* can be rolled up and placed side by side in a buttered casserole dish, making 2 layers. Sprinkle with buttered bread crumbs or your favorite cookie crumbs and reheat briefly, about 5 minutes, in a 325°F oven, and serve with plenty of sour cream.

NOTE: *If you are planning on freezing* nalysnyky, *let them cool completely and stack, layered in between sheets of waxed paper. Wrap the stack in aluminum foil and place in your freezer where they will keep for up to two months.*

Chapter 9

Omelets and Other Egg Dishes

Not just for breakfast ...

In Ukrainian households, eggs form a basic part of everyday meals. They are an absolutely essential in Ukrainian cooking—not only as ingredients, but also as a separate course in their own right. Ukrainians love omelets and prefer a hardy breakfast, so plate-fuls of steaming eggs are in order, even on busy mornings. Throughout Ukraine omelets are traditionally prepared open-style rather than folded, but the omelets listed in this chapter can be prepared in the Western way, too. Ukrainian omelets are usually served with thick slices of fresh tomatoes or hot boiled potatoes dressed with sour cream.

Being the notorious egg-eaters they are, Ukrainians not only enjoy egg dishes as appetizers and for breakfast, but also as side dishes, supper dishes, and novel ideas for special weekend fare, several of which are cited in this chapter.

....

NOTE: *All the omelets here are designed as independent courses, counting 3 extra-large eggs for each person.*

Omelet with Frankfurters

Omlet zi sosyskamy

Makes 1 omelet / 1 serving

Omelets are essential to Ukrainian cookery and frankfurters are a favorite addition and a great way to use up leftovers.

3 extra-large eggs

1 tablespoon light cream

¼ teaspoon salt

Freshly ground black pepper to taste

1 tablespoon unsalted butter

1 cooked frankfurter, skinned and cut into rounds

1 tablespoon chopped fresh parsley

Freshly grated horseradish, if desired

Whisk the eggs, cream, salt, and black pepper together in a small bowl.

Melt the butter in a medium skillet or 10-inch omelet pan over medium-low heat. Add half the egg mixture and then half of the frankfurter slices. Cook without stirring until the edges are almost set, about 4 minutes, running a spatula around the edges of the pan to prevent sticking.

Pour the remaining egg mixture on top and then add the remaining frankfurter slices. Reduce the heat to low, cover, and cook until the eggs are set, about 3 to 4 minutes.

Slide the omelet onto a warmed plate and sprinkle with chopped parsley. Garnish with a bit of freshly grated horseradish if desired and serve immediately.

The Ever Popular Frankfurter

Frankfurters are popular German smoked sausages (or links) made of beef or a mixture of beef and pork. Traditionally, frankfurters (and Vienna sausages which are equally as popular) are used in Ukrainian cookery as in other Eastern European cuisines, in that they are first scalded, skinned, and then cut and served as a main course directly on warmed plates with freshly grated horseradish or mustard. They are also sometimes stewed in sour cream sauces (page 80) along with a few potatoes and a healthy sprinkling of paprika. Remember frankfurters should not be cooked fiercely or kept in hot water for too long, for their skins will split and they will lose much of their attraction that way. Use simmering water and leave the frankfurters soak for about four minutes. Skin them, cut into rounds, and proceed with your recipe.

Omelet with Buckwheat Kasha and Smoked Fish

Omlet iz hrechanoyu kashoyu ta vudzhenoyu ryboyu

Makes 1 omelet / 1 serving

If you like, mix some buttery browned onions and cooked wild mushrooms into the buckwheat kasha before adding to the omelet for an even more robust and authentic flavor!

3 extra-large eggs

1 tablespoon cream

Freshly ground black pepper to taste

1 tablespoon unsalted butter

½ cup cooked buckwheat kasha (page 105)

3 ounces smoked fish (whitefish, trout, salmon, or eel), flaked

1 tablespoon chopped fresh dill

½ teaspoon sweet Hungarian paprika

A sprinkle of apple cider vinegar to serve

Whisk the eggs, cream, and black pepper together in a small bowl.

Melt the butter in a medium skillet or 10-inch omelet pan over medium-low heat. Add half the egg mixture and then sprinkle half of the buckwheat kasha and half of the smoked fish over top of the eggs. Cook without stirring until the edges are almost set, running a spatula around the edges of the pan to prevent sticking.

Pour the remaining egg mixture on top and sprinkle on another layer of kasha and another layer of smoked fish and then the chopped dill. Cover and reduce the heat to low and cook 3 minutes longer or until the eggs are set.

Slide the omelet onto a warmed plate, sprinkle with paprika, and drizzle with some apple cider vinegar. Serve immediately.

Omelet with Fresh Tomatoes and Garlic

Omlet zi svizhymy pomidoramy i chasnykom

Makes 1 omelet / 1 serving

This omelet makes a wonderful brunch dish or light supper when served with boiled new potatoes and a green salad.

Whisk the eggs, cream, salt, and black pepper together in a small bowl.

Melt the butter in a medium skillet or 10-inch omelet pan over medium-low heat. Add half the egg mixture and then the sliced garlic and tomato slices. Cook without stirring until the edges are almost set, about 4 minutes, running a spatula around the edges to prevent sticking.

Pour the remaining egg mixture on top, cover, reduce the heat to low and cook another 2 to 3 minutes or until the eggs are set.

Slide the omelet onto a warmed plate and sprinkle with chopped parsley. Serve immediately.

- 3 extra-large eggs
- 1 tablespoon cream
- ¼ teaspoon salt
- Freshly ground black pepper to taste
- 1 tablespoon unsalted butter
- 2 to 3 cloves garlic, sliced (or more to taste)
- 6 thin slices fresh tomato
- 2 tablespoons chopped fresh parsley

Omelet with Fresh Strawberries

Omlet zi svizhymy polunytsiamy

Makes 1 omelet / 1 serving

In Ukraine, fresh fruit shows up everywhere and here strawberries take center stage in an omelet. Serve with a dollop of strawberry preserves (page 76).

Cut the stems off the strawberries, slice in half and then quarter. Put the strawberries in a bowl and drizzle to taste with honey if desired.

Whisk the eggs, cream, and salt together in a small bowl. Melt the butter in a medium skillet or 10-inch omelet pan over medium-low heat. Pour in the egg mixture. Cover, reduce the heat to low, and cook 3 to 4 minutes or until the edges start to set but the middle is still soft. Run a spatula around the edges of the pan to prevent the omelet from sticking.

Sprinkle the strawberries and brown sugar over top of the egg mixture. Cover and cook another minute and then slide the omelet onto a warmed plate. Serve immediately garnished with a dollop of strawberry preserves, whipped cream, and a dusting of confectioners' sugar.

- ½ cup fresh strawberries
- Honey to taste
- 3 extra-large eggs
- 1 tablespoon cream
- ¼ teaspoon salt
- 1 tablespoon unsalted butter
- 1 tablespoon crusty brown sugar (optional)
- Strawberry preserves, whipped cream, and confectioners' sugar to serve

Eggs Poached in Cream

Yaitsia vareni v smetani

Makes 2 to 4 servings

This is a classic Ukrainian egg dish. I like to garnish my plate with small mounds of sautéed spinach or sorrel and lots of fresh dill. A side of toasted bread is practically unknown in Ukraine, but a side of cooked buckwheat kasha topped with pork cracklings or sliced *kovbasa* (page 124) would be favored accompaniments.

2 tablespoons unbleached all-purpose flour

1 cup sour cream

½ cup (generous) milk

4 extra-large eggs

½ teaspoon salt

½ teaspoon freshly ground black pepper

Finely chopped fresh dill to serve

Whisk the flour into the sour cream. Pour it into a medium saucepan and stir in the milk. Bring the mixture to a boil over medium heat, stirring constantly to prevent scorching. Break 1 egg at a time into a custard cup and gently slip into the hot sauce. If the sauce starts to get too thick, add a little more milk. Cover, reduce the heat to low, and simmer just until the egg whites are firm and a white film has formed over the egg yolks, about 3 minutes. Carefully remove the eggs with a slotted spoon and place on warmed plates. Immediately pour some sauce over top and sprinkle with fresh dill. Serve hot.

VARIATION: *Use halved hard-cooked eggs instead of fresh eggs. Simply place the hard-cooked eggs in the simmering sauce and heat gently for 1 minute. Carefully remove the eggs with a slotted spoon and place on a warmed serving platter. Pour the hot sauce over top and serve immediately with a scattering of toasted breadcrumbs.*

Egg Patties

Sichenyky z varenykh yayets'

Makes 4 to 6 servings

S*ichenyky* is a general term used to describe various ingredients bound together with breadcrumbs, shaped into patties, and pan-fried. In this recipe, these "patties" are made of hard-cooked eggs, breadcrumbs, and a liberal amount of fresh herbs and are really worth a trial. This dish is a favorite stand-by in Ukrainian homes.

⅔ cup dry breadcrumbs

1 cup milk

6 hard-cooked extra-large eggs, chopped

1 small onion, finely chopped

½ teaspoon salt

½ teaspoon freshly ground black pepper

2 tablespoons finely chopped fresh herbs (such as: parsley, tarragon, dill, savory, thyme, etc.)

2 tablespoons unbleached all-purpose flour

1 tablespoon unsalted butter

1 tablespoon sunflower oil

Preheat the oven to 200°F. Put the breadcrumbs in a large bowl and mix in the milk. Let the mixture stand for 5 minutes. Stir in the eggs, onion, salt, black pepper, and herbs.

Wet your hands with cold water and shape the egg mixture into 3-inch patties. Dust both sides of each patty with some flour and make an "X" across the entire top of each patty with the back of a small knife.

Melt the butter in a large skillet over medium heat and add the oil. When the fats are hot, fry the patties about 2 to 3 minutes per side, flipping once with a spatula. Carefully remove to a heatproof casserole and keep the patties warm in the oven until ready to serve.

Serve accompanied by Dill Sauce, Onion Sauce, Mushroom Sauce, Hot Horseradish Sauce, or Creamy Cheese Sauce (pages 80–81).

Scrambled Eggs with Noodles

Yayechnia z lokshynoyu

This popular Ukrainian standby combines home-made egg noodles and fresh scrambled eggs. Always serve this dish hot, perhaps with a cooked vegetable or vegetable salad. Garnishes, while not necessary, could include toasted caraway seeds, chopped fresh herbs, crushed nuts, or another Ukrainian standby—a dollop of thick sour cream.

2 tablespoons unsalted butter, sunflower oil, or bacon drippings

2 cups cooked homemade egg noodles (page 202)

3 extra-large eggs, beaten

½ teaspoon salt

½ teaspoon freshly ground black pepper

Sweet Hungarian paprika to taste

Melt the butter in a large skillet over medium heat. Add the egg noodles and toss until well coated with the melted butter. Pour in the beaten eggs, salt, and black pepper. Cook and stir as for scrambled eggs, about 1 minute, or until the eggs are lightly set. Sprinkle with paprika and serve immediately.

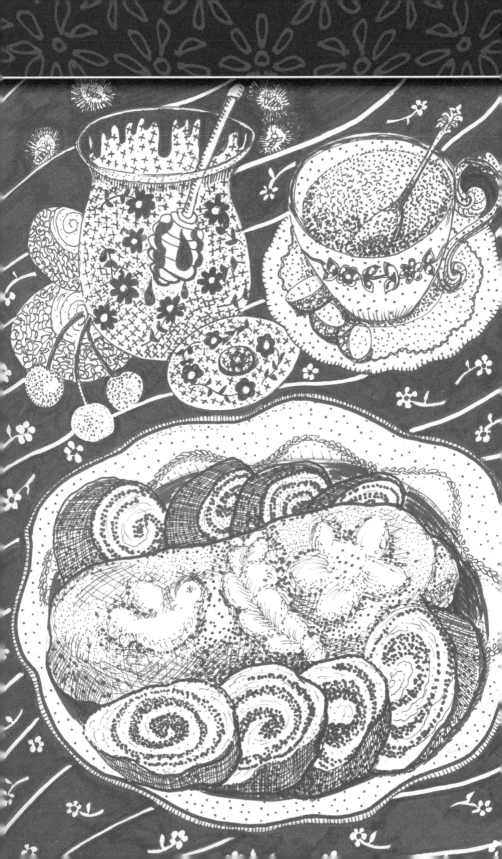

Chapter 10

Desserts

Great culinary extravaganzas ...

There is no doubt Ukrainians have always had a sweet tooth, and as a result, Ukrainian desserts are virtually limitless in their variety. It is not surprising that old Ukrainian cookbooks dedicated large amounts of space to desserts and pastries. Close involvement with other cultural traditions through the ages resulted in different techniques and ingredients being adapted and permanently absorbed into Ukrainian dessert cuisine. Many dessert recipes originated among the common people, but many others were executed by renowned pastry chefs of aristocratic Ukrainian families. For instance, there is certainly a touch of Austro-Hungarian decadence in Ukrainian tortes and cakes, making them all the more worth the guilty indulgence. In western Ukraine there is a definite penchant for Polish and Lithuanian-inspired cheesecakes and puddings. The original Ukrainian name for a long roll of dough with a filling is *vertuta* or *zavyvanets'*, while *strudel* is the more familiar and sophisticated name, with no country being able to claim its origin. What is wonderful is that these contributions from the outside only added greater variety to the art of Ukrainian baking, but at the same time Ukrainian pastries and desserts retained much of their own ingenuity.

Aside from national specialties, Ukrainian households from times gone by kept numerous handwritten notebooks filled with recipes for various desserts, plus their own culinary creations. These notebooks were passed down from mother to daughter and kept as treasured family heirlooms, and since special occasions like holy days and holidays are marked with particular confections, special secret instructions were also included to ensure the baker's success. Honey and nuts are plentiful in Ukraine and featured in many sweet dishes, so these recipes, as well as those for fragrant yeast-raised pastries, were included along with recipes for less formal compotes and gelatin-like custards called *kysil*.

Today the picture has changed somewhat, but Ukrainians still take pride in their baking and many desserts, even those from great-grandma's time, are as popular as ever. I felt it necessary to simplify some recipes—a few old country recipes required up to one hour of hand-mixing or upward of thirty egg yolks be added! The lavishness of some of these recipes is not all that extreme however, for Ukraine at times was a wealthy country, and even the poorest of families most likely had a cow and a flock of chickens. Though several recipes have been updated, I am happy to say there has been no sacrifice of quality to the finished outcomes.

Today in Ukraine, everyday meals still include dessert, though since there may have been two or three other courses, it is more likely to be something light and refreshing—perhaps just a piece of fruit from the perpetually changing fruit bowl or an attractive yet simple to prepare dessert like fruit fritters or compote. Fancier desserts and pastries generally are reserved for weekends, celebrations, or as a special treat with afternoon tea.

Because of limited space, I have included a few perennially favorite desserts that never seem to lose popularity. A few are heirloom recipes. I have embraced a vast confection of styles, tastes, and ingredients and I think readers will find the following exquisite finales more fun than fussy to make, thus making the entire endeavor most worthwhile.

Dried Fruit Compote

Uzvar

This traditional dish made from dried fruits is served on Christmas Eve and also at feasts honoring the deceased. Dried fruit compote is also a favorite wintertime dessert. Feel free to add a few tablespoons of brandy, cognac, or rye whiskey, especially in the winter months. It is just delicious served with a scoop of vanilla ice cream or a generous dollop of whipped cream.

4 ounces raisins

4 ounces pitted dried prunes, halved

4 ounces dried apricots, halved

4 ounces dried pears, chopped

8 ounces dried apple slices

2-inch piece cinnamon stick

3 whole cloves

1 vanilla bean, halved lengthwise

Juice and grated zest of 1 lemon

4 cups apple cider

½ cup honey or more to taste

1 to 2 tablespoons brandy (optional)

Put the raisins, prunes, apricots, pears, apples, cinnamon stick, cloves, vanilla bean, lemon juice and zest in a large, non-reactive saucepan. Pour the apple cider over top and let sit overnight.

Add 4 cups of water to the fruit mixture and bring to a boil. Reduce the heat to low and simmer 3 to 6 minutes or just until the fruit starts to soften and the larger pieces are tender but still whole (do not overcook).

Remove the pan from the heat and stir in the honey and brandy, if desired, and let the mixture cool completely. The mixture will continue to thicken as it cools.

NOTE: *Fresh fruit compote is a popular summertime treat in Ukraine (see recipe page 246).*

Strawberry Kysil

Kysil' iz polunyts'

Kysil is one of the oldest foods known to Ukrainians and it is still a widely enjoyed home-style dessert. *Kysil* is a sweetened fruit puree thickened with potato starch. Any fruit will do, but strawberries, raspberries, and red currants are traditional Ukrainian favorites. Stewed fruit can also be used in preparation, but fresh seasonal fruit is always preferred.

2 cups fresh strawberries, hulled

3 tablespoons honey or sugar, or to taste

2½ tablespoons potato starch

Whipped cream to serve

Put the strawberries and 4 cups of cold water in a large saucepan. Bring to a boil over medium-high heat; then reduce the heat to medium-low and simmer just until the strawberries start to pop or get slightly soft, about 5 minutes. Taste and add honey if needed. (See Note.)

Meanwhile, pour 1 cup of cold water into a small bowl and whisk in the potato starch, making sure there are no lumps. Turn the heat under the strawberries back up to medium and when the strawberries start to boil, slowly stir in the potato starch mixture and continue cooking another 30 seconds.

Remove the pan from the heat and pour the *kysil* into a large bowl. Cover and place the bowl in the refrigerator to chill, stirring from time to time. Serve cold with whipped cream.

NOTE: *If you are making raspberry or blackberry* kysil, *after cooking the fruit in the first step let the mixture cool slightly, and then using the back of a large spoon press the mixture through a fine-mesh strainer set over a large bowl to extract as much juice and pulp as possible, leaving the seeds behind. Return to the pot and reheat before thickening.*

VARIATION: *For a more "sophisticated" flavor, add a little grated orange peel, cinnamon, or freshly grated nutmeg to the fruit puree, or if you are using fresh cranberries or red currants, add a few drops of grenadine.*

Honey-Baked Quince

Medom-zapecheni aivy

Although Middle Eastern in origin, quinces have been enjoyed in Ukraine for centuries. A small, hard, pear-shaped fruit that is golden when ripe they possess a penetrating perfume. In Ukrainian cooking, quinces are never eaten raw, but are most often added to the pan juices when roasting pork and game. Quinces hold their shape well when cooking, not becoming too soft or disintegrating as apples would, and are often added to apple and pear dishes creating a surprising amplification of flavor. Besides complementing meat dishes, quinces are also stewed, poached, or baked, sweetened with honey, and then served as a simple dessert.

6 quinces, peeled, halved, and cored

3 tablespoons honey

1 tablespoon freshly grated lemon zest

Whipped cream to serve

Preheat the oven to 350°F. Place the quince halves in a shallow baking dish cut side up and add just enough water to cover the bottom of the pan. Fill each quince half with some honey and sprinkle with some lemon zest.

Bake 1½ hours, until the quinces are soft, basting occasionally with the pan juices and adding more water if necessary.

Serve on individual plates with a dollop of whipped cream if desired. Simple and healthy eating!

Stuffed Fresh Apricots

Nachyniuvani svizhi abrykozy

This dessert can be whipped up in an instant—however, many times these nut-stuffed beauties are served as part of a *zakusky* (appetizer) spread. I serve this selection as often as I can when apricots are in season and they are always a hit!

½ cup sour cream

1 to 2 tablespoons honey or to taste

¼ cup crushed walnuts or other nut of choice

12 fresh apricots (not overly ripe or soft), halved and pitted

Crusty brown sugar for garnishing

Whisk together the sour cream and honey in a small bowl. Stir in the crushed walnuts.

Stuff each piece of apricot with some of the sour cream mixture and place on a decorative serving platter. Refrigerate until ready to serve. Sprinkle with some crusty brown sugar just before serving.

Creamy Millet Pudding

Pshonianyi pudyng

Makes 6 servings

This creamy layered dessert pudding is made with millet flakes, which can be found in any health food store here in the United States. Millet contains more protein and iron than any other grain and its use is catching on in this country. Ukraine, on the other hand, enjoys millet kasha (porridge) regularly as a savory side dish or sweetened with jam, preserves, or fresh fruit.

1½ cups millet flakes

3 cups milk

1 tablespoon unsalted butter

1 teaspoon freshly grated lemon zest

½ teaspoon vanilla extract

2 tablespoons honey

12 ounces fresh soft fruit: berries, pitted cherries, chopped plums or peaches

½ cup toasted chopped nuts plus a few tablespoons for garnish

Honey-sweetened sour cream or whipped cream to serve

Put the millet flakes and milk in a medium saucepan. Add the butter, lemon zest, and vanilla extract and bring to a boil over medium-high heat. Reduce the heat to low and gently stir the mixture until thickened, about 5 minutes. Remove the pan from the heat and stir in the honey. Leave the mixture to cool for 15 minutes, stirring occasionally.

Put some fruit into 6 individual dessert dishes and sprinkle with some chopped nuts. Divide half of the cooked millet between each dish, then add more fruit and a scattering of nuts; spoon a second layer of millet over each and top with the remaining fruit and nuts. Serve portions warm or cold with a dollop of sweetened sour cream or whipped cream.

Old Country Noodle Pudding

Lokshyna z yablukamy

Makes 8 servings

Made with your own homemade fresh *lokshyna* (egg noodles) and tart apples, similar to a sweet Jewish kugel, this old-time country dessert topped with browned buttered breadcrumbs and crunchy walnuts makes a perfect cap to any late summer meal.

4 tablespoons unsalted butter

⅓ cup dry breadcrumbs

2 cups uncooked fresh homemade egg noodles (page 202)

¼ teaspoon salt

6 Granny Smith apples, peeled, cored, and sliced

1 tablespoon fresh lemon juice

½ cup clover or wildflower honey

¼ cup raisins

½ teaspoon ground cinnamon

Toasted chopped walnuts and a few tablespoons heavy cream to serve (optional)

Melt 2 tablespoons butter in a large skillet until fragrant and bubbly. Add the breadcrumbs and stir constantly until the crumbs are coated and toasted, about 3 to 4 minutes. Set aside.

Preheat the oven to 350°F. Cook the egg noodles in plenty of salted boiling water until just al dente; drain and put into a large bowl. Toss the noodles with the remaining 2 tablespoons of butter and the salt.

Combine the apple slices, lemon juice, honey, raisins, and cinnamon in a large bowl and add half of the buttered breadcrumbs. Add the hot noodles to the bowl and toss gently.

Grease a 6x9-inch rectangular casserole dish with some butter. Spoon the noodle mixture into the pan and sprinkle with the remaining buttered breadcrumbs. Cover the pan with aluminum foil and bake 30 minutes or until the apples are tender. Serve portions warm with a scattering of toasted walnuts and a splash of heavy cream. Homey and delicious!

Cherry Bars

Chereshnyanyk

Makes 6 to 8 servings

In Ukrainian, *chereshnyanyk* is the name for a pastry with a cherry filling. I use my recipe for Sour Cream Pastry Dough to make a sweet pastry base for this dish, reserving some dough to make a lattice top. In a pinch, if fresh sour cherries are not available, drained good-quality canned cherries can be used instead.

1 batch Sour Cream Pastry Dough (page 27), sweet version

¼ cup fine dry breadcrumbs

2½ cups pitted sour cherries

⅔ cup plus a few tablespoons crusty brown sugar

1 to 2 tablespoons milk

Have the sweet version of sour cream pastry dough ready, but keep refrigerated until ready to use. Lightly butter an 18-inch x 12-inch x 1-inch baking sheet. Preheat the oven to 350°F.

Divide the dough into two slightly uneven pieces and refrigerate the smaller portion until ready to make the lattice crust. On a lightly floured board or counter with a floured rolling pin, roll out the larger piece of dough to make a 14-inch x 10-inch rectangle. Carefully drape it over the rolling pin and transfer it to the baking sheet.

Sprinkle the surface of the dough with the breadcrumbs and spread the cherries evenly over the crumbs, leaving about a 1½-inch border all around. Sprinkle the ⅔ cup crusty brown sugar over top of the cherries. Fold up the 1½-inch edges of the dough and crimp decoratively with the tines of a fork.

Roll out the reserved dough to about ¼-inch thickness, cut into narrow strips, and arrange in a lattice pattern or weave over top of the cherries. Brush the dough lightly with milk and sprinkle a little crusty brown sugar over top. Bake approximately 30 minutes, covering with a sheet of aluminum foil to prevent scorching if necessary. Cool completely before cutting into squares or bars.

....

NOTE: *In the United States, canned cherry pie filling is usually a thick combination of sweet cherries, sugar, and gelatin. It can be used as the filling in this recipe in a pinch.*

Peach Fritters

Persyky v tisti

Fruit fritters are a popular dessert in Ukraine and are made from various fruits while in season. My favorite fritters are made with peaches. I opt to pan-fry these fritters instead of deep-frying. Other popular fruits for fritters are apples, plums, and cherries.

1 cup unbleached all-purpose flour

¼ cup granulated sugar

Pinch of salt

1 teaspoon baking powder

2 extra-large eggs

⅔ cup milk or light cream

1 tablespoon brandy (optional)

3 tablespoons melted unsalted butter or sunflower oil

3 large peaches, halved, pitted, and cut into ½-inch slices (do not peel)

Honey to taste

Sift the flour, sugar, salt, and baking powder together into a small bowl. In a large bowl, beat the eggs together, and add the milk, brandy, and 1 tablespoon melted butter, mixing well. Add the sifted ingredients to the liquid ingredients and mix until well-blended. Stir in the peaches, making sure batter covers all the fruit.

Pour the remaining 2 tablespoons melted butter into a large skillet over medium-high heat and fry the batter-coated peaches by the tablespoonful until nicely browned on one side, about 3 minutes; then flip with a spatula to cook the other side. Carefully remove the fritters from the skillet and put on a serving plate. Cover with aluminum foil and keep warm until ready to serve with a drizzle of honey.

Traditional Nalysnyky Cake with Meringue

Tradytsiyinyi tort z nalysnykiv ta pinoyu iz zbytykh bilkiv

Makes 6 to 8 servings

This easy-to-make dessert with its distinctive meringue topping has great rustic charm—it is just as you might find it in a quaint Ukrainian farmhouse. Sometimes fresh fruit is added to the recipe. Let the season, quality, and sense of color be your guide. Fruits that are ripe in the same season are usually good together.

2 cups cottage cheese

2 extra-large egg yolks

¼ cup honey

½ teaspoon freshly grated nutmeg

¼ teaspoon salt

1 batch *nalysnyky* batter (Ukrainian Crepes, page 206)

2 cups fresh fruit or berries (optional)

4 extra-large egg whites

6 tablespoons granulated sugar

Preheat the oven to 325°F. Grease a 6x9-inch rectangular casserole dish with butter and set aside.

Put the cottage cheese in a large bowl and puree with a hand blender. Add the egg yolks, honey, nutmeg, and salt and mix well.

Brush the inside of an 8-inch crepe pan or small skillet with some melted butter. Set the pan over medium-high heat. When a drop of water sizzles and sputters when flicked into the pan, lift the pan from the heat and pour about 2 to 3 tablespoons of *nalysnyky* batter into it, tipping the pan as you pour it in so that the batter runs all over the bottom. Return to the heat and when the top is set (about 15 to 30 seconds), remove the crepe to a flat surface. Spread about 2 teaspoons of cheese filling (and some fresh fruit if desired) over the crepe; roll up like a jelly roll and place in the casserole dish. Repeat with the rest of the batter and filling, placing the rolled crepes side-by-side in two layers in the pan and keeping them warm under a kitchen towel.

Once the crepes are all made, in a large bowl, beat the egg whites until fluffy, gradually adding the sugar until the mixture is stiff and glossy. Pile the meringue lightly over the rolled crepes, spreading it completely to the edges of the dish. Bake the "cake" for 20 minutes or until the meringue is lightly browned. Serve immediately.

Honey Cake

Medivnyk

M*edivnyk* is a honey cake that is truly a symbol of the Ukrainian household. Traditionally honey cake is baked at Christmastime, its flavor bold enough to team with any of winter's dishes and stews. Try to give yourself some time before serving this cake, as its flavor improves with age. It's flavors are best 3 or 4 days after it is made but if pressed for time definitely give it at least 24 hours.

I have experimented with this recipe for years, studding it with raisins, almonds, ground cloves, fennel seeds, and even fragrant tangerine zest—and while all of my remodeled recipes were delicious, I think this humble version is still the best.

- ½ cup packed light brown sugar
- 8 tablespoons (1 stick) unsalted butter, softened
- 1 cup buckwheat or clover honey, slightly warmed
- 5 extra-large eggs, beaten
- 2 teaspoons baking soda
- 1 cup sour cream
- 2 cups unbleached all-purpose flour
- 1 cup crushed walnuts

Preheat the oven to 350°F. Grease and flour a 9x12-inch rectangular pan.

In a large mixing bowl, cream together the brown sugar and butter until well blended, about 5 minutes. Beat in the warm honey. Add the eggs and beat well. In a small bowl, mix the baking soda into the sour cream. Add the sour cream to the batter in 3 parts, alternating with the flour, and beat well. Stir in the walnuts.

Pour the batter into the prepared pan and bake 1 hour or until a toothpick inserted into the middle of the cake comes out clean. Let the cake cool in the pan for about 10 minutes, then remove and place on a wire rack. Let the cake cool completely before wrapping in plastic wrap and refrigerating. Wait at least 24 hours before cutting.

Chocolate Sponge Cake with Blueberries

Shokoliadovyi pukhkyi tort z chornytsiamy

Makes one 8-inch cake

This delicious sponge cake is served on birthdays in Ukraine. Sour cherries, blackberries, raspberries, strawberries, nectarines, or peaches are all delicious substitutes for the blueberries. Cognac or brandy are the traditional accompaniments, but if it is not to your liking, experiment with other flavors such as: anisette, kirsch (cherry), framboise (raspberry), Poire William (pear), or fraise (strawberry)—and if serving children or those who do not imbibe, eliminate the liqueur completely. Please note that this recipe needs to be started two days before serving, so plan accordingly.

Two days before baking, prepare the filling:

Put the blueberries in a large glass bowl. Pour the cognac over them and press down with a large spoon. Pour the granulated sugar over top (do not stir), cover, and refrigerate the berries for 2 days. Do not stir the mixture during this time.

Make the cake:

Preheat the oven to 325°F. Grease 2 shallow 8-inch cake pans and line with greased wax paper. Sift the flour with the baking powder and salt into a medium mixing bowl. Add the cocoa powder, brown sugar, butter, and eggs. Beat everything together until the batter is smooth and glossy, about 2 to 3 minutes. Spoon the batter into the cake pans. Bake, without opening the oven door, for 30 minutes. Test for doneness by a light touch to the center of each cake. If the cake springs back, it is done. Leave the cakes to cool in the pans for about 2 minutes and then turn them out onto a wire rack. Pull off the waxed paper and leave to cool completely.

FILLING:
2 pounds fresh blueberries

¼ cup cognac

2 cups granulated sugar

CHOCOLATE SPONGE CAKE:
1¼ cups unbleached all-purpose flour

1½ teaspoons baking powder

½ teaspoon salt

3 tablespoons unsweetened cocoa powder

1¼ cups lightly packed brown sugar

1 cup (2 sticks) unsalted butter, softened

3 extra-large eggs

TOPPING:
3 tablespoons confectioners' sugar

1 cup sour cream

Grated dark chocolate and confectioners' sugar for dusting

Assemble cake:

When ready to assemble the cake, beat the 3 tablespoons of confectioners' sugar into the sour cream. Remove the blueberries from the refrigerator, uncover, and stir. Put the first layer of sponge cake on a shallow dish with sides, spread with half of the sweetened sour cream, then top with half of the blueberries. Put the second layer of cake on top and gently press together with your hand. Spread the remaining sour cream on top of the cake, and then top with the remaining blueberries. (It is perfectly acceptable for some of the blueberries to fall off to the side). Sprinkle the cake with grated dark chocolate and a healthy sprinkling of confectioners' sugar and serve. This cake is best the day it is baked and assembled.

NOTE: *If using raspberries, blackberries, or mulberries, or berries containing a lot of seeds, sieving will be necessary after maceration. Do this just before assembling the cake. Simply put the macerated berries in a mesh strainer with a bowl underneath and press the berry mixture through with the back of a large spoon. The pulp and juices will be in the bowl and ready to use, while the seeds will be left behind in the strainer.*

Meringue Pineapple Cheesecake

Syrnyk z ananasom ta pinoyu iz zbytykh bilkiv

Makes 8 servings

Cheesecake is a traditional Easter dessert and variations abound in Ukraine. This is my more contemporary cheesecake recipe. It is crust-less, flavored with crushed pineapple, and topped with meringue.

Preheat the oven to 300°F. Generously butter a 6x9-inch ceramic or glass baking dish and sprinkle with breadcrumbs.

Put the 6 egg yolks into a large mixing bowl and beat with an electric mixer until light in color, about 5 minutes. Add the sugar and continue beating about 2 more minutes on medium speed. Reduce the speed to low and beat in the salt, lemon juice, and lemon zest. Add the cheese, a little at a time, and continue beating until well combined. Stir in the flour and pineapple, including the syrup.

In another large mixing bowl, beat the 6 egg whites until stiff and then fold into the cheese mixture. Gently spoon the cheese mixture into the prepared pan. Bake for 1¼ hours. Turn off the oven and let the cheesecake cool in the pan, in the oven, with the door all the way open, for 1 hour.

Remove the cooled cheesecake from the oven. Reheat the oven to 350°F.

Prepare the meringue: Beat 3 egg whites with ¼ teaspoon salt in a large bowl until frothy. Add the sugar 1 tablespoon at a time and beat continually until the meringue is stiff and glossy. Add the vanilla extract and beat just enough to blend.

Pile the meringue on top of the cheesecake and spread all the way to the edges of the pan. Bake about 15 minutes or until the meringue is lightly browned. Remove from oven and let the cheesecake cool completely. Once it is cool, refrigerate overnight. Serve the cheesecake directly from the pan.

2 tablespoons fine dry breadcrumbs

6 extra-large eggs, separated

⅔ cup granulated sugar

¼ teaspoon salt

2 tablespoons fresh lemon juice

2 tablespoons freshly grated lemon zest

2 pounds farmer's cheese

3 tablespoons unbleached all-purpose flour

1 cup sweetened crushed pineapple with syrup

MERINGUE:

3 extra-large egg whites

¼ teaspoon salt

6 tablespoons granulated sugar

½ teaspoon vanilla extract

....

NOTE: *This pineapple cheesecake can be made without meringue. Just make sure the cake is completely cooled and refrigerated overnight before serving directly from the pan.*

Kyiv-Style Cheese Paska

Kyivs'ka syrna paska

Makes 8 to 10 servings

This is a celestial spread of creamy cheeses, dried fruits, and toasted nuts. It is an Easter breakfast tradition in many Ukrainian homes and also a popular Easter dessert. Cheese *paska* is especially savored to mark the end of the long Lenten fast when all meat, eggs, and dairy are forbidden to devout Orthodox believers. To me, it is the perfect gilding for a thick slice of Babka (page 178) or Easter Paska Bread (page 180). Some old country recipes are cooked and others are not. My version of cheese paska requires no cooking.

A special pyramid-shaped, perforated wooden mold called a pasochnytsia, lined with muslin, is often used to mold this spread and leaves an imprint of a cross on the surface of the cheese paska along with other decorations. It is the traditional way of presentation in the more Russian-leaning central and eastern regions of the country. If you do not have a pasochnytsia, an actual clay flower pot can be used to form the dessert's characteristic shape. Wash the flower pot in boiling water that has been flavored with vanilla extract. Also, dampen the cheesecloth that is used to line the flower pot with the vanilla-flavored water.

- 1 pound farmer's cheese
- 1 pound cream cheese
- 6 hard-cooked extra-large egg yolks
- ⅔ cup confectioners' sugar
- 3 tablespoons heavy cream
- 2 teaspoons vanilla extract
- 1 cup dried fruit (chopped apricots, raisins, cherries, etc.)
- ½ cup toasted blanched almonds
- ½ cup toasted walnuts
- A few sheets cheesecloth and a small weight or can
- A clay flower pot or pyramid-shaped mold

In a medium bowl, mix together the farmer's cheese and cream cheese. Add the egg yolks, sugar, heavy cream, and vanilla extract and mix thoroughly until smooth and creamy. Add about two-thirds of the dried fruit and about two-thirds of the toasted nuts to the cheese mixture, mixing well.

To prepare the mold: line the flower pot with dampened cheesecloth and fill with the cheese mixture, covering the top with any extra cheesecloth. Place a weight or can on top of the mixture and put the mold on a small rack with a bowl underneath to catch any draining liquid. Chill the mold for several hours or overnight in the refrigerator.

To serve, unmold your cheese paska and carefully remove the cheesecloth. Position it in the middle of a plate and decorate the outside with the remaining dried fruits and nuts. Delicious!

"*Paska*" is a rich, sweet type of cheesecake/pudding, traditionally made at Easter in Russia to celebrate the end of Lent ("*Paska*" means "Easter" in Russian). This is often confused with the Ukrainian word "*paska*" which refers to a very rich and special Paska Bread (page 180).

Tort Teodoziyi iz chornoslyvu

Makes about 8 servings

In Ukrainian cookery, a torte is usually a fancy cake often composed of anywhere from two to five layers, filled with a rich, satiny filling. If it is a "layered" torte, the end result is much more compact and flatter than the more contemporary versions baked in the United States, which are fluffier and lighter. Ukrainian tortes can use ground nuts or breadcrumbs in place of some of the flour which acts as a thickening agent and when combined with several eggs makes for a heavenly treat!

This is an exceedingly good torte featuring prunes. Prunes have always been, and still are, a popular ingredient in baking in Ukraine. It is a very old family recipe and the perfect accompaniment to an afternoon cup of tea. In the past, tortes were often named after the family member responsible for the creation—this one is my Baba's recipe.

½ pound (2 sticks) unsalted butter, softened

⅔ cup confectioners' sugar

2 extra-large eggs

¼ teaspoon salt

½ cup ground walnuts

½ cup ground almonds

2 cups unbleached all-purpose flour

1 pound stewed pitted prunes, pureed with about 3 tablespoons poaching water

½ cup tightly packed brown sugar

1 teaspoon vanilla extract

2 tablespoons brandy or dark rum

Additional confectioners' sugar for serving

Preheat the oven to 350°F. Grease and lightly dust with flour, five 8-inch round cake pans.

Cream the butter and confectioners' sugar together in a large mixing bowl for about 5 minutes. Add the eggs, one at a time, beating after each addition. Stir in the salt and ground nuts.

Gradually add the flour, mixing thoroughly (the result is somewhat thicker than you may expect). Divide the dough into 5 pieces and pat each piece gently and evenly into each of the 5 pans. Bake the cakes about 15 to 20 minutes, until lightly browned. Remove cakes from the pans while still warm and place on a towel-covered wire rack.

Meanwhile prepare the prune filling: Put the pureed prune mixture in a medium saucepan along with the brown sugar, vanilla extract, and brandy. Place the pan over medium heat and when the mixture is just at the boiling point, remove the pan from the stove and begin to assemble the torte while it is still warm.

Start by placing one cake layer on a cake stand or platter. Spread with some of the prune filling and continue this layering, ending with a layer of cake. Cool the torte completely and then cover. Let the torte rest for at least 24 hours for all the flavors to marry. Dust with some confectioners' sugar before slicing.

Chocolate Cherry Almond Torte

Myhdalevyi tort mokka iz vyshniamy   Makes about 8 servings

This is another way of preparing a temptingly decadent torte. It is common practice to frost some creations.

Preheat the oven to 375°F. Butter a 9-inch springform pan.

Put the cherries in a large mixing bowl. Add the buttermilk, 1 cup of granulated sugar, the eggs, and vanilla extract and mix well. Sift the flour, baking soda, and salt into a small bowl. Add the dry ingredients to the cherry mixture, along with the ground almonds and beat well. Pour the batter into the springform pan and bake 35 minutes or until a toothpick inserted into the middle of the torte comes out clean.

When the torte is nearly baked, prepare the syrup by mixing the remaining 3 tablespoons of granulated sugar with 3 tablespoons of water and the sherry in a small bowl. Pour into a small saucepan and heat gently over medium heat until barely boiling.

After removing the torte from the oven, pierce the top several times with a thin skewer and drizzle the hot syrup slowly over the hot torte. Let the torte cool completely before removing the sides of the pan.

Prepare the Chocolate Frosting: Beat the butter and salt in a medium mixing bowl until creamy. Sift in the confectioners' sugar and beat until light in color, adding 1 to 2 tablespoons of water to loosen the mixture somewhat. Beat the melted chocolate into the mixture.

Ice the entire cooled torte with the chocolate frosting. Sprinkle the top and sides of the torte with some crushed almonds, give the torte a light dusting of confectioners' sugar, and serve.

1 cup pitted sour cherries, well-drained and finely chopped

1 cup buttermilk

1 cup plus 3 tablespoons granulated sugar

2 extra-large eggs, beaten

2 teaspoons vanilla extract

2 cups unbleached all-purpose flour

1½ teaspoons baking soda

¼ teaspoon salt

½ cup ground blanched almonds

⅓ cup dry sherry

Additional ground almonds, confectioners' sugar, and a few stemmed cherries to garnish

CHOCOLATE FROSTING:

4 tablespoons unsalted butter, softened

Pinch of salt

1⅓ cups confectioners' sugar

2 ounces semisweet dark chocolate, melted

....

NOTE: *Jarred or canned cherries can also be used if fresh cherries are not available or in season. In such an instance, adjust the amount of sugar to taste in the cake recipe as bottled or canned varieties of cherries vary in sweetness.*

Perekladanets

My version of *perekladanets* is a layered bread pastry (versus the traditional yeast-raised sweet dough) filled with dried fruits, nuts, and sugar. It is thought of as a festive type of dessert and is traditionally served at Easter celebrations. *Perekladanets* is often referred to as a "coffee cake" because it is usually served with coffee or tea. Any type of dried fruits and nuts will do, so use what you like.

This recipe will take the better part of a day to prepare and the pastry should sit for at least 12 to 24 hours before cutting. It requires three risings and the dough during these times takes longer to rise than most bread-type pastries. Be patient, it is well worth the effort.

½ cup warm water (about 110°F)

2½ teaspoons active dry yeast

¼ cup plus 1 tablespoon granulated sugar

½ cup warm milk (about 110°F)

3 cups unbleached all-purpose flour

2 extra-large eggs

3 extra-large egg yolks

1 teaspoon salt

4 tablespoons unsalted butter, melted

2 tablespoons freshly grated lemon zest

1 teaspoon vanilla extract

2 tablespoons fine dry breadcrumbs

½ cup chopped dried cherries, softened in warm water and drained

½ cup dried apricots, softened in warm water and drained

1 cup finely chopped walnuts

½ cup lightly packed brown sugar

Pour the warm water into a medium glass mixing bowl, stir in the yeast and 1 tablespoon granulated sugar. Mix well and then let the mixture sit until frothy, about 10 minutes. Whisk in the warm milk and add ½ cup flour. Cover the bowl with plastic wrap and let stand in a warm, draft-free place until doubled in volume and the sponge is light and bubbly, about 1 hour.

Break the 2 whole eggs into a large mixing bowl and beat in the 3 egg yolks. Add the remaining ¼ cup granulated sugar, the salt, melted butter, lemon zest, and ½ teaspoon vanilla extract and beat well. Add the yeast mixture and remaining 2½ cups flour and mix vigorously by hand for 10 minutes or for about 5 minutes with an electric mixer on medium-low speed. The dough will be very soft.

Cover the bowl with a kitchen towel and let the dough rise in a warm, draft-free place until doubled in volume, about 1½ hours. Punch down the dough, cover, and let rise again for another 1½ hours.

Meanwhile, liberally grease a 10-inch tube pan with butter and sprinkle with breadcrumbs. Put the softened cherries and apricots and the walnuts in a small bowl, add the remaining ½ teaspoon vanilla extract and the brown sugar.

Pat half the dough into the prepared pan and sprinkle with half of the fruit mixture. Cover with the remaining dough and top with the remaining fruit mixture. Cover the pan with a kitchen towel and let rise in a warm, draft-free place until doubled in volume, about 1½ hours.

Preheat the oven to 375°F. Bake the *perekladanets* for 10 minutes, then reduce the heat to 325°F and continue baking another 35 to 40 minutes. Check part of the way through the baking and cover with a sheet of aluminum foil if necessary to prevent scorching.

Let the pastry cool in the pan for about 15 minutes and then turn it out very gently onto a few layers of soft kitchen towels. Once it is cool, wrap in plastic wrap and let the pastry sit overnight before cutting.

Cherry Cheese Zavyvanets

*Z*avyvanets is yet another type of bread pastry filled with various nuts and fruits, or sometimes with a sweet cheese filling. *Zavyvanets* may be shaped as a long roll (similar to a strudel pastry), a braid, or coiled and baked in a pan.

This recipe for *zavyvanets* is coiled and baked in a pan. It is topped with a delicious mixture of sweetened cheese, cherries, and walnuts.

2 to 3 tablespoons fine dry bread crumbs

1 batch Basic Sweet Dough (page 182)

2 extra-large eggs

½ cup granulated sugar

2 teaspoons vanilla extract

½ teaspoon salt

12 ounces dry cottage cheese

½ cup chopped dried cherries, softened in warm water and drained

½ cup crushed walnuts

Egg wash: 1 egg beaten with 2 tablespoons water

Grease a 9-inch springform pan with butter and sprinkle with the dry breadcrumbs.

Turn the dough out onto a lightly floured board or counter and shape into a long, thin rope. Place the dough rope in the prepared pan, winding the rope in a circular coil beginning at the center of the pan out towards the edges, making sure the last part of the dough touches the sides of the pan.

Make the topping: Break the eggs into a large bowl and beat vigorously until light in color, about 5 minutes. Gradually add the granulated sugar and keep beating until the mixture is pale in color, about 4 minutes. Beat in the vanilla extract and salt. Stir in the cheese and cherries and spread the mixture over top of the dough. Sprinkle the top with crushed walnuts. Lightly cover the pan with a kitchen towel. Let the dough rise in a warm, draft-free place until doubled in size, about 1 hour.

Preheat the oven to 375°F. Brush the top of the pastry with the egg wash. Place in the oven and bake for 10 minutes; then reduce the heat to 350°F and continue baking another 30 minutes or until nicely browned. Check part of the way through the baking and cover the pan with a sheet of aluminum foil if necessary to prevent scorching. Let the *zavyvanets* cool completely before removing the sides of the pan.

NOTE: *Dry cottage cheese is available at most markets. Do not substitute ricotta cheese.*

Christmas Poppy Seed Roll

Makivnyk

Makes about 10 servings

Makivnyk is the specific name given to a *zavyvanets* with a spiral poppy seed filling traditionally served at Christmastime. The poppy seeds have a gritty texture, but when combined with the crushed walnuts, the result is a nice and moist filling.

1 batch Basic Sweet Dough (page 182)

1 cup poppy seeds

2 tablespoons unsalted butter

¼ cup honey

2 tablespoons freshly grated lemon or orange zest

1 tablespoon brandy or dark rum

½ cup finely chopped walnuts

1 extra-large egg yolk

¼ cup lightly packed brown sugar

Egg wash: 1 egg beaten with 2 tablespoons water

Grease a large baking sheet with butter and set aside. Turn the dough out onto a lightly floured board or counter, and with a floured rolling pin, roll it out into a narrow rectangle about 12x6 inches and about ¼-inch in thickness. Cover with a kitchen towel while making the poppy seed filling.

Grind all but 2 tablespoons poppy seeds in a food processor or grinder. Melt the butter in a medium saucepan over medium heat and add the ground poppy seeds, honey, lemon zest, and brandy and cook for 5 minutes. Take the pan off the stove and cool the mixture for about 10 minutes. Stir in the walnuts. Whisk the egg yolk and brown sugar together in a small bowl and then fold into the poppy seed mixture.

Spread the poppy seed mixture on the dough to within 1 inch of the edges. Roll both long ends towards the middle like a jelly roll, ending up with two rolls next to one another. Gently turn the roll over and place on the baking sheet. Cover with a kitchen towel and let rise in a warm, draft-free place until doubled in volume, about 1 hour.

Preheat the oven to 375°F. Brush the top of the roll with the egg wash. Sprinkle with the reserved 2 tablespoons poppy seeds. Put the roll into the oven and bake for 10 minutes; then reduce the heat to 350°F and continue baking 30 minutes longer or until nicely browned. Check part of the way through the baking and cover with a sheet of aluminum foil if necessary to prevent scorching.

Let the *makivnyk* cool for about 15 minutes before placing it gently on a few soft kitchen towels to cool completely before slicing.

Crescent Cookies

Rohalyky

Makes about 2½ dozen

These crescent cookies are usually served during Christmas and Easter.

1 batch Basic Sweet Dough (page 182), made with just 3 cups flour

1 cup ground blanched almonds or hazelnuts

⅓ cup granulated sugar

Lightly grease a large baking sheet with butter. Mix the almonds and sugar together in a small bowl.

Pinch off small amounts of dough and toss lightly in the almond mixture. Shape each piece of dough into a small ball the size of a walnut and shape into a crescent. Place the crescents on the baking sheet, cover lightly with a kitchen towel and let rise in a warm, draft-free place for about 1 hour.

Preheat the oven to 350°F. Bake the crescents about 20 to 30 minutes or until lightly browned. Remove to a wire rack and let cool.

Hazelnut Zavyvanets

This *zavyvanets* recipe features ground hazelnuts which are used extensively in baking throughout Ukraine and rate very high in preference. I usually braid the dough, but feel free to manipulate the dough whichever way you see fit.

2 tablespoons unsalted butter, softened

½ cup plus 2 tablespoons granulated sugar

1 cup plus 2 tablespoons blanched crushed hazelnuts

1 tablespoon brandy or dark rum

1 batch Basic Sweet Dough (page 182)

Egg wash: 1 egg beaten with 2 tablespoons water

Cream the butter and ½ cup sugar together in a medium bowl until light and fluffy, about 5 minutes. Add 1 cup crushed hazelnuts and the brandy and mix well.

Turn the dough out onto a lightly floured board or counter and divide into 3 pieces. Using a floured rolling pin, roll out each piece into about a 3x12-inch rectangle. Spread one-third of the hazelnut mixture on 1 rectangle and roll up like a jelly roll (starting on the long side so the roll is about 12 inches long). Repeat this procedure with the other 2 pieces of dough. Now braid the 3 filled rolls together, starting at the middle; then turn the braid around and finish braiding the other side. Pinch the ends together and turn them underneath the braid.

Grease a baking sheet with butter and gently place the braid on top. Cover with a kitchen towel and let rise in a warm, draft-free place until doubled in volume, about 1 hour.

Preheat the oven to 375°F. Brush the top of the dough with the egg wash. Sprinkle with the remaining 2 tablespoons sugar and 2 tablespoons crushed hazelnuts and place in the oven. Bake for 10 minutes; then reduce the heat to 350°F and continue baking another 30 minutes or until nicely browned. Check part of the way through the baking and cover with a sheet of aluminum foil if necessary to prevent scorching.

Let the *zavyvanets* cool for about 15 minutes before placing it gently on a few layers of soft kitchen towels to cool completely before slicing.

Honey Cookies

Medivnychky

Medivnychky are a distinguished type of honey cookie from days gone by when sugar was not yet known. Bee culture was extensive in Ukraine (and remains so today) and as a result honey played a major role in the preparation of cakes, cookies, and other pastries that have since become traditional treats at Christmastime and New Year's.

This is a very old recipe and yet it is still popular today. It contains no milk, eggs, or fat and the result are cookies much like ginger snaps. Buckwheat honey is preferred because of its deep, rich color and aromatic flavor, but wildflower honey can also be used. As with all honey cookies and cakes, allow a few days for the flavors to develop. These cookies will keep indefinitely in an air tight container or cookie tin.

2 cups buckwheat honey

1 cup soft rye flour

2 cups unbleached all-purpose white flour

2 teaspoons baking soda

Grated zest of 1 lemon

1½ tablespoons brandy

½ teaspoon ground cinnamon

½ teaspoon ground cloves

¼ teaspoon salt

Grease a large mixing bowl and a large baking sheet with butter and set aside. Preheat the oven to 325°F. Pour the honey into a heavy saucepan and bring to barely a boil over medium heat. Reduce the heat to low to keep the honey hot.

Put the rye flour and white flour in a large skillet. Gently toast the flours over medium heat, stirring constantly, just until hot—do not scorch the flour! Add the baking soda to the flour while stirring, then remove the skillet from the heat and set aside.

Quickly stir the lemon zest, brandy, cinnamon, cloves, and salt into the hot honey and immediately stir this mixture into the flour mixture in the skillet. Beat vigorously until thick and then put the dough into the large greased bowl.

Pinch small pieces of dough and roll into balls about the size of walnuts. Place them well apart on the greased baking sheet. Flatten the balls slightly with the back of a teaspoon.

Bake about 10 to 15 minutes or just until the cookies are golden but not brown—not even around the edges (for even a small amount of browning will impart a burnt flavor). Immediately remove the cookies from the oven and place on a wire rack to cool. Even after these cookies are completely cooled, they still need time to develop that "snap." Just pack them into an airtight container and wait 2 or 3 days before eating them.

Syrky

These distinctively Ukrainian chocolate cheese-covered confections are usually stuffed with jam or nuts and are sold in the dairy departments of most Ukrainian grocery shops. This is my adapted version featuring dried fruit and nuts.

1 cup 4% milk-fat cottage cheese

2 tablespoons honey

2 teaspoons heavy cream

1 tablespoon freshly grated lemon zest

1 tablespoon freshly grated orange zest

¼ cup finely chopped dried fruit (any combination), softened in warm water, drained, and blotted dry

¼ cup toasted nuts (any combinations), finely chopped

3½ ounces bittersweet dark chocolate (70% cacao)

In a food processor or blender, combine the cheese, honey, and heavy cream until smooth. Transfer the mixture to a small bowl and stir in the lemon and orange zest. Cover the bowl and place in the freezer for 30 minutes.

Put some water in a small bowl with some ice. Wet your fingers in the ice water and form the cheese mixture into 2-inch balls. Stuff each ball with a bit of fruit and nuts and roll in the palms of your hands until ball-shaped once more. Put all the cheese balls on a waxed paper-lined plate and put back into the freezer for another 30 minutes to firm up.

Carefully melt the chocolate in a heavy saucepan or double boiler over low heat. Remove the pan from the heat and let cool slightly. Retrieve the cheese balls from the freezer. Dip one into the melted chocolate using a thin skewer and covering it completely, and then put back onto the waxed paper-lined plate. Remove the skewer and dab a bit of melted chocolate over the hole. Repeat the process with the remaining cheese balls. Refrigerate until the chocolate is set. Heavenly!

Khrustyky

Also known as *verhuny*, these pieces of twisted fried dough are a personal favorite of mine and my husband, Kevin. Coated with honey or a generous sprinkling of confectioners' sugar, *khrustyky* are just delicious with a big glass of cold milk. Purists would insist on using pig lard for deep-frying them, but sunflower oil works just as well.

3 extra-large egg yolks

2 extra-large eggs

1 tablespoon brandy

½ teaspoon salt

2 tablespoons granulated sugar

1 tablespoon canned evaporated milk or cream

1½ cups unbleached all-purpose flour

About 3 cups lard or sunflower oil for deep-frying

Confectioners' sugar for dusting

In a large bowl, beat together the egg yolks, eggs, brandy, salt, granulated sugar, and milk. Gradually add the flour and knead into a soft dough. Divide the dough into two equal halves, cover with a large kitchen towel and let rest for 15 minutes.

On a lightly floured board or counter, roll out half the dough to a thickness of ⅛ inch. Cut the dough into strips about 2-inches wide and 6-inches long. In the middle of each strip, make a slit and pull one end of the strip through the slit to form a twisted, bow-tie shape. Repeat the process with the remaining dough.

Heat the oil in a deep fryer or heavy pot to 360°F. Fry a few *khrustyky* at a time in the hot oil until golden brown, about 3 to 5 minutes. Drain them on a wire rack and let cool. When all the cookies are fried and cooled, generously sprinkle them with confectioners' sugar and serve.

NOTE: *Adding a dash of brandy, vodka, or rum to the dough helps to lessen the soaking up of fat when frying.*

Nut Bars

Horikhivnyk

Makes about 2 dozen

Horikhivnyk is the specific name given to "nut bars" in Ukraine. But everyone seems to have their favorite recipe. I think of mine as a more contemporary version, but I will let readers be the judge. The thin and crumbly crust is made with both butter and lard, which is typically "old country" and nowadays I opt for turbinado sugar (see sidebar) rather than the usual white sugar because it gives the bars a deeper flavor and a signature crunchy top.

4 tablespoons unsalted butter

4 tablespoons lard

¾ cup turbinado sugar

¼ teaspoon salt

2 extra-large eggs

1⅓ cups unbleached all-purpose flour

1 cup crushed blanched hazelnuts

Preheat the oven to 375°F. Generously grease a 9x12-inch (jelly roll) baking pan with butter and set aside.

In a large mixing bowl, cream the butter with the lard, ½ cup of turbinado sugar, and the salt. Beat in 1 egg. Add the flour and mix just enough to hold the dough together. Press the dough evenly into the baking pan.

Beat the remaining egg and brush over the top of the dough. Sprinkle with hazelnuts and the remaining ¼ cup turbinado sugar. Bake for about 35 minutes or until nicely browned. While still warm, cut into 2-inch square pieces, and serve. Store any leftovers in an airtight container.

What is "turbinado sugar"?

Sometimes called "raw sugar," turbinado sugar is a long-grained sugar that is not as heavily processed or bleached as white sugar. When heated, it gives your baked products a nice, mellow, sugarcane flavor, and when sprinkled on top, gives a nice pleasing crunch. As recently as a few years ago, turbinado sugar was not used in Ukraine. It is available now, but used almost exclusively in bakeries and restaurants.

Easter Fruit and Nut Bars

Velykodnyi horokhivnyk

There are traditional pastries baked for special holy days throughout much of Ukraine. Dried fruit and nut pastries are examples of Easter delicacies and most families have their own favorite recipes, many of which have been passed down from generation to generation. I happen to love the combination of currants and walnuts, but use what you like.

4 tablespoons unsalted butter

4 tablespoons lard

¾ cup turbinado sugar

¼ teaspoon salt

3 extra-large eggs

1⅓ cups unbleached all-purpose flour

⅔ cup black currants

1 cup crushed walnuts

1 tablespoon fresh lemon juice

1 tablespoon freshly grated lemon zest

Preheat the oven to 375°F. Generously grease a 9x12-inch baking (jelly roll) pan with butter and set aside.

In a large mixing bowl, cream the butter with the lard, ½ cup of turbinado sugar, and the salt. Beat in 1 egg. Add the flour and mix just enough to hold the dough together. Press the dough evenly into the baking pan and bake for 10 minutes.

Meanwhile, prepare the filling: Put the currants and walnuts in a small bowl. Mix in the lemon juice and lemon zest. In a large mixing bowl, cream the remaining 2 eggs with the remaining ¼ cup turbinado sugar until light and fluffy, about 5 minutes. Stir in the fruit mixture.

Remove the partially baked pastry from the oven and spread the filling over top. Reduce the oven temperature to 325°F and continue baking another 30 to 40 minutes or until the filling is set. Remove and cool the pastry in the pan. Cut into small 2-inch bars and serve.

Chapter 11

Beverages and Libations

Unique concoctions ...

Hot tea is the number one social drink in Ukraine. Everyday life would just be unthinkable without it. If visiting, tea will be offered to you as soon as you walk in the door. Everyone will gather around the kitchen table and the ritual begins—a scene of endless conversations about anything and everything during which the tea kettle never rests.

Home tea is usually taken quite weak, accompanied by sugar cubes that you bite and mix with tea in your mouth. This is affectionately known as "tea-with-a-bite." Small bowls of homemade preserves will be on the table and whatever flavor you choose, it should be well-stirred into your cup of tea. Sometimes honey and thinly sliced lemon are added to tea, and while milk used to be a popular additive, very few flavor their tea in this way today.

Coffee is the preferred afternoon and after-dinner drink, served piping hot, dark, and sweet. And it is not uncommon to see a person stir a scoop of ice cream into their cup of coffee—a very popular drink in restaurants and ice cream parlors throughout Ukraine! Turkish coffee is also popular and served in homes, coffeehouses, and cafes, usually in regular coffee cups rather than demitasse.

Ukrainians are also partial to buttermilk, sour milk, fruit juices, and fruit syrups mixed with mineral water, and while Western-style soft drinks are gaining in popularity these days, *kvas* is still the number one national drink. *Kvas* is a lightly fermented, nonalcoholic beverage made from wheat, rye, beets, or fruit and sugar. Besides being made in the home, *kvas* is also sold throughout Ukraine in vending machines, at most corner groceries, and by the cupful from small wheeled tanks during the summer months. Beet *kvas* is usually used in the kitchen to flavor soups and in braising meats. For variety's sake, perfectly good *kvas* concentrate is available in most Ukrainian, Russian, or Jewish markets throughout North America if one chooses to try some.

Cognac, champagne, wines, and beer are drunk in Ukraine, but *horilka*, which is Ukrainian for vodka, in all sorts of flavors and varieties, distilled from grains and potatoes, is without a doubt the most popular libation. Vodkas spiked with fresh fruit, herbs, and spices are displayed in huge crocks and served room temperature—along with the fruit. Unlike other nationalities that drink their vodka chilled, Ukrainians prefer warm spirits and there is a ritual surrounding the proper way to drink vodka. It is never sipped. Vodka is downed in a three-ounce shot, followed immediately by something to eat. The term *zakusky* (page 1) takes on literal meaning here. Salty choices are preferable—pickles, olives, herring, or cured pork belly bacon with sliced garlic called *salo* are all good choices. There are also many brands of commercially produced *horilkas* available throughout the country, most touting great medicinal properties, from cold cure to aphrodisiac. If you have a chance, try some, for it promises to be an experience that is hard to describe and one you will not want to miss.

Ukrainians are earnest toastmasters and a get together is not a party without a series of toasts. If you are a guest, you will be expected to join in. Not to worry, if you want to retain your host's respect and not get drunk at the same time, or you simply do not drink, use the state of your health as an excuse. You will be completely understood and supported, but be prepared for much health and healing advice!

Fresh Fruit Compote

Kompot iz svizhykh ovochiv

Makes about 2 quarts

Fruit compotes are usually made in great quantities in Ukraine, using fresh fruit during summer months and dried fruits in the winter months (see page 218). Berries of all sorts, black and red currants, apples, tart or sweet plums, oranges, or even bits of melon are mixed together into a nonalcoholic "punch" of sorts. Fresh fruit compotes are always served in a tall glass with a long spoon—to scoop up all the fruit on the bottom at its conclusion. I have to admit, I like fresh fruit compote made with tart apples and sweet oranges the best. Experiment with several types of fruit though until you find the combination best for you.

2 large Granny Smith apples, peeled, cored, and cut into ½-inch cubes

2 cups fresh orange segments, chopped with juices

About ½ cup honey or more (or less) to taste

1 tablespoon grated lemon zest

Fresh lemon juice if desired

Pour 6 cups of water into a large saucepan. Bring to a boil over high heat. Reduce the heat to low and stir in the apples and oranges with their juices. Simmer for about 1 to 2 minutes, or just until the apples are slightly softened.

Remove the pan from the heat and stir in the honey and lemon zest. Taste and add more honey if desired and some fresh lemon juice if you prefer a more tart taste. Let cool, and then pour the compote into a glass-covered decorative pitcher. Refrigerate until ready to serve.

....

NOTE: *Fresh fruit compote can be spiked with a drizzle of your favorite flavored brandy or dark rum if serving to adults.*

Fresh Watermelon Lemonade

Limoniada iz kavunom

Makes about 1½ gallons

Citrus fruits thrive in the extreme southern climes of Ukraine, along with lush melons of all kinds. This is an especially good summer drink. Sometimes fresh peaches are used in place of watermelon.

7 lemons, washed in hot water

½ cup honey, or more (or less) to taste

8 cups fresh watermelon cubes (seeds removed) and juices

Peel 5 of the lemons with a small knife. Put the skins along with 4 cups of water into a large saucepan. Bring to a boil. Meanwhile, squeeze the peeled lemons to collect their juices. When the lemon mixture comes to a boil, remove the pan from the heat and stir in the lemon juice and honey. Let sit for 10 minutes. Strain and pour into a large punch bowl.

Puree the watermelon in a blender and stir into the lemonade. Taste and add more honey if desired. Refrigerate for several hours until well chilled.

Serve this drink in tall glasses poured over crushed ice. Chop the remaining 2 lemons into small pieces and garnish each glass with extra chopped lemon.

Raspberry Almond Drink

Malynovo myhdalevyi hapytok

This beverage is superior in taste and very nutritious. Serve this "nut milk" chilled in a glass, either as it is—thick and nutty—or strain and top with a dollop of whipped cream. Using a combination of cherries and walnuts in this recipe is also very good.

3 cups milk

1 cup fresh or bottled raspberry juice

1 tablespoon honey

1½ cups coarsely chopped blanched almonds, soaked overnight in warm water to soften and then drained

Whipped cream and a few fresh raspberries to serve (optional)

Put all ingredients in a blender (except the whipped cream and fresh berries). Blend until of desired consistency: the mixture can be thick and wholesome (use more nuts and less liquid), or thin and delicate (use more liquid than nuts).

Pour the mixture into a large saucepan and place over medium-low heat. Simmer gently, uncovered, for about 15 minutes for the flavors to develop. Remove the pan from the heat, cool, and then strain if a smooth drink is preferred (the leftover almond meal can be used in cake, cookie, and bread recipes or frozen for future use).

Pour the remaining "milk" into a covered container. Refrigerate for at least 12 hours or overnight. Serve by the cupful garnished with a dollop of whipped cream and a few fresh raspberries.

Hemp Seed Milk

Konopliane molochko

Makes about 1 quart

The cultivation, use, and consumption of hemp dates back hundreds of years in Ukraine. Hemp seeds were eaten raw, sprouted, made into tea, and ground into meal and used in baking. Hemp seed oil is mentioned again and again in ancient recipes. Hemp milk was made by grinding roasted hemp seeds into a fine powder and mixing with boiling water. It was drunk in times of fasting or when there was a shortage of regular milk. I definitely think hemp seed milk is an acquired taste though.

I have resurrected a recipe for hemp seed milk here since today the medicinal and culinary uses of hemp are enjoying a revival. Hemp seeds are one of the earth's best sources of highly digestible protein and their consumption is a great alternative if one is allergic to soy or dairy products.

2 cups hemp seeds

½ teaspoon salt

Pinch of freshly ground black pepper or more to taste

Put the seeds in a large skillet and place over medium-high heat. Toast until they start to pop and are crisp, shaking the pan continually, or use a spatula to mix the seeds evenly and to prevent scorching. Put the toasted seeds on a plate to cool.

Bring 4 cups of water to a boil in a medium saucepan. When cooled, grind the seeds to a fine powder and stir into the boiling water. Remove the pan from the stove and add the salt and some black pepper to taste. Hemp seed milk can be served warm or chilled by the glassful as is, or you can strain it before serving.

Hemp seeds as aphrodisiac ...

In traditional folk medicine in Ukraine, roasted and salted hemp seeds are thought to possess great medical application as an aphrodisiac. In earlier times, roasted hemp seeds were fed to the bridegroom during the wedding dinner, or added to special wedding bread, or added as an ingredient in the wedding nightcap.

Fresh-pressed Cranberry Juice

Svizhyi sik iz zhuravlyny

Makes slightly more than 2 quarts

Fresh-pressed fruit juice is a popular Ukrainian summer drink. Often sold from kiosks on the street,
lingonberry juice rates as the number one refresher on a
hot day, and by all means use lingonberries in this recipe
if you can find them. But if unavailable, fresh cranberries will work just fine. Fresh-pressed juice of any kind
is usually served over a small bit of crushed ice and occasionally is spiked with vodka if serving adults.

2 pounds fresh cranberries

½ cup honey or more to
taste

Pour 8 cups of water into a large saucepan and add the cranberries. Bring to a boil over
high heat, and then reduce the heat to low. Gently simmer the cranberries until they
start to pop, about 5 to 7 minutes.

Remove the pan from the heat and strain the liquid through a fine mesh strainer,
pressing the cranberries with the back of a spoon to extract all the juices.

Return the liquid to the rinsed-out pan and stir in the honey. Warm gently over low
heat for about 5 minutes. Taste and add more honey if desired. Remove the pan from the
stove, let cool, and pour into a pitcher. Chill and serve by the glassful.

Caraway Tea

Chai z kmynu

Makes 2 cups

A delicious tea served hot and sweet.

2 tablespoons caraway
seeds

Honey, sugar or fruit
preserves served on the
side

Bring 2 cups of water to a boil. Coarsely crush the caraway seeds in a mortar and pestle.
Stir into the boiling water. Cover and let steep for about 5 to 7 minutes. Strain and serve
sweetened to taste.

Ryazhanka

S our milk or "cultured" products are undoubtedly among the staples in the Ukrainian diet. *Ryazhanka* or "baked cultured milk" is appreciated not only for its beneficial health properties, but also for its lovely, delicate taste.

Traditionally, the milk itself is thermally processed overnight in a covered clay pot placed in a turned-off but still hot oven, where it is left to "bake" until morning. I am sure it is still done this way in smaller Ukrainian villages, however, one can make *ryazhanka* just as easily with a thermos or any insulated vessel.

2 quarts (8 cups) raw (unpasteurized) milk
¼ cup buttermilk

Pour the milk into a heavy saucepan and bring to a boil over medium heat, stirring constantly to prevent scorching. Reduce the heat to low and let the milk simmer for 30 minutes, stirring occasionally, until light beige in color. Remove the pan from the stove and let the milk cool to lukewarm (about 110°F).

Stir the buttermilk into the warm milk. Rinse out a lidded thermos or insulated coffee pot fitted with a tight lid with some boiling water. Pour in the milk mixture and seal shut. Let the thermos sit in a warm place for about 10 hours.

Pour the *ryazhanka* into a covered pitcher and chill in the refrigerator before serving.

....

NOTE: *Some people like to sweeten ryazhanka with honey or sugar just before serving.*

Huslyanka

Clabbered milk is milk that has been soured or thickened. *Huslyanka* is simply clabbered milk in drinkable form. I guarantee if you like those "drinkable yogurts" available here in the United States, you will love *huslyanka*! Ukrainians believe drinking *huslyanka* has many health benefits and it is enjoyed throughout the country. While traditionally served as a beverage, many enjoy it as an accompaniment to buckwheat or millet kasha or scooped over mashed potatoes.

I make *huslyanka* with fresh milk and equal parts buttermilk and sour cream. Some prefer a combination of just milk and sour cream. Both are quite good. Friends of mine like to serve their *huslyanka* over fresh fruit or mix it with fresh fruit purees. I do not know what purists would say about that, but I have tried it and it is fabulous!

1 quart pasteurized whole milk

½ cup sour cream

½ cup cultured buttermilk

Pour the milk into a crock or glass container fitted with a lid. Stir in the sour cream and buttermilk. Cover the crock with cheesecloth and secure with sting. Let the crock sit in a warm place for about 24 hours, until the mixture is thick and well-set.

Chill before serving and store covered in the refrigerator.

Chocolate Liqueur

Shokoliadovyi liker

Makes 4 to 6 servings

A rich and delicious libation such as this would be served after dinner. If one is uncomfortable with using raw egg yolks, pasteurized egg substitute can be used instead, however, the end result is not quite as rich and delicious as the original recipe.

5 extra-large egg yolks
¾ cup confectioners' sugar
½ cup chocolate syrup
1 cup good-quality vodka
¼ cup heavy cream

In a medium bowl, beat the egg yolks with the confectioners' sugar for about 5 minutes, until thick and creamy. Gently whisk in the chocolate syrup and vodka.

In another medium mixing bowl, whip the heavy cream until slightly thickened. Stir into the chocolate mixture. Serve immediately in small, stout glasses.

Peperivka

Peperivka

Makes 1 pint

S picing whiskey with fiery peppers to make *peperivka* is an age-old tradition in Ukraine. This is my family's recipe.

2 cups whiskey (rye whiskey preferred)
4 whole cayenne peppers

Pour the whiskey into a glass jar fitted with a tight lid. Prick the cayenne peppers all over with a thin skewer and submerge in the whiskey. Cover and let sit for at least 2 days before serving.

NOTE: *Use rubber gloves when handling hot peppers.*

Flavored Vodkas

Down the hatch ...

Vodka is an essential component of everyday life in Ukraine. Flavored varieties keep life interesting and provide a great way of bringing a delicious taste of Ukraine into your own home. Flavored vodkas are always displayed in pretty glass decanters and households generally offer two or three varieties at a time. Unlike Russians, Ukrainians drink their vodka room temperature—never chilled!

The following are my adaptations. They all make enough for about eight 3-ounce shots or sixteen 1½-ounce shots. Please make note that four to six hours is the limit for infusion—any longer will impart a bitter taste.

Orange-Flavored Vodka

Horilka z pomarancheyu
Pour all of the vodka into a glass pitcher and stir in the zest. Infuse at room temperature for 4 hours. Strain and pour into a decorative decanter to store and serve.

1 bottle (750 ml) Ukrainian vodka

Grated zest of 2 oranges

Coriander and Peppercorn-Flavored Vodka

Horilka iz koriandrom ta pertsem
Pour all of the vodka into a glass pitcher and stir in the coriander seeds and peppercorns. Infuse for 4 to 6 hours. Strain and pour into a decorative decanter to store and serve.

1 bottle (750ml) Ukrainian vodka

1 tablespoon coarsely crushed coriander seeds

2 teaspoons black peppercorns

Dried Cherry and Aniseed-Flavored Vodka

Horilka z vyshniamy ta hanusem
Pour all of the vodka into a glass pitcher and stir in the cherries and aniseed. Infuse for 4 hours. Strain and pour into a decorative decanter to store and serve.

1 bottle (750ml) Ukrainian vodka

3 ounces dried cherries, chopped

1 tablespoon coarsely crushed aniseed

Hot Mulled Plum Brandy

Nalyvka zi slyvok na-horiacho   Makes 4 to 6 servings

While this drink starts out as a hot mulled wine, cupfuls are made even more potable by lacing the brew with plum brandy. Ukrainians love brandies—plum brandy being a particular favorite.

1 bottle (750ml) dry red wine
½ cup honey
Freshly grated zest of 1 lemon
2 cinnamon sticks (each about 2-inches long)
10 whole cloves
1½ cups plum brandy
1 pear, cored and very thinly sliced

Put the wine, honey, lemon zest, cinnamon sticks, and cloves into a large saucepan. Bring to a simmer over medium heat and stir to dissolve the honey. Continue to simmer for 15 minutes. Strain the mixture and pour back into the rinsed-out saucepan. Keep warm over low heat.

Meanwhile, pour the plum brandy into a small saucepan and place over medium-low heat. When the brandy is hot to the touch (not boiling), add the pear slices.

Pour the warm brandy mixture into the wine mixture. Stir to combine and then remove the pan from the heat. Ladle the mulled brandy into warmed mugs and serve immediately.

Ukrainians love brandies, which they so quaintly say "makes a carnation bloom right in your stomach."

Holiday Specialties
of Easter and Christmas Eve

Ancient Traditions

The traditions that originated in pre-Christian times in Ukraine echoed the religious dogma, social structure, and agrarian way of life of its people.

So often helpless in the face of nature's power, "pre-Christian" religion evolved into various cults that worshipped natural phenomena such as the sun, moon, stars, fire, wind, and water. There were also animal cults and cults of trees and magical herbs. By the means of ritual-like dances, incantations, and special offerings, the ancient people thought they could appease and please nature.

The most important season of the year in an agrarian society is spring. Spring was greeted and celebrated when it arrived by the baking of special breads, the coloring of eggs (eggs standing for the renewal of life itself), and the decorating of *pysanky* (ritual symbolic batik-ornamented eggs, not to be eaten). As an example of the special breads, a sign of spring is the return of migrating birds, so to greet the flocks people baked dough birds. They were given to children, who ran through the fields tossing them in the air while singing traditional songs and prescribed sayings.

With the coming of Christianity, the Church merged several of these agrarian seasonal activities and spring holiday celebrations with Easter and so many of the pre-Christian rituals are now part of Ukrainian Eastertime celebrations.

Ukrainian Easter

Preparations for Ukrainian Easter start almost three weeks in advance and with the resurgence of religious practices, it is no wonder many people observe Lent and fast as Easter feasts often consist of some of the richest foods imaginable. It is as if people are trying to make up for all the good foods they abandoned during Lent!

Eggs seem to be the most important symbol of Easter in Ukraine and have made a significant contribution to the national folk heritage. The notable Ukrainian ritual of egg-painting goes back centuries and *pysanky* are deeply pre-Christian in origin and symbolism. Easter egg painting is still today the first concern of Easter preparations, and they are painted the Thursday before Good Friday so they can be taken to church for a blessing.

On Easter eve, many people attend church, which usually starts at about 11:30 p.m. and ends at 4 a.m. During the service, in the countryside especially, worshippers gather with their Easter baskets containing a sampling of foods they will eat on Easter day. Each basket also contains an unlit taper candle to mark the resurrection of Christ. From these tapers, all others are lit and soon the entire church is aglow. The priest will lead a procession out of the church and circle the building three times; finishing the ritual by blessing all the dishes and baskets of food that are arrayed inside and outside the church. Baskets are reclaimed by parishioners after the service is over and all hurry home to begin holiday festivities. The Lenten fast will be broken by the foods blessed by the priest.

On Easter day, as people gather, they exchange *pysanky* and kiss and greet each other exclaiming "Christ has risen!" After eating, there may even be an Easter egg fight with *krashanky* (colored hard-cooked eggs), where everyone tries to break the egg of the person next to them. Tradition dictates that the person whose egg remains intact will be the luckiest all year.

Preparing the Pride and Joy of the Family—The Easter Basket

Paska Bread—the traditional Easter bread, a small loaf will do (page 180)

White or beeswax candle—to be placed in the center of the *Paska* bread; it will be lit during the ceremony

Babka—a small plain or decorated loaf will do (page 178)

Pysanky—inedible batik-decorated Easter eggs (new ones are acquired every year)

Krashanky—dyed hard-cooked eggs; a variety of single-colored eggs is acceptable, however, one must be red which is the color that symbolizes the sun

Peeled, hard-cooked eggs

Salt—just a small amount is appropriate

Butter—softened butter is artfully shaped with one's hands and is placed in a small dish or presented in a mold. Some decorate the butter with whole cloves in the shape of a cross.

Cheese Paska—place a small amount of this "sweet cheese" on the plate next to the butter (page 231)

Horseradish—a piece of horseradish root is acceptable or a small dish of beet and horseradish relish (page 69)

Kovbasa—a piece or small ring of smoked Ukrainian sausage (page 124)

Ham—a wedge or small ham

The basket itself should be lined with a newly embroidered white runner and an embroidered "*servetka*" or runner should be used to cover the basket. Tie a few pussy willows to the handle of the basket (in pre-Christian times the willow tree was thought to have medicinal and magical powers). Periwinkle and a few fresh spring flowers may be added and make sure there is a red ribbon—to ward off evil! Remember, tradition dictates that the mistress of the house will be judged according to the way her Easter basket looks, how it is decorated, and what it contains.

A Typical Easter Breakfast Menu

Hard-cooked Eggs	Liver	Beet and Horseradish Relish
Roast Easter Ham or Smoked Ham	Leg of Lamb	Paska , Babka, and Cheesecake
	Cottage Cheese	
Smoked Sausages	Horseradish	Hot Tea and Coffee

Ukrainian Christmas Eve

The Ukrainians celebrate Christmas on January 7, the Eastern Rite Julian Calendar Christmas day. But I think most would agree the most important moment of the entire holiday would be *Sviata Vecheria* (The Holy Supper), which takes place on Christmas Eve and is preceded by a day of fasting. The meal consists of twelve meatless courses, each representing the annual lunar cycle of twelve months. Everyone present must have at least a bite of each course, including all of the family's animals, for they too participated in the miracle of Christmas.

The festivities begin with the appearance of the first star in the eastern sky on Christmas Eve. Children stroll along door to door singing *koliadky* (Christmas carols) wishing happiness and good health.

The holiday table is set and the first dish to break the fast is *kutia*, a ritual dish consisting of wheat berries, poppy seeds, and honey. After *kutia* some families pass around an offering of *prosfora* (small cubes of bread that have been blessed at church). The *kolach* (page 176) is strictly a centerpiece on Christmas Eve and is a tribute to good harvests. Next several fish courses appear, or perhaps even a whole salmon in aspic! A meatless *borshch* (red beet soup) is next, and then all the traditional favorites, such as: meatless *holubtsi* (stuffed cabbage rolls), meatless *varenyky* (stuffed dumplings), and perhaps sautéed mushrooms and sauerkraut. Ukrainians love their sweets, so several sweet courses will follow, such as: dried fruit compotes, *medivnyk* (honey cake), and *khrustyky* (sugared strips of fried dough). *Pampushky* (small pastries resembling doughnuts) will also be served, some filled with rose petal preserves and some served plain. Hot beverages like coffee and tea will conclude the meal, and even though the meal itself is very solemn, there is plenty of singing, celebration, and merry-making afterwards.

Index

(*var.* = variation)

ALMONDS

Chocolate Cherry Almond Torte (*Myhdalevyi tort mokka iz vyshniamy*), 233

Prune Torte Theodosia (*Tort Teodoziyi iz chornoslyvu*), 232

Raspberry Almond Drink (*Malynovo myhdalevyi hapytok*), 248

APPETIZERS (ZAKUSKY)

Beet Caviar ("*Ikra*" *z buriakiv*), 8

Bell Pepper Paprikash (*Paprykash z pertsiv*), 89

Braised Beef Tongue (*Tushkovanyi lyzen' z yalovychyny*), 130

Champignon Caviar ("*Ikra*" *z hrybiv*), 7

Country Pate (*Pashtet*), 16

Crimean Fish Cakes (*Kryms'ki sichenyky z ryby*), 22

Crimean Tatar Biber Dolmas (*Biber dolma po kryms'ko-tatars'ky*), 21

Duck in Aspic (*Kholodets' z kachky*), 10

Eggplant Caviar ("*Ikra*" *z baklazhana*), 6

Fish Salad Mimosa (*Salata z ryby Mimosa*), 64

Garden Vegetables in Lemon Aspic (*Horodyna v tsytrynovim kholodtsiu*), 11

Garnished Eggs (*Nachyniuvani yaitsia*), 3

Herring Roll Mops Stuffed with Pickles, Mushrooms, and Capers (*Zavyvani oseledtsi, nachyneni kvashenymy ohirkamy, hrybamy ta kaparamy*), 5

Jellied Pig's Feet (*Drahli*), 9

Marinated Mushrooms (*Marynovani hryby*), 18

Mushroom Patties (*Sichenyky z hryby*),19

Pickled Herring (*Marynovani oseledtsi*), 4

Pickled Herring with Sour Cream, 4 *var.*

Poached Chicken with Walnut Sauce (*Tushkovana kurka z horikhovoyu pidlyuoyu*), 136

Potato Spirals with Caviar (*Kartopliani spirali z ikroyu*), 85

Pyrizhky with Cabbage (*Pyrizhky z kapustoyu*), 26

Stuffed Fresh Apricots (*Nachyniuvani svizhi abrykozy*), 221

Sweet Pyrizhky with Cranberries (*Solodki pyrizhky iz zhuravlynoyu*), 27

Ukrainian Cod Fish with Tomato Sauce (*Triska v pomidorovomu sosi*), 15

Ukrainian Meat-on-a-Stick (*Patychky*), 132

Ukrainian Potato Bread (*Pyrih z baraboleyu*), 28

Ukrainian Sausage (*Kovbasa*), 124

Whole Salmon in Aspic (*Losos' v kholodtsiu*), 12

APPLES

Dried Fruit Compote (*Uzvar*), 218

Fresh Fruit Compote (*Kompot iz svizhykh ovochiv*), 246

Meatless Chernivtsi Borshch (*Pisnyi borshch po-chernivets'ky*), 41

Old Country Noodle Pudding (*Lokshyna z yablukamy*), 223

Roast Loin of Pork Stuffed with Apples and Cherries (*Svyniacha pechenia nachyniuvana yablukamy ta vyshniamy*), 120

APRICOTS

Dried Fruit Compote (*Uzvar*), 218

Perekladanets, 234

Spiced Apricot Jam (*Marmeliada iz abrykoz zi spetsiyamy*), 77

Stuffed Fresh Apricots (*Nachyniuvani svizhi abrykozy*), 221

ASPARAGUS

Warm Asparagus with Vinaigrette (*Tepli shparagy u vinegreti*), 88

ASPICS

Duck in Aspic (*Kholodets' z kachky*), 10

Garden Vegetables in Lemon Aspic (*Horodyna v tsytrynovim kholodtsiu*), 11

Jellied Pig's Feet (*Drahli*), 9

Whole Salmon in Aspic (*Losos' v kholodtsiu*), 12

BEANS, NAVY

Bean Fritters (*Slast'ony z fasoli*), 95

BEANS, RED KIDNEY

Beet, Bean and Prune Dish (*Varya*), 94

Roast Leg of Lamb (*Pechena yahniatyna*), 133

BEANS, WHITE

Crimean Tatar Beef with Beans (*Yalovychyna z fasoleyu po-tatars'ky*), 129

BEEF

Beef Patties or Meatballs (*Sichenyky abo Zrazy z yalovychyny*), 128

Braised Beef Tongue (*Tushkovanyi lyzen' z yalovychyny*), 130

Country-Style Ukrainian Borshch (*Selians'kyi borshch*), 34

Crimean Meat Pies (*Chebureky*), 199
Crimean Tatar Beef with Beans (*Yalovychyna z fasoleyu po-tatars'ky*), 129
Crimean Tatar Biber Dolmas (*Biber dolma po kryms'ko-tatars'ky*), 21
Hetman-Style Short Ribs Soup (*Yushka z reber, po-het'mans'ky*), 45
Podillia Stuffing (*Podil's'ka nachynka*), 143
Pounded Steak (*Bytky*), 125
Shish Kebabs (*Shashlyky*), 131 var.
Spicy Beef Soup with Herbs (*Kharcho*), 46
Stuffed Cabbage Rolls (*Holubtsi*), Basic Recipe 97–98
Ukrainian Beef Brisket (*Yalovycha hrudynka*), 126
Ukrainian Sausage (*Kovbasa*), 124
Zaporizhzhya-Style Borshch (*Borshch po-zaporizhs'ky*), 37

BEETS
Beet, Bean and Prune Dish (*Varya*), 94
Beet and Horseradish Relish (*Tsvikly*), 69
Beet Caviar ("*Ikra*" *z buriakiv*), 8
Beet Pickle Salad (*Kholodna salata z tsybuli*), 60
Cold Peasant Borshch (*Kholodnyi selians'kyi borshch*), 43
Country-Style Ukrainian Borshch (*Selians'kyi borshch*), 34
Homemade Beet Kvas (*Buriakovyi kvas*), 35
Meatless Chernivtsi Borshch (*Pisnyi borshch po-chernivets'ky*), 41
Meatless Kvas Borshch (*Pisnyi borshch z kvasom*), 36
Mixed Vegetable Salad with Vinaigrette (*Salata z mishanoyi horodyny, prypravlena vinegretovoyu polykoyu*), 58
Old Country Cabbage-Beet Relish (*Starokrayova pryprava zi svizhoyi kapusty I buriakiv*), 70
Pickled Red Beets (*Kvasheni buriaky*), 66
Poltava Borshch with Chicken and Dumplings (*Poltavs'kyi borshch z kurkoyu ta halushkamy*), 39
Ukrainian Lenten Borshch (*Pisnyi borshch*), 40
Zaporizhzhya-Style Borshch (*Borshch po-zaporizhs'ky*), 37

BELL PEPPERS
Bell Pepper Paprikash (*Paprykash z pertsiv*), 89
Crimean Tatar Biber Dolmas (*Biber dolma po kryms'ko-tatars'ky*), 21
Garden Vegetables in Lemon Aspic (*Horodyna v tsytrynovim kholodtsiu*), 11

BEVERAGES, ALCOHOLIC
Chocolate Liqueur (*Shokoliadovyi liker*), 253

Flavored Vodkas, 254
Hot Mulled Plum Brandy (*Nalyvka zi slyvok na-horiacho*), 255
Peperivka, 253
vodka, about, 245

BEVERAGES, NON-ALCOHOLIC
Caraway Tea (*Chai z kmynu*), 250
coffee, about, 245
Fresh Fruit Compote (*Kompot iz svizhykh ovochiv*), 246
Fresh Watermelon Lemonade (*Limoniada iz kavunom*), 247
Fresh-pressed Cranberry Juice (*Svizhyi sik iz zhuravlyny*), 250
Hemp Seed Milk (*Konopliane molochko*), 249
Huslyanka, 252
Raspberry Almond Drink (*Malynovo myhdalevyi hapytok*), 248
Ryazhanka, 251
tea, about, 245

BLUEBERRIES
Chocolate Sponge Cake with Blueberries (*Shokoliadovyi pukhkyi tort z chornytsiamy*), 228

BOAR
Wild Boar and Sausages with Sauerkraut (*Bigos iz dykym kabanom ta kovbasamy*), 166

BORSHCH
about, 32–33
Cold Peasant Borshch (*Kholodnyi selians'kyi borshch*), 43
Country-Style Ukrainian Borshch (*Selians'kyi borshch*), 34
Meatless Chernivtsi Borshch (*Pisnyi borshch po-chernivets'ky*), 41
Meatless Kvas Borshch (*Pisnyi borshch z kvasom*), 36
Poltava Borshch with Chicken and Dumplings (*Poltavs'kyi borshch z kurkoyu ta halushkamy*), 39
Sorrel or Green Borshch (*Shchavlevyi abo zelenyi borshch*), 42
Ukrainian Lenten Borshch (*Pisnyi borshch*), 40
Zaporizhzhya-Style Borshch (*Borshch po-zaporizhs'ky*), 37

BREADS/ROLLS
Babka, 178–179
Hutsul Corn Bread (*Malai*), 175
Kolach, 176–177
Korovai, about, 177
Paska Bread, 180
Rye Rolls with Cheese (*Zhytni bulky z syrom*), 187

Sour Rye Bread with Caraway Seeds (*Zhytnyi khlib z kmynom*), 171

Sweet Braided Bread (*Pleten'*), 185

Ukrainian Black Bread (*Chornyi khlib*), 173

BRUSSELS SPROUTS

Honey-Glazed Brussels Sprouts and Chestnuts (*Bruksel'ka z kashtanamy u medu*), 92

BUCKWHEAT

Buckwheat Doughnuts (*Hrechani pampushky*), 184

Buckwheat Filling for Holubtsi (*Nachynka na holubtsi z hechanoyi kasha*), 102

Buckwheat Griddlecakes (*Hrechanyky*), 205

Buckwheat Kasha (*Hrechana kasha*), 105

Omelet with Buckwheat Kasha and Smoked Fish (*Omlet iz hrechanoyu kashoyu ta vudzhenoyu ryboyu*), 211

Roast Stuffed Suckling Pig (*Pechene nachyniuvane*), 118

Ukrainian Kulebiak (*Kulebiak po-ukrains'ky*), 155

CABBAGE. *See also* SAUERKRAUT

Country-Style Ukrainian Borshch (*Selians'kyi borshch*), 34

Stuffed Cabbage Rolls and fillings (*Holubtsi*), 97–103

Meatless Chernivtsi Borshch (*Pisnyi borshch po-chernivets'ky*), 41

Meatless Kvas Borshch (*Pisnyi borshch z kvasom*), 36

Mixed Vegetable Salad with Vinaigrette (*Salata z mishanoyi horodyny, prypravlena vinegretovoyu polykoyu*), 58

Old Country Cabbage-Beet Relish (*Starokrayova pryprava zi svizhoyi kapusty I buriakiv*), 70

Poltava Borshch with Chicken and Dumplings (*Poltavs'kyi borshch z kurkoyu ta halushkamy*), 39

Pyrizhky with Cabbage (*Pyrizhky z kapustoyu*), 26

Sweet and Sour Red Cabbage (*Chervona kapusta na kvasno I solodko*), 91

Ukrainian Lenten Borshch (*Pisnyi borshch*), 40

CAKES / TORTES

Chocolate Cherry Almond Torte (*Myhdalevyi tort mokka iz vyshniamy*), 233

Chocolate Sponge Cake with Blueberries (*Shokoliadovyi pukhkyi tort z chornytsiamy*), 228

Honey Cake (*Medivnyk*), 229

Meringue Pineapple Cheesecake (*Syrnyk z ananasom ta pinoyu iz zbytykh bilkiv*), 230

Prune Torte Theodosia (*Tort Teodoziyi iz chornoslyvu*), 232

CAULIFLOWER

Cauliflower with Dill Seed (*Tsvitna kapusta z kropom*), 90

CAVIAR. *See also* VEGETABLE CAVIARS

Garnished Eggs (*Nachyniuvani yaitsia*), 3

Potato Spirals with Caviar (*Kartopliani spirali z ikroyu*), 85

CAYENNE PEPPERS

Chocolate Liqueur (*Shokoliadovyi liker*), 253

CHEESES

Cheese Halushky (Soft Dumplings) (*Halushky zi syrom*), 201

Cherry Cheese Zavyvanets, 235

Farmer's Cheese Filling for Dumplings/ *Varenyky*, 193

Kyiv-Style Cheese Paska (*Kyivs'ka syrna paska*), 231

Meringue Pineapple Cheesecake (*Syrnyk z ananasom ta pinoyu iz zbytykh bilkiv*), 230

Potato and Cheddar Cheese Filling for Dumplings/*Varenyky*, 194

Syrky, 240

Traditional Nalysnyky Cake with Meringue (*Tradytsiyinyi tort z nalysnykiv ta pinoyu iz zbytykh bilkiv*), 226

CHERRIES

about, 196

Cherry Bars (*Chereshnyanyk*), 224

Cherry Cheese Zavyvanets, 235

Chocolate Cherry Almond Torte (*Myhdalevyi tort mokka iz vyshniamy*), 233

Perekladanets, 234

Dried Cherry and Aniseed-Flavored Vodka (*Horilka z vyshniamy ta hanusem*), 254

Roast Loin of Pork Stuffed with Apples and Cherries (*Svyniacha pechenia nachyniuvana yablukamy ta vyshniamy*), 120

Sour Cherry Filling for Dumpling/ *Varenyky*, 196

Sweet Pickled Cherries (*Starokrayova pryprava zi*), 72

CHESTNUTS

Honey-Glazed Brussels Sprouts and Chestnuts (*Bruksel'ka z kashtanamy u medu*), 92

CHICKEN

Baked Chicken with Champignons and Sour Cream (*Pechena kurka z hrybamy ta smetanoyu*), 138

Chicken Kyiv (*Kuriachi kotlety po-Kyievs'ky*), 134

Chicken Pies (*Kuriachi sichenyky*), 135

Country Pate (*Pashtet*), 16

Poached Chicken with Onion Honey Sauce (*Tushkovana kurka z tsybuliano-medovoyu pidlyuoyu*), 137

Poached Chicken with Walnut Sauce (*Tushkovana kurka z horikhovoyu pidlyuoyu*), 136

Poltava Borshch with Chicken and Dumplings (*Poltavs'kyi borshch z kurkoyu ta halushkamy*), 39

CHRISTMAS EVE DISHES
about, 259

Christmas Poppy Seed Roll (*Makivnyk*), 236

Crescent Cookies (*Rohalyky*), 237

Dried Fruit Compote (*Uzvar*), 218

Herring and Mushrooms (*Pisni oseledtsi z hrybamy*), 156

Honey Cake (*Medivnyk*), 229

Jam-Filled Ukrainian Doughnuts (*Pampushky*), 182–183

Kolach, 176–177

Little Ear Dumplings (*Vushka*), 195

Ritual Wheat Berry Dish (*Kutia*), 104

Ukrainian Sauerkraut with Peas (*Kvashena kapusta z horokhom*), 96

Whole Salmon in Aspic (*Losos' v kholodtsiu*), 12

CONDIMENTS
Homemade Mustard, 127

Mayonnaise Relish (*Pryprava z mayonezu*), 13

Traditional Tartar Sauce (*Tradytsiyana tatars'ka pryprava*), 13

COOKIES
Crescent Cookies (*Rohalyky*), 237

Honey Cookies (*Medivnychky*), 239

CORNMEAL
Bukovynian Chicken Broth Cornmeal Dressing (*Bkovyns'ka nachynka na kuriachomu rosoli*), 111

Bukovynian Cornmeal Dressing (*Bukovyns'ka nachynka*), 111

Bukovynian Cornmeal Spoon Bread (*Bukovyns'ka kulesha*), 110

Hutsul Corn Bread (*Malai*), 175

Hutsulian Cornmeal Mush (*Kulesha*), 109

CRANBERRIES
Fresh-pressed Cranberry Juice (*Svizhyi sik iz zhuravlyny*), 250

Sweet Pyrizhky with Cranberries (*Solodki pyrizhky iz zhuravlynoyu*), 27

CREPES
Traditional Nalysnyky Cake with Meringue (*Tradytsiyinyi tort z nalysnykiv ta pinoyu iz zbytykh bilkiv*), 226

Ukrainian Crepes (*Nalysnyky*), 206–207

CUCUMBERS
Crocked Dill Pickles (*Kvasheni ohirky*), 65

Cucumber Salad, Country-Style (*Selians'ka salata z ohirkiv*), 61

Cucumbers with Sour Cream (*Mizeria*), 61

CURRANTS
Easter Fruit and Nut Bars (*Velykodnyi horokhivnyk*), 243

DESSERTS
Cherry Bars (*Chereshnyanyk*), 224

Cherry Cheese Zavyvanets, 235

Chocolate Cherry Almond Torte (*Myhdalevyi tort mokka iz vyshniamy*), 233

Chocolate Sponge Cake with Blueberries (*Shokoliadovyi pukhkyi tort z chornytsiamy*), 228

Christmas Poppy Seed Roll (*Makivnyk*), 236

Creamy Millet Pudding (*Pshonianyi pudyng*), 222

Crescent Cookies (*Rohalyky*), 237

Dried Fruit Compote (*Uzvar*), 218

Easter Fruit and Nut Bars (*Velykodnyi horokhivnyk*), 243

Hazelnut Zavyvanets, 238

Honey Cake (*Medivnyk*), 229

Honey Cookies (*Medivnychky*), 239

Honey-Baked Quince (*Medom-zapecheni aivy*), 220

Khrustyky, 241

Kyiv-Style Cheese Paska (*Kyivs'ka syrna paska*), 231

Meringue Pineapple Cheesecake (*Syrnyk z ananasom ta pinoyu iz zbytykh bilkiv*), 230

Nut Bars (*Horikhivnyk*), 242

Old Country Noodle Pudding (*Lokshyna z yablukamy*), 223

Peach Fritters (*Persyky v tisti*), 225

Perekladanets, 234

Prune Torte Theodosia (*Tort Teodoziyi iz chornoslyvu*), 232

Strawberry Kysil (*Kysil' iz polunyts'*), 219

Stuffed Fresh Apricots (*Nachyniuvani svizhi abrykozy*), 221

Syrky, 240

Traditional Nalysnyky Cake with Meringue (*Tradytsiyinyi tort z nalysnykiv ta pinoyu iz zbytykh bilkiv*), 226

DOUGH, PASTRY
Basic Sweet Dough, 182
Basic Yeast Dough, 24
Dough for Varenyky, 192
Quick Yeast Dough, 25
Rye Yeast Dough, 187
Sour Cream Pastry Dough, 27

DRINKS. *See* BEVERAGES

DUCK
Duck in Aspic (*Kholodets' z kachky*), 10
Roast Wild Duck with Juniper Berries
(*Pechena dyka kachka z yabodamy*
Ukrainian Roast Duck (*Pechena kachka*), 142

DUMPLINGS
Bakhchisaray-Style Steamed Dumplings
(*Manty*), 198
Cheese Halushky (Soft Dumplings)
(*Halushky zi syrom*), 201
Crimean Meat Pies (*Chebureky*), 199
Little Ear Dumplings (*Vushka*), 195
Ukrainian Halushky (Soft Dumplings)
(*Halushky*), 200
Varenyky, 190–197
Farmer's Cheese Filling, 193
Fish Filling, 194
Mushroom Filling, 195
Potato Filling, 193
Potato and Cheddar Cheese Filling, 194
Sauerkraut Filling, 193
Sour Cherry Filling, 196
Sweet Poppy Seed Filling, 197

EASTER DISHES
about, 257–259
Babka, 178–179
Beet and Horseradish Relish (*Tsvikly*), 69
Crescent Cookies (*Rohalyky*), 237
Easter Fruit and Nut Bars (*Velykodnyi
horokhivnyk*), 243
Kyiv-Style Cheese Paska (*Kyivs'ka syrna
paska*), 231
Meringue Pineapple Cheesecake (*Syrnyk z
ananasom ta pinoyu iz zbytykh bilkiv*), 230
Paska Bread, 180
Paska Doves, 181
Perekladanets, 234
Roast Easter Ham (*Pechena shynkka na
velykden'*), 115
Ukrainian Sausage (*Kovbasa*), 124

EGGPLANT
Eggplant Caviar ("*Ikra*" *z baklazhana*), 6
Eggplants Stuffed with Shrimp
(*Nachyniuvani baklazhany*), 93

EGGS
Egg Patties (*Sichenky z varenykh yayets'*), 214

Eggs Poached in Cream (*Yaitsia vareni v
smetani*), 213
Fish Salad Mimosa (*Salata z ryby Mimosa*),
64
Garnished Eggs (*Nachyniuvani yaitsia*), 3
Mayonnaise Relish (*Pryprava z mayonezu*),
13
Omelet with Buckwheat Kasha and Smoked
Fish (*Omlet iz hrechanoyu kashoyu ta
vudzhenoyu ryboyu*), 211
Omelet with Frankfurters (*Omlet zi
sosyskamy*), 210
Omelet with Fresh Strawberries (*Omlet zi
svizhymy polunytsiamy*), 212
Omelet with Fresh Tomatoes and Garlic
(*Omlet zi svizhymy pomidoramy I
chasnykom*), 212
Scrambled Eggs with Noodles (*Yayechnia z
lokshynoyu*), 215
Traditional Tartar Sauce (*Tradytsiyana
tatars'ka pryprava*), 13

FISH. *See also* HERRING; SHELLFISH
Baked Stuffed Salmon (*Pechenyi
nachyniuvanyi losos' — okremi portsiyi*),
154
Crimean Fish Cakes (*Kryms'ki sichenyky z
ryby*), 22
Fish Filling for Dumplings/*Varenyky*, 194
Fish Salad Mimosa (*Salata z ryby Mimosa*),
64
Fried Tench Strips with Creamy Mustard
Sauce (*Smazheni smyzhky lynu iz
smetankovo-hirchychnoyu prypravoyu*), 160
Grilled Bacon-Wrapped Trout (*Smazhenyi
forel', zavynenyi v solonynu*), 151
Grilled Salmon Steaks with Tomato
Dressing (*Pecheni na vuhliakh steiky
lososia z pomidorovoyu polyvoyu*), 152
Lake Trout Pickle (*Marynovanyi ozernyi
forel'*), 161
Omelet with Buckwheat Kasha and Smoked
Fish (*Omlet iz hrechanoyu kashoyu ta
vudzhenoyu ryboyu*), 211
Pike Fillets Baked in Sour Cream (*File
shchuky zapechene v smetani*), 148
Poached Carp Fillets with Yogurt-Scallion
Sauce (*Tushkovani file koropa z pidlyvoyu
iz yogurtu ta tsybul'ky*), 150
Roast Pickerel with Lemon Butter and
Horseradish (*Pechena molada shchuka v
tsytrynovomu masli ta z khronom*), 149
Traditional Ukrainian Fish Soup
(*Tradytsiyna yushka z ryby*), 47
Ukrainian Cod Fish with Tomato Sauce
(*Triska v pomidorovomu sosi*), 15
Ukrainian Fish Babka (*Babka z ryby*), 158

Ukrainian Gefilte Fish (*Ryba po-yevreis'ky*), 157

Ukrainian Kulebiak (*Kulebiak po-ukrains'ky*), 155

Warm Onion Salad with Smoked Salmon Vinaigrette (*Tepla salata iz tsybuli, prypravlena polyvkoyu z vudzhenoho lososia*), 59

Whole Salmon in Aspic (*Losos' v kholodtsiu*), 12

FRANKFURTERS
about, 210
Omelet with Frankfurters (*Omlet zi sosyskamy*), 210

FRUITS. *See* APPLES; APRICOTS; BLUEBERRIES; CHERRIES; CRANBERRIES; CURRANTS; LEMONS; ORANGES; PEACHES; PEARS; PINEAPPLE; PLUMS; PRUNES; PUMPKIN; QUINCE; RAISINS; RASPBERRIES; STRAWBERRIES; WATERMELON

GAME. *See* BOAR; DUCK; GOOSE; QUAIL; RABBIT; VENISON

GOOSE
Goose Cracklings, 145
Holiday Stuffed Roast Goose (*Nachyniuvana pechena huska na sviato*), 144

GRAINS. *See* BUCKWHEAT; CORNMEAL; MILLET; RICE; WHEAT BERRIES

GREENS. *See* SORREL

GRIDDLECAKES
Buckwheat Griddlecakes (*Hrechanyky*), 205
Griddlecakes (*Mlyntsi*), 204
Ukrainian Crepes (*Nalysnyky*), 206–207

HAZELNUTS
Hazelnut Zavyvanets, 238
Nut Bars (*Horikhivnyk*), 242

HEMP SEEDS
Hemp Seed Milk (*Konopliane molochko*), 249

HERRING
Herring and Mushrooms (*Pisni oseledtsi z hrybamy*), 156
Herring Roll Mops Stuffed with Pickles, Mushrooms, and Capers (*Zavyvani oseledtsi, nachyneni kvashenymy ohirkamy, hrybamy ta kaparamy*), 5
Pickled Herring (*Marynovani oseledtsi*), 4
Pickled Herring with Sour Cream, 4 *var.*
Ukrainian Lenten Borshch (*Pisnyi borshch*), 40

HOLUBTSI (STUFFED CABBAGE ROLL)
Beet Leaf Holubtsi, 99
Beet Leaf Holubtsi with Bread Dough Filling, 100
Buckwheat Filling for Holubtsi (*Nachynka na holubtsi z hechanoyi kasha*), 102
Cured Cabbage Leaf Holubtsi, 98
Millet and Salt Pork Filling for Holubtsi (*Nachynka na holubtsi z prosa i sala*), 103
Rice Filling for Holubtsi (*Nachynka na holubtsi z ryzhu*), 101
Sauerkraut Holubtsi, 99
Stuffed Cabbage Rolls (*Holubtsi*), Basic Recipe 97–98

HORSERADISH
Beet and Horseradish Relish (*Tsvikly*), 69
Horseradish Sauce (Cold), 68
Hot Horseradish Sauce, 80
Pickled Horseradish Relish (*Khrin v otsti*), 68

KVAS
about, 245
Cold Peasant Borshch (*Kholodnyi selians'kyi borshch*), 43
Homemade Beet Kvas (*Buriakovyi kvas*), 35
Meatless Kvas Borshch (*Pisnyi borshch z kvasom*), 36

LAMB
Bakhchisaray-Style Steamed Dumplings (*Manty*), 198
Crimean Meat Pies (*Chebureky*), 199
Roast Leg of Lamb (*Pechena yahniatyna*), 133
Rice Pilaf (*Plov/Pilav*)
Shish Kebabs (*Shashlyky*), 131

LEMONS
Fresh Watermelon Lemonade (*Limoniada iz kavunom*), 247
Garden Vegetables in Lemon Aspic (*Horodyna v tsytrynovim kholodtsiu*), 11

LIBATIONS. *See* BEVERAGES, ALCOHOLIC

LIVER
Stuffed Crown Roast of Pork with Old-Fashioned Liver Stuffing (*Svyniacha pechenia reber iz nachynkoyu z pechinky*), 121

MEATS. *See* BEEF; BOAR; CHICKEN; DUCK; FRANKFURTERS; GOOSE; LAMB; LIVER; PIG'S FEET; PORK; QUAIL; RABBIT; SAUSAGE; TURKEY; VEAL; VENISON

MILK/CREAM
Basic Cream Sauce plus variations (*Smetankova pidlyva*), 80–81
Creamy Millet Pudding (*Pshonianyi pudyng*), 222
Huslyanka, 252
Raspberry Almond Drink (*Malynovo myhdalevyi hapytok*), 248
Ryazhanka, 251

Ukrainian Milk Soup with Rice (*Molochna yushka z ryzhom*), 48
Ukrainian Potato Soup (*Kartoplianka*), 49

MILLET
Chumak-Style Millet (*Proso po-chumats'ky*), 106
Creamy Millet Pudding (*Pshonianyi pudyng*), 222
Millet and Salt Pork Filling for Holubtsi (*Nachynka na holubtsi z prosa i sala*), 103
Millet Kasha with Pumpkin and Honey (*Kasha z prosa ta z harbuzom I medom*), 107

MUSHROOMS
about, 17
Baked Chicken with Champignons and Sour Cream (*Pechena kurka z hrybamy ta smetanoyu*), 138
Champignon Caviar ("*Ikra*" *z hrybiv*), 7
Crispy Fried Potatoes with Wild Mushrooms (*Prysmazheni kartopli z dykymy hrybamy*), 86
Dried Wild Mushrooms with Gravy (*Susheni dyki hryby v prypravi*), 87
Grilled Salmon Steaks with Tomato Dressing (*Pecheni na vuhliakh steiky lososia z pomidorovoyu polyvoyu*), 152
Herring and Mushrooms (*Pisni oseledtsi z hrybamy*), 156
Marinated Mushrooms (*Marynovani hryby*), 18
Mushroom Filling for Dumplings/*Varenyky*, 195
Mushroom Patties (*Sichenyky z hryby*),19
Mushroom Sauce, 80
Raisin, Prune and Wild Mushroom Stuffing (for Goose), 144
Stuffed Meat Rolls (*Nachyniuvani bytky*), 123
Ukrainian Kulebiak (*Kulebiak po-ukrains'ky*), 155
Wild Mushroom Soup (*Yushka z dykykh hrybiv*), 50

NOODLES
Homemade Egg Noodles (*Lokshyna*), 202
Maqarne, 203
Old Country Noodle Pudding (*Lokshyna z yablukamy*), 223
Scrambled Eggs with Noodles (*Yayechnia z lokshynoyu*), 215
Suzme, 203

NUTS. *See* ALMONDS; CHESTNUTS; HAZELNUTS; WALNUTS

ONIONS
Chilled Onion Salad (*Kholodna salata z tsybuli*), 60

Onion Honey Sauce (*Tsybuliano-medovoyu pidlyvoyu*), 137
Onion Sauce, 80
Warm Onion Salad with Smoked Salmon Vinaigrette (*Tepla salata iz tsybuli, prypravlena polyvkoyu z vudzhenoho lososia*), 59

ORANGES
Fresh Fruit Compote (*Kompot iz svizhykh ovochiv*), 246
Orange-Flavored Vodka (*Horilka z pomarancheyu*), 254

PANCAKES. *See* GRIDDLECAKES

PASTRIES, SAVORY
doughs for, 24–25, 27
Pyrizhky with Cabbage (*Pyrizhky z kapustoyu*), 26
Ukrainian Kulebiak (*Kulebiak po-ukrains'ky*), 155
Ukrainian Potato Bread (*Pyrih z baraboleyu*), 28
Whole Wheat Bublyky with Poppy Seeds (*Razovi bublyky z makom*), 186

PASTRIES, SWEET
Buckwheat Doughnuts (*Hrechani pampushky*), 184
Cherry Bars (*Chereshnyanyk*), 224
Cherry Cheese Zavyvanets, 235
Christmas Poppy Seed Roll (*Makivnyk*), 236
Crescent Cookies (*Rohalyky*), 237
doughs for, 24–25, 27, 182
Easter Fruit and Nut Bars (*Velykodnyi horokhivnyk*), 243
Hazelnut Zavyvanets, 238
Honey Cookies (*Medivnychky*), 239
Jam-Filled Ukrainian Doughnuts (*Pampushky*), 182–183
Khrustyky, 241
Nut Bars (*Horikhivnyk*), 242
Perekladanets, 234
Sweet Braided Bread (*Pleten'*), 185
Sweet Pyrizhky with Cranberries (*Solodki pyrizhky iz zhuravlynoyu*), 27

PATTIES
Beef Patties or Meatballs (*Sichenyky abo Zrazy z yalovychyny*), 128
Crimean Fish Cakes (*Kryms'ki sichenyky z ryby*), 22
Egg Patties (*Sichenky z varenykh yayets'*), 214
Mushroom Patties (*Sichenyky z hryby*),19

PEACHES
Chilled Fruit Soup (*Kholodnyy sup frukty*), 55
Peach Fritters (*Persyky v tisti*), 225

PEARS
Dried Fruit Compote (*Uzvar*), 218
Hot Mulled Plum Brandy (*Nalyvka zi slyvok na-horiacho*), 255
Preserved Pears (*Zavareni hrushi*), 73

PEAS, DRIED
Ukrainian Sauerkraut with Peas (*Kvashena kapusta z horokhom*), 96

PEAS, FRESH
Fresh Pea Soup (*Yushka iz svizhoho horokhu*), 52

PEPPERS. *See* BELL PEPPERS; CAYENNE PEPPERS

PICKLES. *See also* RELISHES
Crocked Dill Pickles (*Kvasheni ohirky*), 65
Lake Trout Pickle (*Marynovanyi ozernyi forel'*), 161
Marinated Mushrooms (*Marynovani hryby*), 18
Pickled Horseradish Relish (*Khrin v otsti*), 68
Pickled Red Beets (*Kvasheni buriaky*), 66
Preserved Pears (*Zavareni hrushi*), 73
Sweet Pickled Cherries (*Starokrayova pryprava zi*), 72

PIG'S FEET
Jellied Pig's Feet (*Drahli*), 9

PINEAPPLE
Meringue Pineapple Cheesecake (*Syrnyk z ananasom ta pinoyu iz zbytykh bilkiv*), 230

PLUMS
Cooked Fruit Pulp (*Povydlo*), 71
Grilled Pork Tenderloin (*Svyniacha poliadvytsia pechena na vuhliakh*), 116
Hot Mulled Plum Brandy (*Nalyvka zi slyvok na-horiacho*), 255

POPPY SEEDS
Christmas Poppy Seed Roll (*Makivnyk*), 236
Poppy Seed Filling for Dumplings/*Varenyky*, 197
Ritual Wheat Berry Dish (*Kutia*), 104
Sweet Braided Bread (*Pleten'*), 185
Whole Wheat Bublyky with Poppy Seeds (*Razovi bublyky z makom*), 186

PORK. *See also* SALT PORK
Grilled Pork Tenderloin (*Svyniacha poliadvytsia pechena na vuhliakh*), 116
Jellied Pig's Feet (*Drahli*), 9
Pork Cracklings (*Shkvarky*), 81
Roast Easter Ham (*Pechena shynkka na velykden'*), 115
Roast Loin of Pork Stuffed with Apples and Cherries (*Svyniacha pechenia nachyniuvana yablukamy ta vyshniamy*), 120

Roast Stuffed Suckling Pig (*Pechene nachyniuvane*), 118
Shish Kebabs (*Shashlyky*), 131 *var.*
Stuffed Cabbage Rolls (*Holubtsi*), Basic Recipe 97–98
Stuffed Crown Roast of Pork with Old-Fashioned Liver Stuffing (*Svyniacha pechenia reber iz nachynkoyu z pechinky*), 121
Stuffed Meat Rolls (*Nachyniuvani bytky*), 123
Ukrainian Meat-on-a-Stick (*Patychky*), 132
Ukrainian Pork Basturma (*Ukrains'ka basturma*), 117
Ukrainian Sausage (*Kovbasa*), 124
Zaporizhzhya-Style Borshch (*Borshch po-zaporizhs'ky*), 37
Zaporizhzhia-Style Sauerkraut Soup (*Kapusniak po-zaporizhs'ky*), 54

POTATOES
Crispy Fried Potatoes with Wild Mushrooms (*Prysmazheni kartopli z dykymy hrybamy*), 86
Poltava Borshch with Chicken and Dumplings (*Poltavs'kyi borshch z kurkoyu ta halushkamy*), 39
Potato and Cheddar Cheese Filling for Dumplings/*Varenyky*, 194
Potato Babka (*Kartopliana babka*), 82
Potato Filling for Dumplings/*Varenyky*, 193
Potato Pancakes (*Deruny*), 84
Potato Spirals with Caviar (*Kartopliani spirali z ikroyu*), 85
Roasted Potatoes with Caraway Seeds (*Pecheni kartopli z kmynom*), 83
Ukrainian Potato Bread (*Pyrih z baraboleyu*), 28
Ukrainian Potato Soup (*Kartoplianka*), 49

POULTRY. *See* CHICKEN; DUCK; GOOSE; QUAIL; TURKEY

PRESERVES
Cooked Fruit Pulp (*Povydlo*), 71
Rose Petal Preserves (*Rozha z tsukrom*), 75
Spiced Apricot Jam (*Marmeliada iz abrykoz zi spetsiyamy*), 77
Strawberry Preserves (*Marmeliada iz sunyts'*), 76

PRUNES
Beet, Bean and Prune Dish (*Varya*), 94
Dried Fruit Compote (*Uzvar*), 218
Prune Torte Theodosia (*Tort Teodoziyi iz chornoslyvu*), 232
Raisin, Prune and Wild Mushroom Stuffing (for Goose), 144

PUDDINGS

Creamy Millet Pudding (*Pshonianyi pudyng*), 222

Old Country Noodle Pudding (*Lokshyna z yablukamy*), 223

PUMPKIN

Millet Kasha with Pumpkin and Honey (*Kasha z prosa ta z harbuzom I medom*), 107

QUAIL

Crispy Fried Quail with Orange Zest and Honey (*Prysmazhena perepilka iz tertoyu lushpynkoyu pomaranchi ta medom*), 167

QUINCE

Honey-Baked Quince (*Medom-zapecheni aivy*), 220

RABBIT

Braised Rabbit with Red Wine and Capers (*Tushkovanyi zayats' abo krilyk u chervonomu vyni z kaparamy*), 163

RADISHES

Radishes with Lemon and Honey (*Red'ka pripravlena tsytrynoyu I medom*), 62

RAISINS

Dried Fruit Compote (*Uzvar*), 218

Raisin, Prune and Wild Mushroom Stuffing (for Goose), 144

RASPBERRIES

Raspberry Almond Drink (*Malynovo myhdalevyi hapytok*), 248

RELISHES

Beet and Horseradish Relish (*Tsvikly*), 69

Mayonnaise Relish (*Pryprava z mayonezu*), 13

Old Country Cabbage-Beet Relish (*Starokrayova pryprava zi svizhoyi kapusty I buriakiv*), 70

Pickled Horseradish Relish (*Khrin v otsti*), 68

RICE

Raisin, Prune and Wild Mushroom Stuffing (for Goose), 144

Rice Filling for Holubtsi (*Nachynka na holubtsi z ryzhu*), 101

Rice Pilaf (*Plov/Pilav*)

Stuffed Cabbage Rolls (*Holubtsi*), Basic Recipe 97–98

Ukrainian Milk Soup with Rice (*Molochna yushka z ryzhom*), 48

ROLLS. *See* BREADS/ROLLS

SALADS

Beet Pickle Salad (*Kholodna salata z tsybuli*), 60

Chilled Onion Salad (*Kholodna salata z tsybuli*), 60

Creamy Shrimp Salad (*Salata z krevetok v smetani*), 63

Cucumber Salad, Country-Style (*Selians'ka salata z ohirkiv*), 61

Cucumbers with Sour Cream (*Mizeria*), 61

Fish Salad Mimosa (*Salata z ryby Mimosa*), 64

Mixed Vegetable Salad with Vinaigrette (*Salata z mishanoyi horodyny, prypravlena vinegretovoyu polykoyu*), 58

Radishes with Lemon and Honey (*Red'ka prypravlena tsytrynoyu I medom*), 62

Sauerkraut Salad (*Salata z kvashenoyi kapusty*), 62

Warm Onion Salad with Smoked Salmon Vinaigrette (*Tepla salata iz tsybuli, prypravlena polyvkoyu z vudzhenoho lososia*), 59

SALT PORK

Millet and Salt Pork Filling for Holubtsi (*Nachynka na holubtsi z prosa i sala*), 103

SAUCES. *See also* CONDIMENTS

Basic Cream Sauce (*Smetankova pidlyva*), 80

Brown Cream Sauce, 81

Creamy Cheese Sauce, 81

Creamy Mustard Sauce (for fish) (*Smetankovo-hirchychnoyu prypravoyu*), 160

Crimean Yogurt Sauce (*Kryms'ka pidlyva z yogurtu*), 23

Dill Sauce, 80

Dried Wild Mushrooms with Gravy (*Susheni dyki hryby v prypravi*), 87

Horseradish Sauce (Cold), 68

Hot Horseradish Sauce, 80

Mushroom Sauce, 80

Onion Honey Sauce (*Tsybuliano-medovoyu pidlyvoyu*), 137

Onion Sauce, 80

Spinach-Sorrel Sauce (*Shpinatovo-shchavlevoyu pidlyvoyu*), 140

Tart Sour Cream Sauce, 80

Tomato Dressing (for fish) (*Pomidorovoyu polyvoyu*), 152

Traditional Tartar Sauce (*Tradytsiyana tatars'ka pryprava*), 13

Walnut Sauce (*Horikhovoyu pidlyuoyu*), 136

Yellow Cream Sauce, 81

Yogurt-Scallion Sauce (for fish) (*Pidlyvoyu iz yogurtu ta tsybul'ky*), 150

SAUERKRAUT

Fresh Homemade Sauerkraut (*Kvashena kapusta*), 67

Sauerkraut Filling for Dumplings/*Varenyky*, 193

Sauerkraut Salad (*Salata z kvashenoyi kapusty*), 62

Sauerkraut Soup (*Kapusniak*), 53

Ukrainian Sauerkraut with Peas (*Kvashena kapusta z horokhom*), 96

Zaporizhzhya-Style Borshch (*Borshch po-zaporizhs'ky*), 37

Zaporizhzhya-Style Sauerkraut Soup (*Kapusniak po-zaporizhzhs'ky*), 54

SAUSAGES

Ukrainian Sausage (*Kovbasa*), 124

Wild Boar and Sausages with Sauerkraut (*Bigos iz dykym kabanom ta kovbasamy*), 166

SEAFOOD. *See* FISH; SHELLFISH

SHELLFISH

Boiled Crawfish (*Vareni richkovi raky*), 159

Creamy Shrimp Salad (*Salata z krevetok v smetani*), 63

Eggplants Stuffed with Shrimp (*Nachyniuvani baklazhany*), 93

SORREL

Roast Turkey Breast with Spinach-Sorrel Sauce (*Pechena hrudynka indyka iz shpinatovo-shchavlevoyu pidlyvoyu*), 140

Sorrel or Green Borshch (*Shchavlevyi abo zelenyi borshch*), 42

SOUPS. *See also* BORSHCH

Fresh Pea Soup (*Yushka iz svizhoho horokhu*), 52

Hetman-Style Short Ribs Soup (*Yushka z reber, po-het'mans'ky*), 45

Rich Ukrainian Chicken Broth (*Kuriachyi rosil*), 44

Sauerkraut Soup (*Kapusniak*), 53

Sauerkraut Soup, Zaporizhzhia-Style (*Kapusniak po-zaporizhzhs'ky*), 54

Spicy Beef Soup with Herbs (*Kharcho*), 46

Traditional Ukrainian Fish Soup (*Tradytsiyna yushka z ryby*), 47

Ukrainian Milk Soup with Rice (*Molochna yushka z ryzhom*), 48

Ukrainian Potato Soup (*Kartoplianka*), 49

Wild Mushroom Soup (*Yushka z dykykh hrybiv*), 50

SPINACH

Roast Turkey Breast with Spinach-Sorrel Sauce (*Pechena hrudynka indyka iz shpinatovo-shchavlevoyu pidlyvoyu*), 140

STRAWBERRIES

Omelet with Fresh Strawberries (*Omlet zi svizhymy polunytsiamy*), 212

Strawberry Kysil (*Kysil' iz polunyts'*), 219

Strawberry Preserves (*Marmeliada iz sunyts'*), 76

TOMATOES

Country-Style Ukrainian Borshch (*Selians'kyi borshch*), 34

Grilled Salmon Steaks with Tomato Dressing (*Pecheni na vuhliakh steiky lososia z pomidorovoyu polyvoyu*), 152

Meatless Chernivtsi Borshch (*Pisnyi borshch po-chernivets'ky*), 41

Omelet with Fresh Tomatoes and Garlic (*Omlet zi svizhymy pomidoramy I chasnykom*), 212

Poltava Borshch with Chicken and Dumplings (*Poltavs'kyi borshch z kurkoyu ta halushkamy*), 39

TORTES. *See* CAKES/TORTES

TURKEY

Breaded Turkey Cutlets (*Obkacheni kotlety z indyka*), 139

Roast Turkey Breast with Spinach-Sorrel Sauce (*Pechena hrudynka indyka iz shpinatovo-shchavlevoyu pidlyvoyu*), 140

TURNIPS

Roast Leg of Lamb (*Pechena yahniatyna*), 133

VARENYKY. *See* DUMPLINGS

VEAL

Beef Patties or Meatballs (*Sichenyky abo Zrazy z yalovychyny*), 128

Country Pate (*Pashtet*), 16

Stuffed Meat Rolls (*Nachyniuvani bytky*), 123

VEGETABLE CAVIARS (IKRA)

about, 5

Beet Caviar ("*Ikra*" *z buriakiv*), 8

Champignon Caviar ("*Ikra*" *z hrybiv*), 7

Eggplant Caviar ("*Ikra*" *z baklazhana*), 6

VEGETABLES. *See* ASPARAGUS; BEETS; BELL PEPPERS; BRUSSELS SPROUTS; CABBAGE; CAULIFLOWER; CUCUMBERS; EGGPLANT; MUSHROOMS; PEAS; POTATOES; PUMPKIN; RADISHES; SALADS; SORREL; SPINACH; TOMATOES; TURNIPS

VENISON

Venison Sirloin with Cherry Mustard Butter (*Steiky z oleniny iz chereshnevo-hirchychnym maslom*), 162

VODKA

about, 245

Chocolate Liqueur (*Shokoliadovyi liker*), 253

Coriander and Peppercorn-Flavored Vodka (*Horilka iz koriandrom ta pertsen*), 254

Dried Cherry and Aniseed-Flavored Vodka
(*Horilka z vyshniamy ta hanusem*), 254
Orange-Flavored Vodka (*Horilka z
pomarancheyu*), 254

WALNUTS

Easter Fruit and Nut Bars (*Velykodnyi
horokhivnyk*), 243
Perekladanets, 234
Prune Torte Theodosia (*Tort Teodoziyi iz
chornoslyvu*), 232
Walnut Sauce (*Horikhovoyu pidlyuoyu*), 136

WATERMELON

Fresh Watermelon Lemonade (*Limoniada iz
kavunom*), 247

WHEAT. *See* BUCKWHEAT

WHEAT BERRIES

Ritual Wheat Berry Dish (*Kutia*), 104

YOGURT

Crimean Yogurt Sauce (*Kryms'ka pidlyva z
yogurtu*), 23
Poached Carp Fillets with Yogurt-Scallion
Sauce (*Tushkovani file koropa z pidlyvoyu
iz yogurtu ta tsybul'ky*), 150